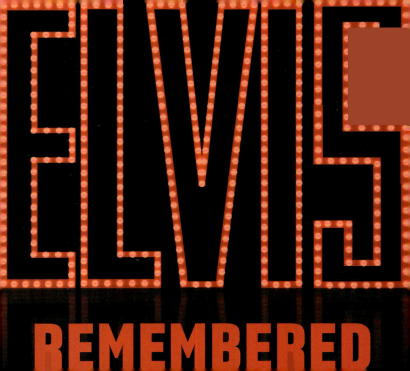

A FIREFLY BOOK

Published by Firefly Books Ltd. 2023
Copyright © 2023 Moseley Road Inc.

First printing

Library of Congress Control Number: 2023935012

Library and Archives Canada Cataloguing in Publication
Title: Elvis remembered : intimate interviews from the Elvis international archives, with the
  people who knew him best / Shelly Powers.
Names: Powers, Shelly
Identifiers: Canadiana 20230225160 | ISBN 9780228104506 (hardcover)
Subjects: LCSH: Presley, Elvis, 1935-1977. | LCSH: Presley, Elvis, 1935-1977—Friends and
  associates. | LCSH: Presley, Elvis, 1935-1977—Anecdotes. | LCSH: Rock musicians—United States—
  Biography. | LCGFT: Biographies.
Classification: LCC ML420.P74 P88 2023 | DDC 782.42166092—dc23

Published in Canada by
Firefly Books Ltd.
50 Staples Avenue, Unit 1
Richmond Hill, Ontario
L4B 0A7

Published in the United States by
Firefly Books (U.S.) Inc.
P.O. Box 1338, Ellicott Station
Buffalo, New York
14205

Written by **Shelly Powers**
Project Management
Moseley Road Inc.
Picture research, art direction, and design
Adam Moore at Moseley Road Inc
Duncan Youell at Oiloften.co.uk

Printed in China

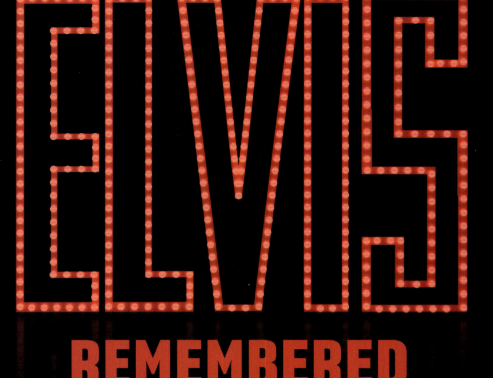

REMEMBERED

Intimate Interviews from the Elvis International Archives, With the People Who Knew Him Best

Shelly Powers

FIREFLY BOOKS

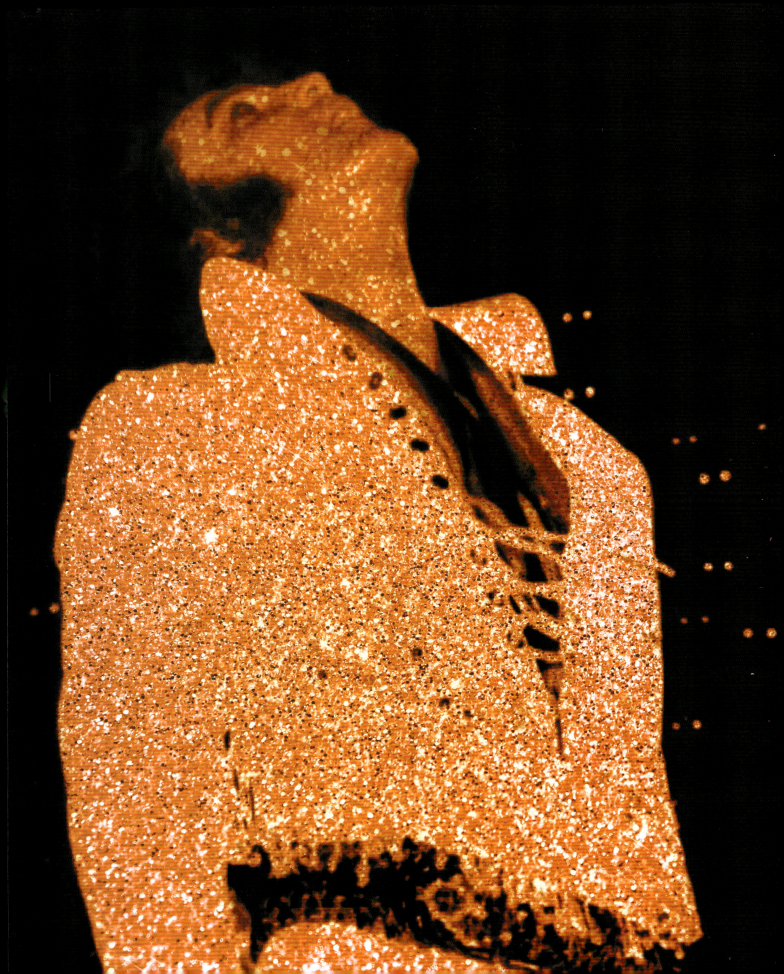

Elvis Remembered

Contents

Foreword

I am truly very honored that Shelly has asked me to write the foreword for this amazing Elvis International interviews book.

Shelly and I first met "virtually," as seems the norm these days, through our shared love and respect for Elvis Presley, back in 2006 when we both became members of Elvis International, an online official fan club. Shelly was married to Eddie Powers, a Las Vegas based Elvis Tribute Artist (ETA), so she was ideally placed in Las Vegas for Elvis connections.

Shelly and I eventually met face to face in April 2007, when she traveled over to the UK with Elvis's official photographer, the late Ed Bonja. I was so honored to spend some quality time with someone so close to Elvis. Shelly got the idea to interview Ed Bonja and, from memory, Ed helped Shelly connect with more Elvis insiders.

Shelly is such a beautiful lady inside and out, and her easy-going attitude to life makes her such an excellent interviewer—she gets her subjects to relax and warm to her and open up with some truly amazing revelations, which you will discover as you read this great book.

Very sadly, most of these Elvis people have now passed on, which makes this book even more of a treasure. Shelly has captured so many glorious Elvis stories, which through hundreds of hours of transcribing her interviews, are now preserved forever in this beautiful book.

Michael Comley

Michael Comley, with Priscilla Presley

Introduction

Elvis has always been a huge part of my life.

From as far back as I can remember, Elvis's songs echoed throughout our house—either on the radio, or crackling through our old record player, or Dad belting them out in the bathroom.

I recall seven-year-old me, telling my mum I was going to marry Elvis Presley when I grew up and that's exactly what I did; not the Elvis we all know and love, but a tribute artist from Minnesota who I encountered on a trip to Las Vegas, the place where I ended up residing for almost 12 years.

I have to say that moving from Manchester, England, to Vegas changed my life in more ways than one, and although our marriage wasn't to last, I will forever be grateful to the rhinestone-clad American who swept me off my feet with sweet renditions of "Love Me Tender" on a daily basis. Had fate not brought us together I would never have had the opportunity to meet so many amazing people connected to Elvis's world. So for that, Eddie . . . Thank you, thank you very much!

During my time in Vegas I was introduced to an Elvis fan club through a dear friend of mine. She too loved Elvis and talked about this particular club with such enthusiasm that I felt I had to check it out. Fast forward a few months and a couple of Elvis conventions later, not only had I become a member but I'd landed my first interview with Elvis Presley's personal photographer, Ed Bonja.

What started out as just one interview quickly turned into much more than I had anticipated. As the fan club grew in numbers so did my interviews.

I feel so honored to have had the opportunity to meet and become close to some truly amazing individuals who had spent a lot of time with the man himself. I learned so much about the kind of

man Elvis Presley really was—as Cynthia Pepper said, "chosen for this earth and a truly special man." I learned even more about those that were close to him, with a number of them ending up dear friends of mine.

Sadly a few of those dear friends have now passed on, their personal experiences with Elvis no longer in living memory, so it's never been more important to me than now to be able to pass on the stories that they so generously shared with me.

One thing that has become so apparent to me is how Elvis touched so many people's lives and continues to do so today. He would often state, fearfully, "Nobody will remember me."

How ironic that almost six decades after his death he is more popular now than he ever was. I've never met one person who does not know the name Elvis! He really is eternal.

The following transcripts are taken directly from these interviews—words directly from the people who knew him best.

I hope you enjoy them as much as I did.

Shelly Powers

TOP RIGHT: The author during her interview with Darlene Tompkins, March 2007; **ABOVE, TOP TO BOTTOM:** The author in her Elvis jumpsuit, 2006; with Darlene Tompkins; and with Jimmy Velvet; **OPPOSITE:** Elvis onstage during his 1968 TV Comeback Special.

"He was very edgy back then, when he was really young, and it really worked with the whole persona..."

JERRY SCHILLING ON THE YOUNG ELVIS PRESLEY

Jerry Schilling

Jerry Schilling, best known as Elvis's confidant and part of the inner circle of the Memphis Mafia, is an American talent manager. His clients have included the Beach Boys, Jerry Lee Lewis, and Lisa Marie Presley. His *Me and a Guy Named Elvis: My Lifelong Friendship with Elvis Presley*, published in 2007, is an intimate memoir of a friendship with the greatest artist in rock and roll history. In this frank interview, Jerry discusses his close relationship with Elvis.

OPPOSITE: A moody portrait of Jerry, taken during the interview.

Interviewing Jerry...

Born February 6, 1942, in Memphis, Tennessee, Jerry is an American talent manager, but I wanted to meet him because of his close friendship with Elvis over many years. The interview was recorded at the home of Patti Parry in Los Angeles, on August 31, 2009. Patti—who sadly died in October 2011—was the only acknowledged female member of the Memphis Mafia, and she spent 17 years being a "little sister," and hairdresser to Elvis. Ed Bonja was also present during the interview. Ed was Elvis's photographer during the seventies. Sadly, Ed too has died since the interview, passing away in September 2019.

TOP: Jerry and Elvis, in Hawaii during the filming of *Paradise, Hawaiian Style*, circa 1965; **ABOVE:** Jerry with Elvis, running through the setlist and preparing for that evening's gig during his acclaimed 1972 Spring tour.

I found Jerry to be charming, attentive, and friendly. In fact, listening to the interview after the recording, I quickly discovered that I was flirting with him a little bit during that time. He was easy on the eye and extremely charismatic; however, I tried to remain professional throughout the interview.

He was honest to a fault and spoke his mind. He didn't hold back or try to gloss over anything when talking about his time with his friend Elvis.

We recorded the interview with Jerry in the living room of Patti Parry's home in Los Angeles, while Patti and Ed Bonja were both present. I didn't know I was going to interview Jerry, but he turned up, so I seized the opportunity. There was good banter between the three of them at times and especially before the interview kicked off. It was a lot of fun,

and yet there were moments when we talked about Elvis that were tinged with great sadness.

I immensely enjoyed the time I spent in Patti's living room with her, Jerry, and Ed. It was one of the most enjoyable and interesting interviews I held—along with being extremely moving and emotional at times. During the interview Patti became visibly melancholy regarding Elvis, and it was lovely to see Jerry's genuine concern for his friend—the only female member of the Memphis Mafia, and Elvis's "little sister." Jerry himself I found to be extremely easy to talk to. He was relaxed, thoughtful. He made me feel comfortable, like I was chatting with an old friend, and his history with Elvis I found to be very interesting. A dear, charming man, just like his friend Elvis Presley.

SP: Jerry, thank you so much for allowing me to interview you today for Elvis International.

JS: Yes, and you're welcome. I am familiar with Elvis International. I didn't mean to imply that I wasn't... I just wasn't sure where you were located.

SP: So you've heard of Elvis International? That's great! Well, we are big and growing. That's fantastic. I'm really pleased.
[To Patti] **Turn around, and face me. I don't like talking to the back of you!**

PP: Well, he doesn't want me to! [Everyone starts laughing.]

JS: Well, if she turns around, I'll get depressed. [More laughter.]

SP: We love Patti!

PP: You love me, don't you Jerry?

JS: Well . . .

SP: How can you not love Patti?

JS: Okay, let's start.

PP: Enough of Patti!

SP: Moving swiftly on!

JP: By the way, you look nice. [acknowledging Patti.]

PP: Thank you, Jerry.

SP: She does look beautiful, doesn't she? Ed showed me a picture of her on the way up. I've seen Patti loads of times, but Ed showed me a pic, and I said, "Yeah she's lovely." But when I arrived and saw you, I thought Patti, you look so slim and healthy!

JS: Let's not overdo it.

PP: Well, this is his interview—so let's go to Jerry.

[We now got on with Jerry's interview.]

SP: Let's start with how you met Elvis in the beginning. See, I have been reading your book... how you met Elvis in Guthrie Park?

JS: Very good. Yeah, back in 1954—same year that Elvis had recorded his first professional record. It was the same week that it had been played as well, and I had heard it for the first time it had been played on the radio. I went to the local playground that weekend, and there was some older guys trying to get a football game going. That's how unpopular Elvis was, as he couldn't get five people his own age to play football with him back then. So they needed a sixth player, and I got to play it, and I realized that that was the guy I had heard on the radio. I got to the huddle, and he was like the quarterback, so that started a twenty-three-year relationship.

TOP: Shelly Powers talking with Jerry during the interview in Los Angeles, 2009; **CENTER:** Jerry and Patti; **ABOVE:** Ed Bonja, Elvis's photographer in the 1970s.

13

TOP: Shelly (left), Jerry and Patti Parry, during the interview; **ABOVE**: Whilst on the cusp of stardom, Elvis still loved playing football in his hometown. Pictures taken in 1956.

SP: My goodness! So when you were playing football with him, were you not in awe of him?

JS: Absolutely.

SP: Did you not feel a little bit intimidated?

JS: I was in awe. He was nice enough that I wasn't intimidated—he knew that I was the youngest, and he had a way of making you feel kind of comfortable and at the same time keeping his distance and his edge. He was very edgy back then, when he was really young, and it really worked with the whole persona. He was kind of like a James Dean type, ya know? He wasn't the boy-next-door—he was different.

SP: He was always different... always a little bit different.

JS: I think so, yeah.

SP: He kind of left you wanting more, if you like; so I know where you're coming from.

JS: Exactly, exactly. Well put, yeah.

SP: So now after you had got acquainted with him during football and stuff like that... what happened then? How did you become firm friends?

JS: It takes a while with Elvis, ya know. Especially at this time, because all of a sudden he's going from being somewhat a recluse to now overnight almost like everyone wanting to be with him or give him trouble. You know he was as much disliked as liked! It was all, I think, a matter of trust with Elvis. The more you were around and worked in or whatever the more he would have you back. At the end of the football game that day, he said, "Do you guys want to play next Sunday?" And so we played the following Sunday, and at that point his record was HOT in Memphis. And then the following week, we played again, and I mean a lot of people showed up, and I thought I was out at that point because these were all eighteen and nineteen-year-old guys, and I was twelve.

SP: Aghhh! You were a baby, weren't you!

JS: Well, I was twelve [laughing]. Almost a teenager! That was again the sensitivity of Elvis Presley. I think he kind of knew I was in awe of him—I liked him before he was popular, and he knew I wanted to play football and stuff, so he just kept me on the team when he didn't have to, so it was really nice.

SP: So did he kind of take you under his wing because you were young?

14

"At the end of the football game that day, he said, 'Do you guys want to play next Sunday?' And so we played the following Sunday, and at that point his record was HOT in Memphis..."

JERRY SCHILLING ON ELVIS'S LOVE OF FOOTBALL

JS: No, I think that's me projecting too far. I'm still a little kid—I'm not his best friend. He's being nice to a little kid—the poor little kid in the neighborhood. It's not like he's taking me under his wing and taking care of me and all that stuff.

SP: When did you actually start hanging out?
[Jerry turns to Patti, without answering my question.]

JS: He would have liked her. [Referring to Shelly.]

PP: He would have LOVED her [laughing]. I tease her about her accent.

JS: Yeah! It's great!

SP: Really? Well, thank you. That's very nice.

PP: I'm shutting up.

SP: You can talk Patti—it's more fun.

PP: No, this is Jerry's.

SP: Its okay. It's allowed. I'm Shelly Powers!

PP: And I'm Patti Parry, and that's Jerry Schilling, my brother.

SP: Yes, and that's Jerry Schilling... there you go. Now, where was he living?

JS: That's a good question... Well, when we were playing football, he was living in Lauderdale Courts. Yeah, which was a government project where I was from, where I lived. I went to a school, and if you stood in my playground and you looked over, you could see Humes High School. It was a great school—Catholic boy-girl up to the eighth grade,

and there was also an all-girls high school, and on a Saturday night at Holy Name, they would have a dance, and a lot of the Humes High guys would go, because it was an all-girls high school, and Elvis would go, and all my cousins would go also.

SP: At what point did you really get close to Elvis?

JS: I think that over the years in Memphis, there were times I felt close, and then because of his career taking off, I wouldn't see him for a long time, and then he was gone to the army for two years. I knew he knew me—I knew he felt comfortable around me. I knew I was invited if he was having people around, but the drastic changes were in 1964, when I went to work for him, when we left driving from Memphis to Los Angeles and on that bus drive. It's chapter four in my book, and it's what I sold the book on. The night I went to work for Elvis... and that's where the relationship went from casual to friends. We talked about fun things but deep things. There was nobody around—just five of us guys. First time there were really just good one-on-one long conversations with nobody around. Elvis and I playing football, truck stops late at night, so it was very special. I had known him for ten years before that, and that's where things changed.

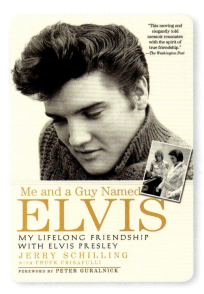

TOP LEFT: Elvis running with the ball, 1956; **ABOVE:** Cover of Jerry's 2007 book, *Me and a Guy Named Elvis. The Washington Post's* review states: "This moving and elegantly told memoir resonates with the spirit of true friendship."

TOP LEFT: Elvis loved his cars. This one is his 1956 Lincoln Continental; **CENTER:** His 1962 Ford Thunderbird Sports Roadster, bought in Memphis. The car was driven to California so that Elvis had transport to and from the movie shoots; **ABOVE:** Elvis as the Panhandle Kid in the Comedy Musical Western *Tickle Me*, released in June 1965; **TOP RIGHT:** Elvis surrounded by adoring and swooning girls in *Tickle Me*.

SP: I remember a part I had read in your book, you were about to start another job or go in a different direction when he came with this job offer?

JS: I was getting ready to be a history teacher. I had one semester left in school, and then I got the offer I couldn't refuse.

SP: Absolutely, who could refuse an offer like that!

PP: And then he met me [laughing].

SP: And then your life changed again!

JS: Yeah [laughing].

SP: So, then you went to work for Elvis as a bodyguard, was it?

JS: Well, kind of... that was part of it—traveling companion—whatever he needed. I didn't know; we never discussed what I was going to do. I'd been around the guys for ten years, and I kind of knew we would fall into what he needed. I really didn't care.

SP: You just wanted to be around Elvis?

JS: Yeah, sure... you know. I had gotten over that after ten years, and there were times in the fifties that I couldn't wait. Gosh, you know, I grew up in Memphis, and these guys were doing films in Hollywood and going to Vegas and things. And I dreamed about it. But, then, you know, I went on with my life. He was

gone for long periods of time, so whatever. I had, you know, kind of a plan for a life.

SP: A normal life—really as a history teacher and a football coach.

JS: Yeah, because I went to college on a football scholarship.

SP: And then Elvis changed everything? I remember in part of your book, you said you noticed when he was back in town because of his car.

JS: Around the movie theater.

SP: Yeah, and then there would be swarms of teenagers?

JS: No, no... because it was late at night. That was the whole purpose. It was after the movie was closed, and nobody knew, and maybe there would be three or four cars—Elvis's cars—there would be nobody around. When he was performing, it was a whole different thing. He couldn't do anything when it was advertised that he was performing. It was hard to get around. Tons of people, as opposed to—and Patti can tell you—on a day-to-day thing around town or whatever, people weren't following him around every day.

SP: So, he asked you to go work for him. Were you working for him when he was doing the films?

JS: When I came out it was right in the middle of '64. The first movie that I was with Elvis on was *Tickle Me*. We did a number of films after that.

SP: Did you get any cameo roles?

JS: More like an extra. Then, because of the connections I made, I got a Screen Actors Guild card. I did other shows, like *Charlie's Angels, Mod Squad, T.J. Hooker*, and so forth.

SP: Speaking parts?

JS: [Laughing.] Yeah, speaking parts, not as an extra.

SP: Tell me about *Charlie's Angels*.

JS: They did an episode, where there were sexual situations, where the girl would get killed, and I played the killer.

SP: You were the bad guy!

JS: Yeah, I was the bad guy. You were always the bad guy, unless you were a regular. Everything I played was a bad guy.

PP: I didn't know that.

JS: Then on Elvis's movies, I stood in for him on seven movies. I was the stand-in. On three movies, I was his photo double, but it's distant stuff you know, like horseback riding, climbing on ships in *Easy Come, Easy Go*. All you have to do is be about the same size, and they dyed my hair black because I stood in every day, and I had to wear makeup every day, because of the lighting. And there's where I learned a lot, believe it or not, standing in for Elvis. I learned a lot and had this passion to do filming and eventually quit working for him and went into film editing.

SP: That must have been a really tough decision to make.

JS: The biggest... the biggest. That was the toughest decision I ever made in my life—really tough.

SP: So how long were you apart from Elvis after you made that decision?

JS: Well, what happened is... So when I made that decision, I didn't have a job, because I didn't want to be working for Elvis, and go looking for a job. I knew what I wanted to do, but I didn't have a job, so I was trying to get into film editing, and people didn't take me seriously because I was working for Elvis Presley, you know. The guy who eventually hired me later told me this.

First, what happened before that, about six weeks into after I had left, Elvis didn't like to be said no

to, so he called me, and said, "Are you doing that editing stuff on the weekends?" I said, "No." He said, "Okay. I'm on my way to pick you up. We're going to Palm Springs." I was so glad to hear from him. Normally, back then, when somebody quit working for Elvis, the relationship was pretty over—you go. You don't go for a weekend or take a trip with Elvis—it's done, and he just did that with the people that were hired and that he worked with.

SP: He must have really liked you.

PP: He did, he did.

JS: Well, I hope so. So that kind of started me going, ya know. And then after that, he was saying, "Well look, if you haven't got a job yet, we're doing a film in Arizona, *Stay Away, Joe*. Do you want to come and stand in for me and whatever?" Which was really great, because at nighttime, there was this director, and he had this great editor, and they let me sit in while they edited the film in the evening after shooting the film in the daytime. So I was still learning my profession—and I was making money. And I was still being friends with Elvis and still getting to hang out with the guys. So it was the best of all worlds.

TOP, LEFT AND RIGHT: Elvis in the 1969 movie *Charro!* and right, Jerry as his stand-in; **ABOVE:** Still from the Elvis movie *Easy Come, Easy Go*, 1967.

TOP: Elvis and Jerry in the early 1970s.

TOP: Elvis and Jerry in the early 1970s; **ABOVE:** Jerry in front of a wall of gold and platinum Elvis records.

OPPOSITE: The Colonel and Elvis on set for *The Trouble with Girls*, 1969.

SP: That's fantastic. So you were filling in your weekends with Elvis. At what point did you think "I'm going to ditch the directing, and I'm going to go back with Elvis full time"?

JS: Well, I did film editing for five years.

SP: Film editing—sorry.

JS: But I worked for ABC and Paramount to do some independent things.

SP: So you were quite independent weren't you! Actually, this is very admirable. This is my personal opinion, okay?

JS: Which means a lot to me [Laughing].

**SP I like you [Laughing.] He's nice, isn't he!

PP: He's lovely.

SP: He looks good, too! [Laughing.] You look fantastic.

JS: Thank you. I will take one glass of wine now, Patti.

SP: I've lost track now. [Yes, I was blushing in his presence but hoped he hadn't noticed.] I mean, if you were lucky enough to be a part of EP's entourage, group... whatever... you would never leave. It would take a lot of courage to leave? It would take a lot to do that. Because when you're a friend of EP's—then am I right in saying this— you're more or less probably secure for the rest of your life, right?

JS & PP: No, not really.

JS: No, but, you know, I mean, luckily, he was a very loyal bond. But I think all the guys had to be very strong, because not only was it your job, not only was it where you lived, not only was it because he was your best friend, but one big argument... I mean you were starting back at birth almost; everything that you did in your life centered around Elvis Presley, and that was a wonderful thing, and he didn't abuse that. In fact, he made us feel welcome. He made us feel a part of it.

SP: When I said, "secure for the rest of your life," I was referring more to friendship. When you were a friend of Elvis, and you had his best interests at heart, and you were a loyal friend.

"He was a gentleman. He was a gentleman in a disguise. The Colonel was a gentleman... he was honest, he was brilliant..."

JERRY SCHILLING ON COLONEL TOM PARKER WHO WAS ELVIS'S MANAGER

"I think he is a creative genius. If they would had let him, it would have been unbelievable what he would have accomplished as a producer, as an actor, and all these things..."

JERRY SCHILLING ON ELVIS'S SUPPRESSED TALENT

TOP RGHT: Jerry with Lisa Marie; **ABOVE:** Jerry with Priscilla.

JS: You had to prove it from time to time. Things came up in that situation—there's always jealousies, there's always outside influences. No, you don't feel secure. In one way you do, I wouldn't use the word secure.

SP: What word would you use? So you mean Elvis could turn, maybe?

JS: Well, yeah. He was a human being. I mean, I could have turned on him. We're all human beings, but let's face it, when push came to shove, he was sharing his life with us, and he did that very graciously. But... there's sometimes, you know what, when he couldn't speak out to the public, and he had tremendous creative frustrations and stuff, and some days he wasn't in a great mood, and you didn't feel secure on those days.

SP: I hear what you're saying.

JS: Then some days there may be some big thing with him, and the Colonel—and you know the Colonel—would be saying you need to cut your staff in half. And I was packing, and Elvis would come in and say he was talking about you, but you know, there goes your feeling secure, so I felt more secure actually.

I never wanted to be a burden on Elvis. I wanted to be his friend first of all, and the job is second. When I trained myself to do various things, that's where he came back, and said Jerry, "Why don't you come back, and work as a film editor on my films?" And there's where I started to feel secure. And that was really great., because I got to talk to him on those levels. I think he is a creative genius. If they would had let him, it would have been unbelievable what he would have accomplished as a producer, as an actor,

and all these things, and I got to talk to him on those levels. Like when I was working on *Elvis on Tour* as an assistant film editor, that's about as low as you can get. I could go and talk to Elvis, you know. I wasn't even working for Elvis at that point. I was on tour with him, and I really liked the filmmakers of this, and asked Elvis if he would mind if I asked if I could work as a film editor for them, and he said, "No. It's okay with me." And when I went to meetings with them, I realized they probably thought I was some spy for Colonel Parker or the Elvis camp, and so I said, "You know what, guys, maybe if there's another project that you do these music things, maybe could I come back and talk to you." And then they realized—they knew I had done my apprenticeship and everything, and they said, "No. You know what? You come back tomorrow and work for us." So then I was working for them, but I was still seeing Elvis on a friendship basis, and in those conversations, we got to talk about audio review, voice, still pictures, montages, and whatever, which eventually led to when he was going to produce his own karate film. God what a thrill... what an honor, right?

PP: Shame he didn't.

SP: I know, I know.

JS: We got halfway through it.

SP: So now that footage—you say you got half way through it? Was it ever released?

JS: It's been bootlegged. You've heard of it, right Ed?

EB: Yes.

PP: He was really excited about doing it, and it was before they even started making karate movies.

JS: He was ahead of his time.

PP: He was way ahead of his time.

JS: There was actually two projects: one was a dramatic karate film, and the other was a documentary. And it was always the powers-that-be who were always trying to undermine him as a businessman, because they thought they might lose him if he got too much experience—they knew he was smart. My log line in my book, one underlying theme was, we lost Elvis Presley through creative disappointment. The drugs were the band-aid, not the... that's the bottom line... and you know what? He had a great career, but the bottom line is it's not a happy ending. We lost him a half life—we should be still sitting with him."

SP: Exactly. Like what we were saying about Tom Jones—he is still doing really well, and Engelbert Humperdinck.

PP: Yeah, that's what we talked about.

SP: You know, I don't know. I've read so many times that nobody could help Elvis but himself. What do you think about that?

JS: I think Elvis was very hard to help, because he always thought of himself as the helper, and he liked that. But if you really, on rare occasions, and you knew what you were talking about, and you really went on one-on-one with him, and were honest with him, you could, you know, help. But it was very rare, and you picked your time, and he didn't need help all the time. But that was his role—he helped, and it was hard, very hard. Because what happened is, he had done so much for us and helped us and shared his career and his life and everything with us, and then for us to go to say, "Well, I want to talk to you about this problem," it was very hard for him to accept. And I understood, and it was very hard to have that conversation.

SP: Joe Esposito said to me the other week that you know Elvis was really great at solving other people's problems and giving advice, but he used to bottle up a lot himself.

JS: No, that's true.

PP: Well, also as I said before at the end—Jerry was gone, Joe wasn't there, he lived here, we were

TOP: Jerry, during his interview with Shelly; ABOVE: Publicity still from *Stay Away, Joe* of 1968.

21

"Jerry was gone, Joe wasn't there, he lived here, we were all gone. He had a bunch of young kids with him; he had nobody left to play with, you know, he was lonely..."

PATTI PARRY ON ELVIS'S FINAL YEARS

TOP RIGHT: Promo shot of Elvis for the 1958 musical drama *King Creole;* **BELOW:** Elvis Presley with actress Vera Tschechowa.

all gone. He had a bunch of young kids with him; he had nobody left to play with, you know, he was lonely.

JS: He had no... no peers so to speak. No friendship peers.

PP: Exactly. Really. And he was just lonely, and with people that he couldn't enjoy his life with. He couldn't have fun, and I think that was part of it.

SP: How did that happen—that you had all gone? The people that he loved so much.

JS: Well I think, ya know... lifestyle changes, you know. That's what Elvis told me... basically Sonny and Red had nothing in common anymore. I just think it was a terrible rough time for Elvis. There were three major things going on in his life, he didn't like the idea of turning forty.

SP: Really?

JS: No, and if he could have gotten through that, he would have been a great looking sixty-year-old, seventy-year-old guy. He didn't like that. I think he had major regrets about losing his family. This guy, he worked hard. I mean, artists today could not and do not work hard like Elvis did. He started basically as a kid. I mean if you look at 1956 and go day by day, it's amazing, and then when he's in Vegas two shows a night—he worked very hard.

SP: Were you with him when he worked two shows a night in Vegas every night?

JS: Yeah.

SP: Did he enjoy that, going out to two shows a night?

JS: Yeah, I think he enjoyed it. I think there was a point, though, where after he had conquered Vegas, and after he had done it for three or four month-long engagements, and he was on to year three... ya know, that's where he wanted to tour overseas. I think there becomes a point where it's not as exciting as it was when he was first doing it.

SP: It kind of loses its appeal a little bit?

JS: He still loved performing every night, but he knew he had a worldwide audience.

SP: There were other people waiting.

JS: Yeah, yeah. I mean he could even see that in Vegas, think he wanted... I know he wanted to travel. I mean look at my conversations with the Colonel, his anger at me and my conversations with Elvis in my book.

SP: So would you say that your relationship with the Colonel was a good one?

JS: Yeah.

SP: It was always a good one?

JS: No [laughs].

SP: I remember in your book, you said you were a little bit wary of the Colonel, and he was always in a rush.

JS: Well, he was intimidating.

SP: Very intimidating.

JS: There are two relationships with the Colonel—there was the relationship during Elvis. The Colonel in a lot of ways was like Elvis—he had held his own... You had to kind of prove your loyalty or whatever, and I was loaned out one day a week from Elvis to the Colonel in the studios, so I kind of got to know him and whatever. And I'd be going, "God, I'm going to have to be loaned out to the Colonel—breakfast at seven o'clock," and that type of stuff, but I always enjoyed it. The Colonel was very interesting to be around. I really liked him a lot. He's not this typical carney; he was not a guy with foul language.

SP: He was a gentleman?

JS: He was a gentleman. He was a gentleman in a disguise. The Colonel was a gentleman... he was honest, he was brilliant.

SP: Do you think he had Elvis's best interest at heart?

JS: I do think so. I think from his perspective, I know he had Elvis's best interest at heart. I think the only problem, I think there was a period later on where Elvis outgrew him. He wanted to play the drunk in a *Star Is Born,* the washed-up drunk, and I don't think the Colonel saw him that way. And when Elvis wanted to do the '68 comeback special, ya know, and the Colonel wanted it to be a Christmas show, and I don't think you can blame the guy for his taste and what he thought was best.

SP: Was it because of his era?

JS: Yeah, a big part of it. And then there's the relationship with the Colonel after Elvis. I was probably, according to his wife, the closest guy to him. I would talk to him almost every day. That relationship went from where he didn't speak to me

for a year, which was pretty cruel, where a new guy came on and came up, and said, "Colonel"... and he gave him that stare... and he said, "You gotta break him in Jerry." *[Laughing]* I miss the man tremendously. I have a certain love for the guy.

SP: Nice to hear.

JS: People who really knew him, like Joe Esposito, Ed. That really spent time with him. Could he be intimidating? Yes, he could. Could he be overbearing? Yes. Could he be manipulative? Yes. But damn it—it was all honest.

PP: When I brought my parents for the first time to Las Vegas, and I brought them backstage, he walked over to my mom and dad and introduced himself. Now, he didn't really hang out with us at the house, but he was a nice, nice man. Business was business.

SP: He had a really good business head on his shoulders didn't he? I mean he made some mistakes, bad decisions.

JS: Long-term creative decisions.

SP: Wasn't there another film... *West Side Story*?

PP: No!

JS: This is my interview *[laughing]*.

PP: I forget. I'm sorry.

JS: I've just been hearing that like the last few

TOP: Jerry, left, stands with Priscilla Presley, Olivia DeJonge, Austin Butler, and Baz Luhrmann, Cannes Film Festival 2022; **ABOVE:** Deborah Walley, Joe Esposito, Larry Geller, and Jerry Schilling flank Elvis on his 1966 Harley-Davidson FLH Electra-Glide in Cornell, California, circa spring 1966.

ABOVE: Jerry, at left, stands with Baz Luhrmann and Austin Butler in the back row. In front, from left to right are Finley Lockwood, Lisa Marie Presley, Priscilla Presley, Riley Keough, and Harper Lockwood at a handprints ceremony to celebrate the film *Elvis* at TCL Chinese theatre in Los Angeles, California, June 21, 2022.

years, but I think I would have heard about this from Elvis.

SP: So this is just one of those things?

JS: Yeah. It's a fun story. I like it—but I don't think it's true.

SP: I can imagine him in *West Side Story*. He would have been fantastic in it.

JS: He would have been fantastic in anything.

SP: He was a natural-born actor, he was. It was just the roles he was given.

JS: You know he had some good roles.

SP: *Love Me Tender, King Creole*, and I also loved his last movie *Change of Habit*. It was a bit cheesy in parts, but I loved Elvis in that movie.

JS: Oh, Elvis could make anything look good, almost anything. There are certain things that he would be the first one to say... and he did. And I have it on tape saying that Hollywood never got who he was. I have his voice on my audio book saying that... right from the horse's mouth.

SP: So you have an audio book?

JS: Yes. It's on tantor.com. Tantor is one of the big audio book companies.

SP: I'll check that out. I'd love to listen to that. Now, I've booked to go on this Elvis cruise.

JS: The one I'm hosting?

SP: Yes.

JS: You're kidding!

SP: I've got one of those lovely suites.

JS: That's funny. What I've been doing is my future contracts all morning.

SP: Yeah, I'm so excited!

JS: It's gonna be huge.

SP: I've been looking at this on the internet, and it sounds fantastic.

JS: Yeah, we are going to have the TCB band, the Jordanaires, the Imperials, and Ruby Wilson—she's the queen of Beale Street.

SP: I was trying to get Ed Bonja, to come but he says he gets seasick. Are you coming Patti?

PP: I've not been invited.

SP: Well, you can go... I'm inviting you. I just want to ask you about Priscilla. You were very close to Priscilla, were you not?

JS: I still am.

SP: I was just going to say that, yes, and you still are. You're still very good friends. I love Priscilla. I've never met her, but I'm really looking forward to meeting her. I really admire her. She's a wonderful lady, and I think she's done a lot for Elvis Presley's memory.

JS: More so than people realize, I've had the opportunity on a day-to-day basis to work with her in many capacities. I was on the board of Elvis Presley Enterprises for years. Elvis would be big without any of us, without Priscilla, whatever, but to an extent, if you don't have an organization, if she hadn't opened up Graceland. It seems like very together today, but it was very controversial at the time, and everybody thought it would last six months.

SP: She was very nervous about it wasn't she?

JS: Of course, She wanted to make sure it was all in the spirit of Elvis; she wanted it to be successful. Her main motivation, she wanted to keep Graceland until Lisa was of age. She felt her father wanted her to have that. She learned a lot; she made a lot of the right decisions. She cared about everything, from what color were the original carpets. She talked to me and Joe and asked, "What do you think? I'd love to show the house to people, and here are the circumstances." And I think she is the lady of rock 'n' roll.

SP: That's beautiful. That's a really lovely sentiment, and I've never heard that before.

JP: *[Laughs]* Well, I've never said that before.

SP: I'm glad you've said that to me, Jerry.

SP: Well, I don't want to take up more of your time, but where do you think it's going to go from here with the whole Elvis legacy? We're all not going to be around forever.

JS: We're not?

SP: No. It's a shame, isn't it? Say years from now, where do you see Graceland and Elvis, where do you see things?

JS: There will be certain times when it will be larger than other times, but what I'm seeing with CKX [majority owner of Elvis Presley Enterprises] buying the 85 percent of the image and likeness, is I'm looking at some of the long-term things that he is planning. I think we are just on the brink in the next few years of Elvis reaching a higher level with the Cirque show and Vegas. There will be traveling shows; there are other projects that are in the works.

SP: So you think that CKX is a good thing, a good move?

JS: I will say this: if I had my choice for my friend's image and likeness to be in somebody's hands, I would prefer the family. If the family want to take it to another level, I would say they made the right choice in Robert Sillerman, because he has the expertise, the knowledge, the connections, the property—he knows what to do with the brand name... Yeah, I think that's how I would answer that. *[Note: Sillerman died in 2019].*

SP: And you did it very well.

OK, Final question: When you think about Elvis, how do you like to remember him?

JS: Sitting up late at night, sitting about, like talking about nothing, everything. If somebody said, "Look, if you had one thing, one wish, one night left in life, what would you do?" it would be nothing, but sit around talking with him, like we did so many nights.

SP: If you could go back to one day, is there a particular day you would go back to?

JS: No, no... there were too many... to pick one just wouldn't cut it. *[Jerry turns to Patti, and says, "Are you okay, hon?" as Patti becomes quite emotional.]*

PP: The one day was when he met me. Every minute, every hour, every day, my life was Elvis's. I'm sorry.

JS: Yeah. Patti was very instrumental in the whole thing. One of the few people out here that was. Once he trusted you, it was total. There were no secrets. That's pretty good.

SP: You were all very privileged, but then, so was he to have such wonderful friends.

JS: You know I think so. I don't want it to be imbalanced on the friendship level—on the creative level, it was way-y-y unbalanced. I mean this guy was... he was a giant. Even on the friendship level, he was a bigger guy than me, I gotta tell ya. He had the choice, pretty cool.

SP: Well, Jerry, thank you so much for allowing me to take up some of your time for Elvis International. I will be looking forward to listening to your audio book.

JS: If I have it in my gym bag, I'll pull it out.

SP: And thank you, Patti.

PP: You're welcome, doll.

SP: Thank you from the bottom of my heart—to both of you.

JS: Well, thank you. You did a great interview. I'm glad you weren't prepared.

SP: I'm quite proud of myself, actually. I was thinking when you arrived, "Oh my goodness, I have nothing prepared for Jerry Schilling!"

JS: It's unusual that I get to do interviews with such a beautiful girl.

PP: Are you talking about me? *[Laughing]*

SP: Thank you so much, Jerry. It's not often I get to sit with such a hunk like yourself!

ABOVE: Shelly Powers during her interview with Jerry.

ELVIS
REMEMBERED

"Elvis is a truly great vocalist, and you can hear why on this song. His phrasing, his use of echo, it's all so beautiful. It's the way he sings it, too. As if he's singing it from the depths of Hell. It's a perfect example of a singer being in command of the song."

Paul McCartney

On "HEARTBREAK HOTEL"

27

"He said to me once, 'Do you think the fans will remember me when I've gone,' and I said, 'What do you mean? Of course, they'll remember you!' And I'm not the only person he said that to, and I know he would be very surprised if he could look down, and he'd say, 'Wow! What's all the fuss about!'"

CYNTHIA PEPPER ON ELVIS

INTERVIEW **TWO**

Cynthia Pepper

Cynthia Pepper starred in the movie *Kissin' Cousins* as PFC Midge Reilly opposite Elvis in 1964—a role she didn't even have to audition for. These days, Cynthia resides in Las Vegas and is often invited to Memphis by Elvis Presley Enterprises to meet and greet Elvis fans, sign photos, and give talks about her experience working opposite The King.

OPPOSITE: Cynthia reminisces about Elvis, taken during the interview.

Interviewing Cynthia...

The interview with Cynthia Pepper took place at the home I shared with my then-husband, Eddie, which displayed floor-to-ceiling Elvis memorabilia. Her reaction was one of shock and delight; she thought it was all wonderful. Sitting down with Cynthia and chatting about Elvis over a cup of English tea felt like chatting with an old school pal. She clearly had a genuine respect and admiration for this man and freely shared her memories of working on the set of *Kissin' Cousins* as the character of Midge.

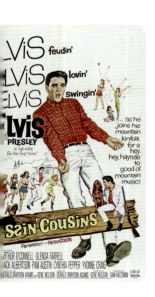

On the whole, I found her to be a very sweet lady—cute as a button, full of fun—and I quickly discovered that she had a cheeky side to her that surfaced when we talked about the kissing scenes with Elvis. Cynthia was the type of person that I would call a friend, and I am so grateful for meeting her—we did become friends and are still friends to this day. Cynthia was four years old when she landed her first role on Broadway. Both her parents were in show business: her mother was a dancer and showgirl and her father a singer/entertainer, who knew a lot of people in the show business world, including Bob Hope, who was a good buddy at the time. His other connections proved fruitful, too, including a friend who worked on the set of the 1956 film *Giant,* starring Rock Hudson and

Elizabeth Taylor. One day, in September of 1955, her dad called her and said, "Hey, honey, I've got someone who wants to talk to you." This someone got on the phone, and said, "Hi, is this Cynthia?" She replied yes, and then she heard, "Well this is James Dean, and I just want to wish you a happy birthday!" He then asked, "How old are you?" She told him fifteen, so he said, "Well, happy birthday!" Two weeks later, Dean was gone, killed in a fatal car accident. Later in life, when Cynthia landed her role in *Kissin' Cousins,* she relayed this story to Elvis, as she knew he loved James Dean and even emulated him. Elvis was blown away that she actually got to speak with this icon. It was an absolute joy to interview Cynthia—we giggled and cooed over Elvis like two lovestruck teenagers, and she made me blush

Soldier Elvis and Country Cousin Elvis forget their differences with some rousing singin' and dancin'.

Metro-Goldwyn-Mayer presents "KISSIN' COUSINS" in Panavision® and Metrocolor

crimson with her coy reply when I tried to find out if she and Elvis had continued kissing after the scenes were cut. Following are some excerpts from my interview with this dear woman.

CP: It's good to be here.

SP: How's the tea?

CP: So good. Thank you.

SP: Okay, so before we get down to business regarding Elvis, can you tell me a bit about yourself, Cynthia—the roles you have had leading up to your part in the Elvis movie?

CP: I was married quite young, and I had small parts in various things, but I did 11 episodes of *My Three Sons* in 1960 . . . that was my first big role. I auditioned for a show called *Margie* on ABC, and I would be the lead, and I got it. It ran from 1961 to 1962.

I was under contract to 20th Century Fox, so I would be loaned out for different things, did a lot of different shows: *Perry Mason, Wagon Train, The Addams Family,* etc. . . . [Cynthia and I then began singing the theme tune to *The Addams Family* and clicking our fingers, where upon we both broke out into fits of giggles. This was what Cynthia was like—a lot of fun to be around!]

So I came home one day, and I remember at that time we had a woman who cleaned for us once a week. I lived in West Hollywood, and she said, "You better get on the phone. Your agent called." (This was in 1964.) I said okay . . . and an actor thinks his last part is his *last* part, and he will *never* work again, and it had been kinda slow, so I called, and my agent said, "Are you sitting down?" I said yes, and he replied, "Well, I want you to go out to the MGM studios. It's for a movie called *Kissin' Cousins,* and if you can wear the uniform, you've

OPPOSITE, TOP: Shelly Powers with Cynthia; **OPPOSITE, LEFT & TOP:** *Kissin' Cousins* promo posters; **ABOVE:** A still from *Kissin' Cousins.*

"He was almost the opposite of Elvis. In other words, Elvis I saw many times offer his seat to a lady. 'Would you care to sit down?'... and I never saw that politeness with the Colonel..."

CYNTHIA PEPPER ON COLONEL TOM PARKER

got a part, costarring with Elvis Presley." And I thought, "Oh My God!" In high school, I'd listened to Elvis records, and I was in love . . . like every other teenage girl. So I ran over there—this was a Friday—and I got the part and was told, okay, we start shooting on Monday, up in Big Bear [*in the San Bernadino Mountains east of Los Angeles*], and I didn't even have to audition.

SP: You didn't have to audition?

CP: No, because what happened was someone told me that Elvis had seen me on something I had done, and they were looking for someone for Midge. And he said she might be right for this part—why don't you check her out.

SP: So actually Elvis had recommended you?

CP: So to speak in a way . . . so when I first met him I thought I was going to faint. He had roses in the dressing room with a note saying, "to Cynthia, Love EP," and right away, I thought, "Oh my gosh, he's got a crush on me!" But you know he didn't—he did that with all leading ladies. He was just so dear when I first met him.

SP: Wow! So tell me what it was like when you first met him?

CP: The morning before we shot, we were introduced, and I said hello, and he said, "Hey, honey," and he gave me a big old hug. And that's the way he was: he made you feel comfortable. From then on, he was; just... I wouldn't say one of the guys, but he didn't stand out as a big shot."

SP: Did he make your knees go weak and your heart beat faster and all that?

CP: Yes, always.

SP: Did you get to spend much time on the set with Elvis?

CP: Well, we only shot for three weeks. Most of the movies were like that, I think. He did thirty-one films in nine years, so it was very quick. I got to know him afterwards, mainly until he started touring. He was quite insecure, I found, because when we were doing the kissing scene, when he sang to me—and it was kind of drizzling that day up in Big Bear—and I'll never forget this either—there's a lull in the shooting, and he said to me "Cynthia," and I said, "Yes, Elvis" . . . can you imagine saying "Yes, Elvis"? Oh my god, when I look back! I said, "What," and he said, "I don't know what I'm doing here, making these films." I said, "What do you mean?"

SP: He kind of opened up to you?

CP: Yeah, and he said, "I should be back home driving a truck." And what can I say to that? And then we started shooting again.

Other things I remember, like I found a cat up there because I'm a big animal lover. I found this stray cat that came to my motel door almost every morning, so I was bound to take it home, and I told some

TOP LEFT: Cynthia in *Margie*, 1962; **ABOVE AND OPPOSITE:** Cynthia with Elvis on *Kissin' Cousins*.

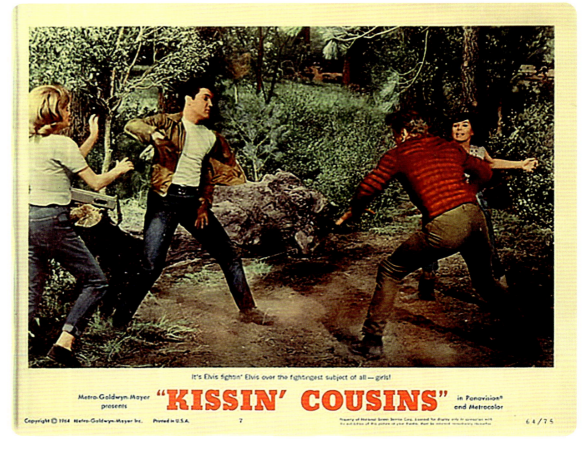

It's Elvis fightin' Elvis over the fightingest subject of all — girls!

Metro-Goldwyn-Mayer presents "KISSIN' COUSINS" in Panavision® and Metrocolor

TOP LEFT: *Kissin' Cousins*;
TOP RIGHT: A promo poster for *Kissin' Cousins*; **ABOVE:** Cynthia, circa 1964.

of the guys, and I told Elvis about it, and he said, "Well, I hope you get it," and we were kind of out there in the woods all looking for this cat, and he's looking for this cat.

SP: Elvis is out there looking for your cat?

CP: Yes, and finally they all found the cat for me, and I was happy. And I got to take it home with me, but I didn't call it Elvis because it was a girl, and I named her Cally, because she was a calico cat.

SP: That is so wonderful—Elvis out there in the woods looking for this cat for you!

SP: I have a question here for you from a dear member of Elvis International, Michael Comley. He wants to ask you, did you prefer the blond Elvis or the dark-haired Elvis?

CP: To be honest, it didn't matter to me. He was just Elvis. I think he looked better with dark hair—I like the blue eyes and dark hair on a lot of people, so yeah on Elvis.

SP: What was it like having Elvis sing "Tender Feeling" to you? I was watching this scene last night, and I was trying to capture how you were actually feeling. If that was me, my legs would turn to jelly.

CP: Well, first place, you're doing a film, and you're a professional, and you have to do what the director says. And then he told me before this scene was shot that I have to kind of look all starry eyed, and now I look back, and I think how silly I look. Also, I had to watch my footing, as I'm walking backwards and thinking where my next move is. I know it's Elvis, but you have to remember what you're doing. Elvis was walking towards me; I had to make sure I didn't trip, and of course when we stopped shooting and were talking that's when I tried to absorb everything he said and his presence.

SP: And that's when the real chemistry starts?

CP: Yeah.

SP: During the filming, there were a cast of other beautiful ladies present. Did you witness any cattiness or jealousy?

CP: No. We all became friendly then, and basically, I wasn't in any of the scenes with the other girls. But we got to know one another, and, no, I didn't see anything like that at all. But, you see, I was isolated, and in the scenes, I was basically with him and a few other people.

SP: So how accessible was Elvis to get to? For

example, could you just go knock on his dressing room door for chat at any time, or was he kind of a private person off set? I mean, you did talk about that earlier . . . how you used to chat, and he opened up to you.

CP: He had his friends around all of the time—his buddies—and you respected anyone's privacy, and he may be going over his lines—he knew everyone's lines. It was a simple movie to do, and, yeah, you would go in and talk, but you wouldn't be invasive, as I wouldn't be with anyone else. But it's been said before: he knew his lines, your lines, and everybody else's lines.

SP: So how close would you say you got to him then. I mean [Cynthia's face changes with this cheeky grin, and we swiftly move on] you became friends, right?

CP: [Cynthia smiles and nods.]

SP: One of our Elvis International members from Down Under wants to know if you could remember what Elvis smelt like?

CP: Brut. He wore Brut cologne. I love Brut—he smelt fresh.

SP: Did you ever get to meet the Colonel [Elvis's manager Colonel Tom Parker]?

CP: I met the Colonel on the set, and I didn't really know him.

SP: How was he?

CP: He was almost the opposite of Elvis. In other words, Elvis I saw many times offer his seat to a lady. "Would you care to sit down?" . . . and I never saw that politeness with the Colonel. But I don't have anything really negative to say about Parker, because I didn't really know him.

SP: Okay.

SP: Now, it's no secret that Elvis dated some of his leading ladies, and the majority of these women just fell under his spell, and indeed some have admitted to falling in love with Elvis. So how was it for you, Cynthia, as a young girl spending time with Elvis, getting up close to him and sharing intimate scenes . . . would you say that you fell in love with him?

CP: Well, you fall in love. I mean you don't *really* fall in love like you do with someone you would marry for the rest of your life. You're infatuated. I was infatuated; I wouldn't say I fell in love.

SP: Did you ever feel after the filming had all finished and ended, when it was all finished, did

you keep thinking about him and wishing that you were back in that situation, or was it more like, well it's all done now?

CP: Well after that film I just kept on working. I worked a lot in the '60s. We kept in touch, but it was going on to the next thing. It's very funny when you're doing a film—and I know it's only three weeks—but when you do a film, and you go away on location, it's a very tight quarters, and you become very friendly. And you become like you're a thousand miles away, so you might do things you wouldn't do if you were at home. That's why some of these show business marriages break up . . . because you're in close proximity to someone who is very attractive and . . . *errr* . . . it can get carried away. So I mean, let's say I had a crush, and that's the best way to put it.

SP: And who didn't! I mean they all had a crush on Elvis Presley.

CP: As a human being, I could say I was in love with him, because he wasn't perfect—obviously—but as a person, he was the best. One of the best.

SP: Was he always a gentleman towards you when you were together?

CP: Yes, always. Always respectful. He called me his "little speckled pup" during rehearsals, so they put

TOP: Magazine cover; **CENTER:** Cynthia in *The Addams Family*; **ABOVE:** Still from the Elvis movie *Kissin' Cousins*.

TOP: Cynthia with Peter Brooks starring in *The Addams Family*; **ABOVE:** Cynthia fronts a magazine cover, 1962; **OPPOSITE:** Cynthia with Elvis in *Kissin' Cousins*.

it in the film. They said, let's put it in the film. I was never the vamp, never the femme fatale, more like the girl next door. Doris Day kind of look.

SP: I'd say so, Cynthia, you're really cute for sure.

CP: We are what we are. It was easier for me growing up in the business. I never had the casting couch thing going on. The only thing is—which was really crazy—the same cast man produced this *Kissin' Cousins*, and he would joke with me in the morning. He was a real card. And his wife was on the set. She was a character, and he would say in the morning, in front of everybody, "Did you have a good sleep?" And I'd say, "Yes." Then he would say, "Well, Cynthia, why didn't you nudge me when you got up?"—*Oh my God*—no way would that happen. But I would be mortified. I was twenty-four years old, for goodness sake, and he would keep doing that. And finally Elvis had had it, and he stepped in, and said, "Don't do that. She's not enjoying that anymore." So he stepped in and stopped it in a nice way.

SP: So Elvis came to your rescue and was almost protective of you, and he could see you were uncomfortable.

CP: Back then, I was mortified. But I would handle it very differently today, as I'm older. Yeah, he kind of came to my rescue.

SP: I remember recently you shared a fab story that involved your gorgeous son. Would you like to relay that story for the members of Elvis International?

CP: Yes . . . well, the story is my son is a grown man now: he lives in Los Angeles, Studio City, and they have a coffee house where they all hang out. Actors, directors, and so forth—they go hang out there and solve the world's problems. Well, my son has never really talked to me about Elvis or my career, so to speak. It's just taken for granted. So he called me up quite a while ago, and he said, "Mom, I want to talk to you about something . . . well, I want to ask

"He wasn't perfect—obviously—but as a person, he was the best. One of the best..."

CYNTHIA PEPPER ON ELVIS

"I could see there was a lot more to him . . . the depth and spirituality and, um, the beauty. He was beautiful. He was, as you know. He was a beautiful man..."

CYNTHIA PEPPER ON ELVIS

THIS PAGE: Cynthia with Elvis in *Kissin' Cousins.*

you something." So I said, "Yes what?" So he said, "Am I Elvis's son?" I said, "WHAT!!!?" Now, this is someone who has never, you know, had an Elvis record or anything. He likes him, but anyway, I said, "Why do you ask?" "We were sitting around the coffee house, and the guys said, "Hey, you got blue eyes and full lips and the time is right," so he said, "Hey, I'm gonna ask my mom." So he said, "I want to ask you two questions: did you have a thing with Elvis, and, the second, am I his son?"

So after I'd picked myself up off the floor, I said, "The first question I won't answer, and the second one—no you're not." And he went on to say, "OHHH . . . gee whizz, it would really be cool. It would be great, and besides Dad wouldn't mind!" I said, "What! I think Dad would mind."

That was the power of Elvis. He's since asked me, and said, "Are you sure?" and I've said, "Drop it. No, you're not!"

SP: Does he resemble Elvis?

CP: Well, he doesn't look like me, and he has blue eyes and full lips, and I could see where someone would think that. And the timing is right. But, no, he's not. It was a shock because it came from him. He said who wouldn't want to be Elvis's son!

SP: Absolutely. Golly . . . I mean Lisa Marie is just the image of him, isn't she?

CP: Oh, I have to tell you a story about that . . . After we had finished shooting, we used to go to a park called West Hollywood Park. It's no longer there— it's a big mall now, and Priscilla and I would sit while Lisa Marie and Michael, my son, would play.

SP: Were you friends with Priscilla?

CP: Well, I'd see her on the set sometimes, but mainly she would be back in Memphis. But she

would come out on the set now and again and later, after the film, a number of times. I'd see her and Lisa Marie at the park. She would come out, and we would talk, and the kids would play. He was about two or three years older than Lisa Marie, and now my son would say, "I don't remember that, Mom, but why didn't you keep in touch?" I said, "Well you don't . . . you don't realize the impact down the road." So they used to play together.

SP: Now during the dance scenes of *Kissin' Cousins*, did you dance? Did you get involved with the dance scenes?

CP: I know how to dance.

SP: Were you always the character Midge in the film? There are scenes where all the girls are dancing. Did you dress up and dance with them?

CP: No. No. I just had the two costumes, and when you do a film they shoot twelve to fourteen hours a day, and by the time they cut it, you might be in this scene and not in this one.

SP: So how many takes were required to complete the first kiss on the ground?

CP: Well, listen . . .

SP: I'm listening . . .

CP: I hadn't done this for quite a while . . . so I kept messing it up.

SP: On purpose?

CP: On purpose. So I could keep doing it . . . enough where I didn't get fired, you know.

SP: You little fox. Do you think Elvis knew?

CP: Yeah, he knew. I'd say, "Am I doing it right." He would say, "Noooo—mess it up again!"

SP: What was your perception of Elvis before

TOP: Cynthia in *Margie*, 1962;
ABOVE: Cynthia in *Kissin'
Cousins*.

you met him and after you met him, as you got
to know him better? And did your perception
change?

CP: Only I didn't know him when I was a teenager—
other than he was a singing idol—and when I got
to know him, I could see there was a lot more to
him . . . the depth and spirituality and, um, the
beauty. He was beautiful. He was, as you know.
He was a beautiful man. What I liked about him
was he didn't think he was special. We all have
different versions of him—like Ed Bonja would have
a different idea of him, because he's a man. I saw
him as someone who was beautiful but didn't flaunt
it and didn't act like the big man. He knew who he
was, but he didn't flaunt it.

**SP: Would you say that Elvis almost had a sort of
low self-esteem? Would you go that far?**

CP: I think Elvis was one of us—this is my opinion.
I think Elvis was born to be who he is—and of
greatness—but I think he also saw himself as a
regular guy. He wasn't perfect, and people who put
him on a pedestal should not do that, because there

is no one perfect.

Like I said before, as a human being, he was one
of the best, he had a good heart. As far as perception, I just got to know him, obviously. I was
comfortable with him, and I didn't feel like I was in
the presence of someone where I was going to faint,
because I knew him. When you know somebody,
the intimidation has gone—if you're intimidated at
all. And I just think that he thought himself as one
of us and a regular guy. It's an unusual life, though.
I can't imagine as they do today, going through
that! You and I can walk down the street; we can do
different things. And they're prisoners. And I think
what happened is he became a prisoner in his life,
and that's sad. He paid a price—they all do who are
in that position, but especially Elvis being so huge,
hugely popular.

**SP: Do you think that it ever bothered Elvis that
he had to sing over the soundtrack?**

CP: Well, he actually sang you know. They do that;
they do the soundtrack with the orchestra, but he
was actually singing to me and everyone else so

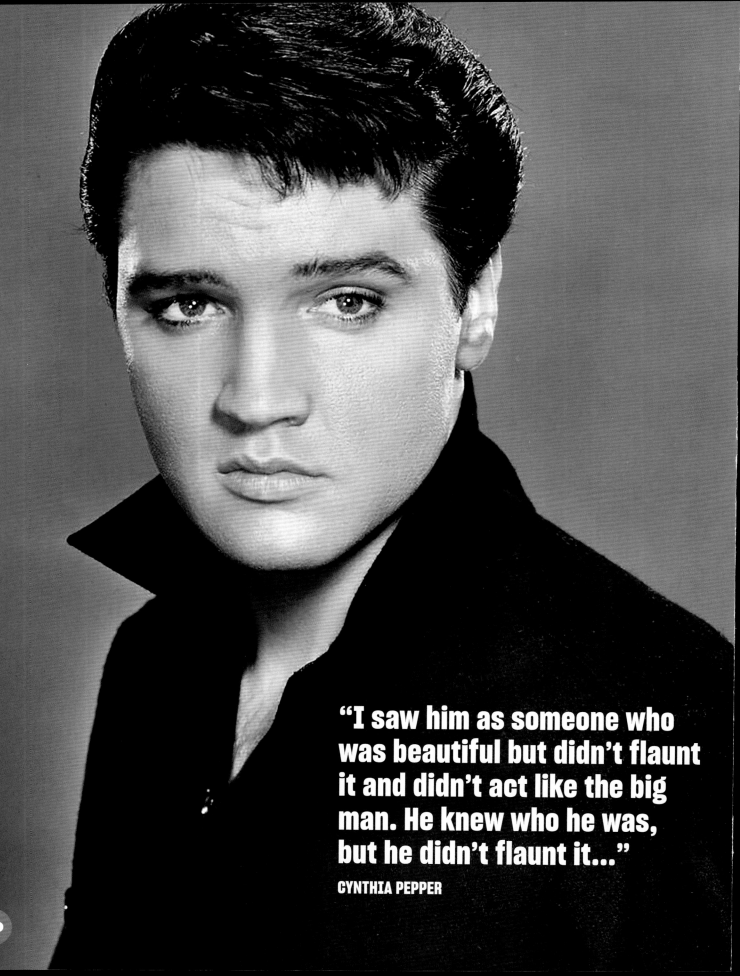

"I saw him as someone who was beautiful but didn't flaunt it and didn't act like the big man. He knew who he was, but he didn't flaunt it..."

CYNTHIA PEPPER

that it would look like he was singing. Because you couldn't do it live in those day, because there was too many distractions. Especially when we were shooting in Big Bear—overhead, like planes, or when the rain came down. And we were out in the Jeep, and we would have to stop, but I never saw Elvis complain about anything. Now maybe he did with his guys, but I never saw that. The star of a film or TV series . . . I believe this . . . sets a tone for the atmosphere, and if they're grumpy or if they're a diva, whatever, then it's not a happy film. But I never saw that. People say he hated his movies, but I never saw that either.

SP: Elvis was known to be a practical joker. Can you remember him pulling any stunts on you during the filming of *Kissin' Cousins*?

CP: Well, we're going back about forty-five years ago. My gosh, he did one, because I had to throw him over my shoulder in the film. In the film, it's so fast, and he taught me how to do that. And we had to rehearse it, and rehearse it, and this one time, we were by ourselves, and he said let's go over this again. And I said okay, so I threw him, and he went out flat, flat on his back with his eyes shut, and I said to myself, "Oh my God, I've killed Elvis. They're gonna shoot me. I'm going to have to leave the country, because I've killed Elvis Presley." And he let me go for what seemed like a long time, but it was about a minute and a half, and I was leaning over him saying, "Elvis! Elvis, are you alright?" and he just lay there! And finally he opened his eyes and said, "I got ya!" And I never figured out how to get him back! He loved to play jokes, and they played them on him also.

SP: In your opinion, what was Elvis's most beautiful feature?

CP: Hmmm . . . his eyes. I'd have to say his eyes. I like eyes, and his skin was beautiful. He had that beautiful skin, but, yes, his eyes . . . blue.

SP: What about his most beautiful personality trait?

CP: Two things: being humble, modest. And kindness. But he also loved to have a good time too. He is almost what you would want for a spouse . . . you know, almost perfect. No one's perfect, but, boy, that's what I want. I mean we all have our demons and things—we are not perfect obviously—but he came pretty close, and he was chosen for this life.

SP: Now, you don't have to answer this question if you don't want, Cynthia...

CP: Oh my God. And, by the way, I don't like that...

you're blushing. She's blushing... It's not a hot flush, is it? Because I get a lot of them. [Lots of laughing.]

SP: Someone [from Elvis International] has sent a question in, and if I don't ask you, she will be very upset. . . . Now Elvis was known to get close to a lot of his leading ladies, so on the set of *Kissin' Cousins* did Elvis ever try to seduce you or you him?

CP: I don't want to answer that. No comment. Not being coy, but no comment, (with a smile) I never kiss and tell.

SP: So we will move swiftly on. . . . What are your views about Elvis as an actor? Do you think he was a good actor?

CP: I think he was a better actor than the movies would let him be. I think he had it in him. He had a raw talent, he wanted to break out, he had the potential, but he never had the opportunity, as we know.

SP: Well, this is the thing—I'm sure that's what made Elvis so frustrated. Because of the roles he was given—all the same character.

CP: It's all about money now. But before—I loved the movies of the thirties and forties, and I think the big studio people knew how to put out the movies and keep stars stars. That's showing my age, but that's how I feel. It's a whole different game now, but they

TOP: Scene from *The Addams Family*; **ABOVE:** Cynthia in *Kissin' Cousins;* **OPPOSITE:** Studio publicity still.

TOP: *Margie*, Cynthia Pepper, Johnny Bangert, Wesley Marie Tackitt, 1961-62; **ABOVE:** Cynthia during interview.

homed them and protected them, and they were very special.

SP: For all the lady members of the Elvis International fan club and myself, tell me a little bit more about the kissing, because his lips looked so soft and inviting. How did you contain yourself?

CP: Well, like I said before, I contained myself as much as I could without getting fired. I wanted to kiss him, and he did have soft lips, as a matter fact. And in those days, they kissed nice. His kiss was very sweet and long. I think each time now, when I think about that, I can't believe it. And I was getting paid for it! I appreciate that part of my life 100 percent more than I did when I was living it. You have your life, and you don't realize the impact Elvis was going to have down the road. Who would have thought? He said to me once, "Do you think the fans will remember me when I've gone," and I said, "What do you mean? Of course, they'll remember you!" And I'm not the only person he said that to, and I know he would be very surprised if he could look down, and he'd say, "Wow! What's all the fuss about!"

SP: Now, acting in the same movie as Elvis

Presley must have been a terrific boost for you. Do you think it helped you in your chosen career?

CP: Honestly, no. But now, it's helped me because the mystique is there. In the sixties and early seventies, I did a lot of work, but it wasn't like, "Oh, she did an Elvis movie, so let her do this." No . . . but now it's a bigger impact. You have to remember in '64, he was a big star, but the Beatles were coming in, and so he was concerned about that, and he wasn't the big, huge icon that he is now. So all I have to do now is mention Elvis to people, and the doors open in a positive way.

SP: Were you shocked when you heard that Elvis had left this world and was no longer with us?

CP: Yes. I was up in San Francisco. My ex-husband and my son, and we were on the freeway with some friends, and we had the radio on. And I was completely shocked. People didn't know how sick he was. I certainly didn't know how ill he was, and I couldn't believe it. He has touched so many people's lives, and I hope it'll go on and on.

SP: Fun question for you. If you could have starred in any film with Elvis as his leading lady, what movie would it be?

CP: I think *Casablanca,* because it's such a classic, such a love story . . . even though she went off with her husband, and he knew that was best, and we are little specks in the world. That love from afar—I think that's very romantic—and that longing that you know you can't be with that person. I could be Ingrid Bergman.

SP: If they were to create a film about Elvis's life, who do you think should play Elvis, and why?

CP: You know I think because of the looks, Brad Pitt. Because of his popularity, his acting talents, and he could look like him . . . I mean that essence. So, yes, Brad Pitt.

SP: Do you have a favorite Elvis song?

CP: Yes, I do. "I Remember You." People don't sing it often, but I love that song—I just love it.

SP: What do you miss most about Elvis Presley, and how do you like to remember him?

CP: I miss that he's not here. I miss that he's not around, and we can't call him or see him perform. I miss his presence. I miss him not being here on this earth. I feel honored to have known someone like him. It's almost unbelievable when you think about it, as there are not many of us left who knew him. He was special . . . but what was special about him was that he didn't think he was special . . . and that made him special.

A huge thank you to Cynthia Pepper for taking part in the interview, a very special lady that I love dearly.

ELVIS
REMEMBERED

"I never saw Elvis perform 'Sweet Caroline.' I did see him perform live in Vegas, I had never seen him before. You know, he was Elvis Presley, and I was awed. He was an amazing, amazing live performer.

He was electric and he was wonderful and halfway through his show, he introduced me. I was in the audience and he introduced me and it's like worshipping a god and that god is saying, 'Oh, stand up. I like this person. World, why don't you meet him?' My God. So I stood up and the audience started to cheer and they started to say, 'Get up on stage. You know, sing together.' No, I couldn't possibly. It's - and he saw I was uncomfortable with it. He said, 'Well, he's on holiday now, so leave him alone. Let him enjoy the show.' And they did."

Neil Diamond

"He said, 'Pull over,' and that one minute in time changed my whole life. We bonded, and it changed my whole life..."

PATTI PARRY ON HER FIRST ENCOUNTER WITH ELVIS PRESLEY

INTERVIEW **THREE**

Patti Parry

Patti Parry spent 17 years being a little sister to Elvis and was sometimes noted as being the only female member of the "Memphis Mafia." In fact, Patti was one of a small number of girls who hung out with Elvis and the guys for many years in L.A. from the time they were young in the early 1960s.

OPPOSITE: A portrait of Patti, taken during the interview.

Interviewing Patti...

I instantly liked Patti the first time I met her. She made me feel welcome from the minute I walked through the door. She had an edge to her that could be misconstrued as brusque, however; but I quickly realized that this impression may have had something to do with her being the only female member of the Memphis Mafia and spending years in the company of a group of men and Elvis himself.

TOP: Patti with Shelly; **ABOVE:** Patt during her interview; **OPPOSITE:** Patti with Elvis.

The interview took place at her home in Los Angeles, just off Sunset Boulevard. Ed Bonja escorted me to Patti's home, and I brought along our own wonderful Elvis International photographer, Rudy Aveytia, who captured some brilliant shots during all the interviews I held for the fan club. Patti, who suffered from Crohn's disease, looked healthy and well-groomed and was in good spirits, for the most part. During the interview we laughed a lot—she didn't take herself too seriously, only when it came to Elvis. Patti was fearlessly protective of her friend's name. After the interview with Patti had finished, along with the interview with Jerry Schilling (Jerry had showed up at Patti's house that day), she kindly drove me around to some of the places where Elvis once lived and hung out. His house in

Palm Springs, the beautiful retreat Lake Shrine in the Pacific Palisades, where he would visit and seek sanctuary in the garden while he prayed in silence. We finished our little tour, and on Patti's recommendation, we sampled one of the best hot dogs on Sunset Boulevard. It was a fantastic day—moving and by far one of the most amusing interviews I have held and one I will never forget.

Patti and I became friends after this, and we remained in touch. Patti was a straight shooter— very funny, witty with a dry sense of humor. She had the ability to make you laugh long and hard, but she never minced her words, and if Patti wasn't happy with you, she would let you have it and didn't hold back! Sadly, we lost Patti in 2011. I miss her, but I'm pretty sure she's happy now and at peace somewhere in the afterlife,

ABOVE: Some of Patti's souvenirs, including a personal, handwritten note from Elvis.

joking around and hanging out with her dear friend Elvis. I will never forget the time I was meant to meet up with Patti for dinner after the Larry Geller interview had finished. I gave her a rough estimate of time, and she booked a couple of tables. I hadn't planned on Larry's interview going on for as long as it did. Larry... can talk the hind legs off a donkey. It was a great interview but it ran way over schedule. I think Patti must have called at least three times... to see what I was up to, but I couldn't just drop everything and wrap it up as Larry was still talking about his friend Elvis. By the time we arrived at the restaurant Patti was fit to be tied and not happy with me at all. She blew a fuse because I had kept her waiting for so long. Of course I was apologizing profusely, but she was having none of it. I was so exhausted from the extended interview that I broke down in tears, and even then she was still mad at me. There was a large group of people for that meal and Patti refused to sit at my table. I learned that if you made arrangements with Patti Parry, you better not be late. Like she told me, she was Elvis's little sister, and she waited for no one. This may give the impression that Patti was high maintenance, but

she wasn't. She was a great lady, and I loved her company and all her little quirks. Later that night Patti called me and her demeanor had completely softened. She apologized to me and I instantly forgave her. You couldn't help but love Patti, and you knew exactly where you stood with her at all times. You could count on her, she wouldn't let you down, and she expected the same in return if you were her friend.

I will never forget on one visit to her home she told me she had something special to show me. Patti retreated to her bedroom and soon returned carrying a small box. Inside the box was a ring made up of a thick platinum band that held two huge pear-shaped diamonds. I cannot even imagine how many carats those diamonds were but she placed it in my hand to hold and said, "Elvis gave me this ring. He was so generous he always gave his friends beautiful gifts." The ring was heavy in weight and as I admired it, and thought about the fact that Elvis had chosen this ring for Patti, the hairs on the back of my neck stood up, and I tell you this, at the moment I felt another presence in the room right next to me. I looked up at Patti, and it was if she knew what

"The first time I cut his hair—well Larry Geller was his hairdresser—but that's another story. The first time I cut his hair he gave me $750. I threw it back in his face, and I said, 'You give me gifts every day. I'm not taking your money.' I loved the man, and he loved me…"

PATTI PARRY ON ELVIS

I was thinking, for as I made her aware of my feelings, Patti's nonchalant reply was, "Girl, Elvis comes to see me all the time. He talks to me, you know, what can I say?… I was his little sister."

Sometimes during the early hours of the morning while I was still sleeping I would be awoken with a phone call from Patti. She would start the conversation with, "Hey, girl, are you awake?" and my response would be, "Well, I am now, Patti."

Patti would love to talk, she was quite lonely at times, especially during the evening, so she often wanted to reminisce about her brother Elvis—she would refer to him as "her brother always"—and there seemed to be a deep sadness to Patti at times that I could feel because of the loss of her friend. She genuinely loved and missed Elvis greatly. He was her world, and when Elvis passed it left a huge void in Patti's life.

When I think of Patti I smile, the memory of her and me walking along Santa Monica promenade on a hot sunny day, sipping from her bottle of "Patti water" as she called it (and if you were a friend of Patti's you will know what I'm referring to), talking on the phone late at night for over an hour about her friend and life in general until I had to say, "Patti, I need to sleep, darling."

SP: So, let's start off at the very beginning. Just tell me every little detail about the day you met Elvis

Presley for the very first time all those years ago.

PP: It was November of 1960. I was with a girlfriend, and we were in an old clunker Buick driving down Santa Monica Boulevard. We were going to a fraternity party, and we were driving down, and we saw a black Rolls Royce, and I said, "Let's go see who's in that Rolls Royce." We pulled up, and I said, "That's Elvis Presley! Let's pretend we don't know who it is." He was actually on his way to go record "Flaming Star." So we pulled up next to him, and I was very attractive in those days. He said, "Hey, girls." And I said, "Gee, you look familiar. Do I know you from somewhere?" And he knew we knew who he was, so he said, "Pull over."

SP: He told you to pull over?

PP: He said, "Pull over," and that one minute in time changed my whole life. We bonded, and it changed my whole life. We laughed you know, because I was funny. He said, "You gotta come up to the house. I'll send a limo to pick you up." So I said, "Are you crazy! My parents would kill me." So he said, "Well, call, and I'll meet you at the Bel Air gate." So that

TOP LEFT: Patti during her interview; **ABOVE:** Patti with Ed Bonja and Shelly.

ABOVE: Elvis with Patti (right) and Linda Thompson center. Circa 1973.

was the next day.

SP: So you were really cool?

PP: Well, yeah. I wasn't an Elvis fan.

SP: So he asked you to come up to his house!

PP: Well, we just bonded, ya know—our personalities bonded.

SP: So you were totally relaxed with him?

PP: Yeah, I didn't care, you know. And so anyways, the next day, I went up to the gate, and there was an east gate and a west gate, and I went to the wrong gate, naturally. We were waiting, and my friend said, "They're not coming, they're not coming." Then all of a sudden, this big white limo pulls up, and it's Charlie Hodge. He says, "You're at the wrong damn gate." So then he took me to the house— there was no party, just Elvis and a bunch of guys, [Joe] Esposito, Charlie Hodge... can't remember who else... and then Elvis takes me on a tour of his house. But I'm like seventeen, a nice little virgin, and that's all he needed to hear because after that

day, I was his little sister. Nobody could come near me; nobody could touch me. Later, when I was in my thirties, and guys would hit on me, he would say, "Patti doesn't fool around." And I'd say, "Elvis, I fool around!" It's true. He would be on stage with Joe Gercio, and he would say, "There she is Joe. You can't have her." He totally protected me.

SP: Sounds like he was very protective of you [laughing].

PP: Well, his mom had passed. He didn't have a little sister, so I became his little sister. I told him the truth you know; I was honest with him.

SP: He trusted you.

PP: The first time I cut his hair—well Larry Geller was his hairdresser—but that's another story. The first time I cut his hair he gave me $750. I threw it back in his face, and I said, "You give me gifts every day. I'm not taking your money." I loved the man, and he loved me.

SP: Can you remember how he looked that day when you saw him?

PP: He looked bloody gorgeous. He was a handsome man. There never was and never will be anybody that looked like Elvis Presley, sang like Elvis Presley, or was as generous to his fans and family like Elvis Presley was. He was an incredible human being.

SP: Now, like we said, Patti, you were known as his little sister and one of the boys—not that you resembled one of the boys.

PP: Well, the girls or wives knew me as one of the boys.

SP: How did that come about?

PP: I don't know. Those boys brought me up, ya know. That's why I have a such a big mouth! I was seventeen. I gave up my life to these guys—seven guys and me—you know, and it changed my life.

SP: You must have been attracted to Elvis at some point. There isn't any woman around that I know who doesn't find Elvis attractive, okay. So were you and Elvis ever more than just friends? Didn't you say that he was the best kisser? Or was this just hearsay?

PP: Oh, he was a great kisser! He gave wet kisses. Elvis was my brother ya know.

SP: He gave you wet kisses?

PP: Well, when he gave you a little kiss, they would be wet kisses.

SP: Yeah?

PP: Let me explain something to you. Elvis was a nineteen-year-old truck driver over in Memphis, and overnight, he became a super, superstar, a super stud. He was a nineteen-year-old truck driver; he didn't know how to deal with this life either. That's why he had us around him; that's why we were there. That's why I was there to look after him, rub his back, cut his toenails. He didn't know how to deal with that stuff, you know; you have to realize Presley was a prisoner of his own fame. He had us all around him because he was lonely. We all had great times with him; we all had great fun. He trusted everybody; we were his secret society, basically, behind closed doors, but me being attracted to Elvis? He was gorgeous. I was cutting his toenails, but I'm not going to have sex with him. He was my brother, you know—he was my brother. He was gorgeous.

SP: You could appreciate his beauty but...

ABOVE: Memorabilia adorns the shelves in Patti's home.

PP: Let me tell you something—I wasn't as beautiful as those girls he dated. I wasn't stupid—I was his sister. He loved me. When I see all those girls, they would jump on me, they would hug me and kiss me—they know I was his sister, and they had no problem with me at all.

SP: Elvis was known to be a joker. Did he play many practical jokes on you, Patti?

PP: No, darling. He never played any practical jokes on me. I would have killed him. He played them on a lot of the guys, in Vegas, especially. You have to remember we would go from the suite to the show, from the suite to the show. We couldn't do anything! He was a prisoner of his own fame, so we played jokes, you know. Debbie Reynolds' brother, they put a snake in his trailer and closed the door because they knew he was afraid of snakes—stuff like that—but he played practical jokes mainly on the movie sets. [Laughing]

SP: So what was the atmosphere like at Graceland

ABOVE: Shelly and Patti chatting before the interview; **OPPOSITE:** Elvis Presley in concert at the Fox Theater, Detroit, Michigan, May 25, 1956.

"Elvis was a wonderful, wonderful son. A wonderful friend. He was a wonderful grandson. He was good boy! Nobody else like him in the world..."

PATTI PARRY ON ELVIS

in the early days? Did you hang out there quite a bit? Was it a fun place to be?

PP: I have to tell you, though, the only time I went to Graceland was at Christmas.

SP: Really?

PP: Elvis lived here, he lived here, and I'm going to show you some of his houses today. He lived on Perugia Way, Hillcrest, and Rocco Place, but Elvis said, "Patti, do you wanna come to Graceland for Christmas?" I said, "I'd love to come to Graceland for Christmas." So I went there, and it was pristine. It was beautiful—there was the church next door that was called Graceland. There was nothing around—there was Highway 51 South; it was gorgeous, but nothing around. So we went in there, and it was so cool, and every morning we would get up, and he would take me down to see his Grandma Dodger to say hello... every morning. Elvis was a wonderful, wonderful son. A wonderful friend. He was a wonderful grandson. He was good boy! Nobody else like him in the world. He had monitors all around the house. I slept in that big, round, fuzzy bed that they show at Graceland, but they have monitors there, so I had to get dressed in the closet. [We all crack up laughing.] He loved being there; he just loved being there. That was his home, but I just went there for Christmases.

"Steve Bender said, 'I want him to do it a Christmas special,' and Elvis said, 'I want to do it my way.' And, honey, he did it his way…"

PATTI PARRY ON ELVIS'S SUPPRESSED TALENT

SP: So how was Elvis just before he was about to go on tour? What was his demeanor like? Was he excited about another tour? What was it like being on tour with Elvis? Did you go along sometimes?

PP: Well, I was there for the '68 special. I met Elvis when he was doing the movies. He was doing the movies, but he really didn't care for the movies. He said, "They got me singing to animals and little kids, you know?" He would come home, and it would really frustrate him. The most excited I ever saw him get was, first of all, when he did that Famous Young Man thing. He practiced that speech over and over again, and when he went on stage, he stuttered—you know Elvis stuttered a little bit—and then the '68 special, he was really excited about that, because he wanted to get back in front of an audience—that's what he loved to do. He needed to be in front of an audience, and they wanted it to be a Christmas special, but they changed their minds, and Steve Bender said, "I want him to do it a Christmas special," and Elvis said, "I want to do it my way." And, honey, he did it his way. And who else dressed like that? He dressed in black leather—it was '68, and I went there with Priscilla and Joe Esposito's wife and Jerry Schilling's first wife, and they said, "Go sit next to him on the stage," because he was nervous. And that's my picture right there sat next to him [Patti motions to a photo of Elvis on her shelf unit]. I looked good. I was twenty-five years old…

take me back; I wanna go back, baby." [We all start laughing.]

SP: I have to look out for you in that. Can we see you at the front of the stage?

PP: Do you have the DVD?

SP: Yes, of course I do.

PP: Okay, the second show, the outtakes, I'm all over it. When he's singing "Baby, trying to get to you," I'm there, but I look good. I was twenty-five years old, God dammit! Anyway, he was most excited about that show, and that show was amazing. And then we started Las Vegas. I worked—I would never go on payroll. I wanted to have my own life, but

ABOVE: Elvis portrait; **TOP RIGHT:** Patti (in white) at the Elvis Comeback Special.

"And who else dressed like that? He dressed in black leather—it was '68, and I went there with Priscilla and Joe Esposito's wife and Jerry Schilling's first wife, and they said, 'Go sit next to him on the stage,' because he was nervous. And that's my picture right there sat next to him…"

PATTI PARRY ON ELVIS

ABOVE: Elvis enjoying a joke on set.

my life was Elvis. But every day after work, I would go there. I'd have dinner and about one o'clock he would have one of the guys follow me home.

SP: To make sure you got home okay?

PP: Yeah. He was very good—a good boy—and every weekend, wherever he was—Palm Springs, Vegas—I would fly in, and I had the best time.

SP: Amazing! I bet you look back, and you just can't believe it all.

PP: I can't believe he's gone. I can't believe it all happened, but let me tell you something—that changed my life. I have no children: I gave up my life to Elvis Presley, but it was worth it. I have no kids, no kids, you know, but it was worth every minute.

SP: You have family and kids in your friends. People who love you... there's one big kid sat over there [referring to Ed Bonja, who was sitting in an armchair listening to the interview].

PP: But you have to realize, you know, Elvis Presley he was a phenomenon—everybody that he touched, everybody he touched, clung to him. He was a special man; he was a baby boy, he talked baby talk, and he needed his friends, and I was the only girl, and I was so lucky. Let me tell you something, as I say, Priscilla and all the girls, they know that I was his sister... they knew I was his little sister. They never had any confrontation with me: there was no competition. They would walk in, and say, "Who is this girl," and they would say, "That's Patti. She's part of the family," and I was. Seventeen years was a long time. I was seventeen and with him 'til the day he died. I was with him for seventeen years, until the day he died. I got the call here that morning when he passed, and I called Jerry Schilling, and that was the worst day of my life.

SP: You did? So he didn't know. We will go to that in a minute.

"Priscilla was a lovely, lovely girl. I was there the day that he brought her to California. We used to have parties at the house, and he said listen, 'I'm bringing this little girl, so the parties are going to stop'..."

PATTI PARRY ON PRISCILLA

PP: No. And I talked to Elvis on the phone the day before, but I wasn't with him when he passed... worst day of my life. Am I doing good?

SP: You're doing great, Patti. Fantastic.

PP: Now let me tell you something... I'm just Patti. I was lucky to be with Elvis, but this is all about Elvis Presley. None of us—not Jerry Schilling, not Joe Esposito, Sonny West, and all those guys—none of us would be ever recorded. The man has been dead for thirty years—it's all because of Elvis Presley. And when anyone gets into any arguments, I say it's not you, it's Elvis Presley.

SP: I'm so glad you said that.

PP: Thank you.

SP: I couldn't agree more.

PP: And also, all you guys, you know, here I go! Isn't it amazing. It's thirty years he's gone. He's bigger now than he ever was. Bless his heart!

SP: [Laughing] She's on one now!

PP: I mean, bless his heart, ya know? His memory will never die, and we are dwindling you know. My Memphis Mafia are dying you know, and the young people, the tribute artists, whether they are good or bad, I say thank you. They are honoring my friend. They're all keeping his memory alive.

SP: Absolutely, I agree. They really do, and the majority of them are doing it because they love Elvis.

PP: There are a few idiots, though.

SP: I know.

PP: Well, you married one! Some who are a few idiots.

SP: Yeah. I've seen a few down at the Mardi Gras.

PP: Yeah, there are a few idiots, and if they put Elvis Presley down, I lay there. Butt out, man. And the other guys know me; they would hold me back, and I'd say, "Don't you talk about my friend. Don't you ever say anything bad about Elvis Presley." I say to them, "If it wasn't for Elvis, you wouldn't be here, so don't you ever say anything bad about Elvis! Not in front of me!"

SP: What did you think of Dodger [Elvis's grandmother]? Did you spend much time with Dodger?

PP: No, Dodger was an old lady. I spent time with... what's her name?

SP: Aunt Delta?

PP: Yeah, Aunt Delta. I mean Elvis would get up at five. I would get up at ten in the morning when I was in LA. So I would hang out with Aunt Delta, her dogs, and the cooks.

SP: I bet that was fun.

PP: Yeah, they made me grits. I never had grits in my life, I came back here to Beverly Hills, and I said do you have grits? They were like, "What?" And they made me red-eyed gravy.

SP: Southern food.

PP: Yeah, but sometimes Elvis wouldn't get up until the afternoon.

SP: Were you not originally from England, Patti?

PP: Yeah, I was. Then I came here in 1954 on the QE 1. I was eleven.

SP: Eleven years old?

PP: Eleven when I moved from England to California, and when I was seventeen, I met Elvis.

SP: And you never looked back, and how your life changed! Did you ever think when you boarded that ship that your life would change so drastically?

PP: When I boarded that ship, I thought I was going to see cowboys and Indians. That's all we ever saw in England, remember? I remember Muffin the Mule and The Flower Pot Men.

SP: You remember The Flower Pot Men? [Laughing.] Andy Pandy? Little Weed in the Flower Pot Men! [At this point, Patti is cracking up laughing.]

PP: I came to America—it was a whole different world. When I came from England all I expected to see was cowboys and Indians, ya know. I was eleven. I remember The Flower Pot Men, Muffin the Mule... but you're younger than me, darling. [At this point, Patti asks me how old I am. So I lean in to whisper my age privately in her ear, and she immediately blurts it out.]

PP: She's forty-five! I'm nineteen years older than you, darling. So it was a different world. I still watch *Are You Being Served?* all the time. I liked the blonde lady that smoked cigarettes.

SP: Oh, yeah, she's a character, isn't she?

PP: Are you going to edit this?

SP: No, I'm not! Take out all the good bits? You're joking!

PP: You're not—you're not going to put this in.

SP: Absolutely... its all natural and genuine. This shows your personality shining through, so no we are not going to change a thing. They're going to love you even more after listening to this.

PP: What?... I need a drink! I'm drinking my Patti water—I drink a lot of milk, darling [laughing].

"So she came, and, you know, I combed her hair for her; I did her hair. That big boomba. You have to know, Priscilla loved Elvis a lot, she did. She is a wonderful woman..."

PATTI PARRY ON PRISCILLA

[We all start laughing, as we know that Patti has had a few tipples during the interview.]

SP: Do I look like a woman you can trust?

PP: No. [More laughing]

SP: Ask Cynthia [Pepper].

PP: I gotta tell you this story. I travel around a bit, and I go up to the Smoky Mountains, and there's this tribute artist, a friend of mine, Lou Vuto. And he worked with Charlie Hodge. I loved to see Charlie, bless his heart. I loved Charlie—I miss Charlie so much. Charlie was so fun, so I said Charlie, "I'll see you in the morning, about twelve," because we were up late. And its ten o'clock in the morning, Charlie calls, and I say, "I'm downstairs having coffee." So anyway, they're all like Bible people there, so I'm like—well, I have a mouth you know—so they say you can't say "God damn"; you have to say "gosh darn." So you have to be very careful. So anyway, I went to one of their fellowships, and I'm reading scriptures, and I'm Jewish, so I say, "Okay you guys, if I'm going to read scripture, you all have to learn a Jewish word. So I had them all saying, "oy vey." So I've got all these people saying, "Oy vey, Patti."

SP: What does that mean?

PP: Oy vey means "oh my goodness." I'm a crazy lady—why, can't I tell you.

SP: How close were you to Priscilla?

PP: Priscilla was a lovely, lovely girl. I was there the day that he brought her to California. We used to have parties at the

OPPOSITE, TOP RIGHT: Priscilla Presley speaks to invited guests at the opening of 'Elvis at the O2,' an exhibition of Elvis Presley memorabilia at the O2 Arena, London; **OPPOSITE, BOTTOM LEFT:** Elvis Presley with his wife Priscilla and their daughter, Lisa Marie, 1973; **ABOVE:** Patti.

TOP: Elvis in concert in the late 60's; **ABOVE TOP:** Elvis signs for fans; **ABOVE:** Elvis, Tupelo, USA, 1956

house, and he said listen, "I'm bringing this little girl, so the parties are going to stop." So she came, and, you know, I combed her hair for her; I did her hair. That big boomba. You have to know, Priscilla loved Elvis a lot, she did. She is a wonderful woman.

SP: I love Priscilla.

PP: She was a wonderful girl.

SP: I'd love to meet her one day.

PP: Who's talking here? [We all start laughing again.]

SP: No, sorry, go on... just say, "Shut up, Shelly."

PP: You know, you have to realize she loved Elvis a lot, and Elvis loved Priscilla, but it's not conducive to a normal marriage when you have seven guys, their wives, their girlfriends, and me around every day. I mean she wanted a life with Elvis, but Elvis Presley had his own genre. She's a fabulous girl; she gave him a lovely daughter, and she loved Elvis, and she knows I'm loyal to Elvis, and we never had a problem. I think the world of her, bless her heart. She stuck with him until she couldn't do it anymore. It's very hard living that kind of life.

SP: I can imagine.

PP: You can't imagine. Elvis was a fantastic guy, but he should have never been married, you know.

SP: I know—he just wanted to love everybody.

PP: He did.

SP: Okay, now I have some questions from some of the members from Elvis International. Jason

Edge, our amazing president wants to ask you what was the happiest you saw Elvis and what was the saddest?

PP: The happiest I ever saw Elvis was when he was on stage, that's when he was the happiest. Let me tell you something, there were two different Elvises... there was the Elvis at home and the Elvis on stage. When Elvis was on stage that's when he just blew it all out, that's when he was the most happy, he loved it. And when his daughter was born. The saddest I ever saw him was when that book was written about him (Should we mention the title of the book? I think it was *Elvis: What Happened?*). That broke his heart. These were our family, and they broke the silence, ya know? After 25 years I talked to some of those guys, and I talked to Charlie (Charlie Hodge) and I said, "Charlie, Elvis would forgive and forget," and he said, "Patti, he would forgive, but he would never forget." You know I'm friends with those people. I don't know maybe I shouldn't do this.

SP: No, it's okay to talk Patti. I've spoken to Sonny and his wife, and she said when Elvis died she lost her husband for a good year.

PP: It was a mistake. [Patti then whispers to me] But that killed him, that book killed him.

SP: I mean they have regrets, everybody makes mistakes.

PP: Anyway, listen, that's the saddest, you know.

SP: Okay. So what is the one unique thing about Elvis Presley's personality that you will always remember?

PP: The unique thing about Elvis Presley is, let me tell you something, if Elvis walked in a room and your back was to him, you would feel him come in that room, it was his charisma. There was this magnetism that he had. You knew he was there. I mean, I don't know, he was a God-given gift, ya know? ... but he didn't realize it, he didn't know. He kept searching, "Why me, why me, why me?" but he was a special man, and as I say, his generosity, he let us live his life. He didn't care about the money; whatever he got we all got, we were his family.

SP: He wasn't materialistic.

PP: He wasn't materialistic; whenever he got something we got it. Whatever he got he shared with us, and we lived like millionaires you know. We all came from nothing but so did he, you know.

SP: I have another question.

PP: I wasn't finished yet but go on... [Laughing.] No go on... She loves me, doesn't she?

SP: I do love you, Patti, you're wonderful.

SP: Another question here from our dear friend Marion, who comes from Bonny Scotland but she lives in Northwich, Cheshire. She's just an Elvis nut this girl, and she wants to ask you, "What was it like running your hands through Elvis's hair when you cut it?"

PP: Hmmm. [Laughing.] Well, let me tell you a story. I'm a professional hairdresser. Larry Geller was his hairdresser, but I cut his hair for the Aloha special. In fact I got a call... he was there during the rehearsal, and he needed a haircut, and they said get over here now. I made him look gorgeous and did on special occasions when Larry wasn't working, but I don't claim to be Elvis's hairdresser. I was his little sister. Elvis didn't have really thick hair, we used a lot of hairspray, and Elvis had sandy blonde hair and we used to dye it... and all these girls used to come up and say they have Elvis's love child with black hair and blue eyes. I'd say "Excuse me, number 51 Clairol!"—he used that to dye his hair. But it was good, you know, he wouldn't go to the barber shop, he would be watching television, and I would cut his hair. I was scared to death the first time, but I used to cut the guys' hair, so he said, "Patti, you gotta cut my hair."

SP: Were you scared you would make a mess of it?

> **"...Let me tell you something. Elvis wore a Jewish star and a cross always, because he didn't want to get shut out of heaven on a technicality..."**
>
> **PATTI PARRY**

PP: I would never make a mess of it, I'm a good hairdresser.

SP: Who decided when Elvis needed a haircut, you or him?

PP: As I said I was not his hairdresser but he decided.

SP: How did Larry come to cut his hair then?

PP: Larry worked at... well, there was this hairdressers' shop. What's that guy that got killed with Manson, what's his name? The Manson killing—Jay Sebring! A guy named Sal Orfice worked there, and he started cutting Elvis's hair during the movies but when Elvis went on tour, Sal didn't want to go so he turned him over to Larry Geller. Larry worked at Jay Sebring. [Jay Sebring was a celebrity hair stylist.] I went to beauty school with Larry Geller. I've been cutting hair for 45 years.

SP: Who did the better haircut, you or Larry?

PP: I don't know, whoever, look at the Aloha special.

SP: [Laughing.] Yeah, Larry Geller was probably overrated.

PP: Don't say that. He doesn't cut hair anymore, he's a spiritualist.

I went on to tell Patti a story about how when we were kids my mum would cut our hair, and I looked like one of the Three Stooges. Patti replied, "Whats this got to do with Elvis?" and we all cracked up laughing. There were a lot of

ABOVE: Patti with Jerry.

ABOVE: Elvis in playful mode signing autographs.

moments during this interview that we spent laughing. I loved Patti's sarcasm and dry wit. She was very funny.

SP: Freda, our lovely U.S. manager from Elvis International, asked me to tell you she met you during Elvis Week last year. Freda and Donna, her daughter, were seated next to you during the gospel show, and you both talked; she said you may not remember but you both cried lots and held on to each other.

PP: Oh, she was lovely! I do remember, and yes we both cried. She was a very, very nice lady. She looked after me because I got upset. Especially after seeing Donny Sumner there, and some of these guys had gotten old, and it upset me. He used to come up to the suites every night and sing "The Lighthouse" with [his group] the Stamps. Donny and I were really good friends, and when I saw these guys again it made me cry.

SP: Freda also sent me an email; she was very hurt by some clip she had seen on the internet. It was Red West, Sonny, Lamar Fike, Larry Geller, and David Stanley all going on about Elvis and his Christianity, and it kind of made out that he had occult powers and that he believed he was a prophet and he referred to them as his disciples.

PP: That's baloney. That's Larry Geller nonsense.

PP: I've never heard that.

SP: When I listened to it, I was completely outraged myself, but we all know that Elvis read a lot of books on spiritualism, and he wanted to know more about life after death as a lot of us do, and it seems so unfair that he allowed these men to come into his life, into his home, he took care of them and they had such negative stuff to say about him then. I'm saying then... Now what's your opinion on Elvis as a Christian, Patti?

PP: Let me tell you something. Elvis wore a Jewish star and a cross always, because he didn't want to get shut out of heaven on a technicality. He believed in every religion. When I got married he said, "Well, I wanted to step on a glass, you know." I'm a Jewish girl. He had Jewish people, he had Christian people, he had Catholic people, he had black people. Elvis was open to everybody. There was never any religious problem with him. He got involved in a lot of the spiritual stuff because Larry Geller turned him on to that, which I don't want to go into, but he was just searching for something, self-realization. He didn't like Scientology, he wasn't

into that. Elvis loved every religion, he loved every person, every race and creed. He was an incredible man so that's a bunch of nonsense, and I don't care for that, and we weren't his disciples, we were his friends, his family, so I don't care about that.

SP: Exactly!

SP: Now he and J.D. Sumner were really extremely close and so too were Elvis with Charlie Hodge. Elvis was fortunate enough to have some really good friends, like the lovely Joe Esposito, Jerry Schilling, and yourself of course. Out of all those guys would you say there was one in particular that he was closest to?

PP: I think he was close to all of us, you know, and we all used to spend every day with him and every night with him; we all shared his life, and he shared his life with us. Everybody had different jobs, everybody had different things to be there for. We are mostly there to be his friend and keep him company. You have to realize he was a prisoner of his own fame. We couldn't go anywhere, so we all had the same mindset, and we used to have so much fun. Some worked harder than others. Joe worked really hard... Joe did all the personal reservations and stuff. Richard Davies did the wardrobe, but I think we were all equal in his life and his love for us, you know, and his caring for us.

SP: Now, Patti, were you around Graceland during the time of Elvis and Priscilla's separation, when she took Lisa Marie and left?

PP: No, I wasn't but I saw him in Las Vegas after she left, and he was heartbroken,

SP: Did you notice a change in him?

PP: Well, no, there was no change, he realized... but I can't do this, you know, I don't want to talk about that. But you know... listen, Priscilla was a wonderful girl, and it was not conducive to a normal life, and Elvis had his own life... but there are things I'm not going to discuss because they're private. Fun things are okay. People ask me to write a book and I'm not going to write a book. I've got a job, I don't need to write a book. There are things that are private about my life with Elvis, but the fun things, that's when I travel around and I tell wonderful stories, I make them laugh. I tell the sad stories, when they got the death threat in Las Vegas—that was the worst thing that ever happened in my life with him—but some things I don't want to talk about.

SP: Being his little sister, did you ever feel protective toward Elvis, say for example when these women were swarming around him wanting a piece of the action. Did you ever think "Hey, this is my brother?"

PP: No, darling, no. The fun times were when we would sit on the couch and I would be sat next to him, and I'd get up, and the fun thing to see was who was the first girl to run and sit next to Elvis. You know I didn't have to protect him, he had seven guys. I was just there; you know, all these girls, they remember me, they know me, he was my brother.

SP: So now I've got a question here from the sweetest man. His name is Michael Comley. He's our U.K. manager for Elvis International.

PP: Hi, Michael.

SP: He's lovely, he's our U.K. manager, and we love him to bits, don't we, Ed?

EB: Yes.

PP: You're LUVLY. [Patti starts taking the mickey out of my accent.]

SP: He said he met you briefly in 2002 at the Great

Britain Fan Club event in Tunica, and the great Ed Bonja was there, along with Richard Davies.

PP: I never went to Tunica! Did I? Where is Tunica?

EB: 30 miles from Memphis.

PP: Oh yeah, yeah at the casino. Hey, listen, I'm getting old, dude! I don't know about THE great Ed Bonja, but Ed Bonja was there [laughing].

PP: I love Richard Davies. I miss Richard Davies so much. Richard Davies was one of the most wonderful friends of Elvis. When we would travel sometimes I'd got to share a room with Richard, with a bunch of them. Joe Esposito, Richard. They were my brothers, you know. But I miss Richard Davies so much; he was an incredible man. They were my boys.

SP: Michael said the Sweet Inspirations and the silly Suzanna Leigh was there. Sorry, Patti, but she irritates me so much. You came across as a very lovely down-to-earth lady.

PP: Well, that's what I am! [Laughing.] Thank you.

SP: Would you describe yourself as a bit of a tomboy, Patti?

PP: No, I'm not a tomboy, but I was brought up by

ABOVE: Patti far left, next to Linda Thompson and Priscilla 2nd right; **BELOW:** The Memorial Service cover for Patti Parry.

PATTI PARRY

February 4, 1943 – October 27, 2011

A Celebration of Life

November 18, 2011   1 - 3 pm

seven guys, you know? I've got a big mouth, and I swear a bit, that's my personality. I grew up with Joe and Jerry and Sonny and Charlie you know, so they brought me up, but when it comes to Elvis Presley I got big mouth, so don't mess with me when it comes to Elvis Presley. I will lay your butt out, man, but I'm not a tomboy. I'm a lovely, beautiful, feminine woman, right, Ed?

EB: I agree.

PP: Thank you.

PP: But when it comes to Elvis Presley, don't mess with me. I have a big mouth, I tell the truth, you know, and if people will put my friend down I will just lay their ass out. I don't care!

[I turn to Ed.]

SP: She was good to have around, wasn't she?

PP: I layed his ass out a lot, too. That's why he loves me. [Referring to Ed Bonja.]

SP: You did?

SP: Tell me a bit more about the good times with Elvis, Patti. You went to the theme park and he rented out the movies didn't he, stuff like that?

PP: I never went to the theme park, but we went to the movies all the time, we went to the Memphian. I was there when he met Linda Thompson actually.

SP: You were?

PP: I spent 17 years with Elvis.

SP: Did you ever receive gifts from Elvis?

PP: Are you kidding me!

SP: Yeah, what kind of gifts would he give you?

PP: Let me tell you something, whenever Elvis went shopping everybody got something. He would go to a jewelry store, everybody got something. He'd put his hands behind his back and say, "Pick a hand," and he would give you a diamond ring. He bought me a car, he gave me a fur coat, he was very very generous, you know, whatever he got we got. He shared everything with us, that's why I mean, who could put down this man? This man shared his life. We all had nothing, and we got to live like millionaires. We had amazing cooks and limousines. I mean he shared everything with us, and we were really lucky to be part of his life... and he was lucky to have us as a part of his life too.

SP: He was, absolutely.

PP: Otherwise he would have been very alone.

SP: Okay, another good question here.

PP: Hey how long is this going on for?

TOP, RIGHT: Elvis posing with fans; **ABOVE:** Patti during her interview with Shelly.

OPPOSITE, TOP: Elvis in action; **OPPOSITE, BOTTOM:** A very rare picture of Elvis with Roy Orbison.

SP: It could go on forever. Now listen... when was the last time you saw Elvis?

PP: Elvis moved back to Memphis. I was married, and he got really lonely because Joe was out here, that book was written, and I was out here, and he had all these young kids with him—Billy Smith, he loved Billy Smith, David Stanley—but he had nobody to play with, nobody left to play with, and he was very lonely. He had this woman living with him that I do not acknowledge. [Patti was talking about Ginger Alden.] And if Linda was with him, he would still be alive. He was very lonely, and he was in Memphis, and I think that was his demise, you know.

SP: I've just got a few more questions here, Patti.

PP: What! That's all right, carry on.

SP: I don't want you to get fed up, just a few more.

PP: I'm not fed up. I get sad.

SP: Aghhh... I don't want you to get sad, but you are allowed to get sad, okay.

SP: Now, Elvis dated a lot of beautiful woman. Linda Thompson was known to be very good for Elvis. How was your relationship with Linda?

PP: I have a great relationship with Linda. She was a wonderful, wonderful lady. She was a terrific girl, and she's come into her own, but she married an idiot! I'm sorry, but she was very happy, and she was very good for Elvis... she loved Elvis.

SP: Now, we know Elvis gave Ginger Alden a huge diamond ring.

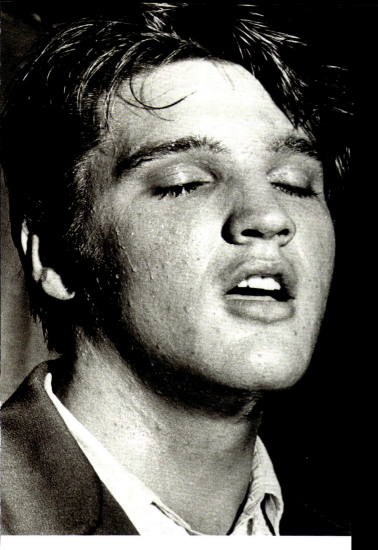

ELVIS
REMEMBERED

"His energy was incredible, his instinct was just amazing... I just didn't know what to make of it. There was just no reference point in the culture to compare it..."

Roy Orbison

PP: Who, who?

SP: Who, who? [Laughing.]

SP: Ginger Alden.

PP: Who? I don't acknowledge that woman, I don't acknowledge her. Don't want to know, no.

SP: I was just wondering if Elvis would have married her?

PP: She was there, she should have kept him alive. I don't acknowledge her.

SP: Okay, its okay.

PP: Sorry.

SP: Did you suspect that the end was near during that year, in 1977, Patti?

PP: No, I didn't. The only sad thing is that if we were all with him he wouldn't have gone. Listen, he would have still been alive. Like I said, he had nobody left to play with, he was alone, he had a bunch of young kids, he had some woman there that didn't care about him.

SP: I know that, you could see it in clips, I know she didn't care about him. She was so young, and she was just there for the ride.

"…Myrna Smith and I were watching this Elvis thing on TV and the lights started going on and off, on and off, and we were watching and then this commercial came on and it said Jimmy Velvet was having a big auction, and the light kept going on and off, on and off, then all of a sudden the phone rang and who was it but Jimmy Velvet…"

PATTI PARRY

PP: I don't know that. I don't acknowledge her, but no I didn't expect that. Listen, look at Englebert today [Englebert Humperdinck]. Look at Tom [Tom Jones]. I mean Tom Jones just sold out the Hollywood Bowl. Elvis liked Tom Jones.

SP: Now, Patti… okay.

PP: Yes, dear? [Patti laughs.]

SP: It's nearly done.

SP: It's August 17th, the day after Elvis left this earth and went on his journey to be with Jesus, his body was at Graceland, and he would lie in state for one day. I read during that evening after 75,000 people paid homage to the king, a soft, warm rain began to fall as the world mourned this beautiful, talented, special man.

PP: Let me tell you a story, six months ago I went to Memphis to visit a friend, and I called and I wanted to go see Elvis on my own just to say hello, you know. I was there for the 25th anniversary. I did the Sirius satellite radio show with Doc Walker, and he came with me and we drove through the gates of Graceland, as we drove through the gates I swear to God, it started to rain, it started to pour rain. I stood by his grave, I started talking to Elvis, and I had a little cry, I told him he had left me. We drove out of Graceland, the rain stopped. Let me tell you something, when they walked him out of Graceland in the casket, a branch from the tree fell over to stop him. I don't know what it is about this man, he was a God-given gift and someone said to me "Patti, when you die and go to heaven what do you think Elvis will say to you?" I said, "Well I hope I'll be in my 80s

and Elvis might not recognize me." [She laughs.] I dream about him.

SP: You dream about him?

PP: I dream about him. Constantly!

SP: Vivid dreams?

PP: Vivid dreams.

SP: He comes to see you?

PP: He cooms and he comes. [Patti imitates my northern British accent.]

PP: I tell you, Myrna Smith and I were watching this Elvis thing on TV and the lights started going on and off, on and off, and we were watching and then this commercial came on and it said Jimmy Velvet was having a big auction, and the light kept going on and off, on and off, then all of a sudden the phone rang and who was it but Jimmy Velvet.. and Myrna got so nervous she jumped up and ran out of the house. I believe in spirits.

SP: Oh, I do too.

PP: I believe in spirits totally. I believe Elvis's spirit is with us, well he will always be with me.

SP: Do you believe in angels?

PP: I don't know about angels, but Elvis was an angel.

SP: I do.

PP: I dream about my mum and dad, and my friends that I have lost. I hope when I pass that I will meet all these people again, but I hope I look as good as I look now!

SP: You will. They say when you go to Heaven you look like you did when you were in your prime. So I think I'd like to be 21.

PP: 30 was good, I'm 64 now but I still look good. Sorry… I'm 35!

SP:… and I'm 23!

SP: Well, I do believe in angels, I'm sure that the angels that day must have wept tears of joy because—

PP: Tears of joy?

SP: Yes, because Elvis was going to be with them.

PP: I guess.

PP: His mum, his mum would be happy.

SP: Yeah, and no more, no more pain to endure.

PP: He had no pain, he was just lonely.

SP: So when you think of Elvis, your dear friend, how do you like to remember him, Patti?

PP: My brother, my friend, the best person I ever knew

in my life, that was the most generous wonderful man, boy. He changed my life, and I wouldn't change it for a minute. I mean as I say, I gave up my life to that man, and I wouldn't change that in a heartbeat. I was a very lucky girl but he was lucky to have us too. All of us. Don't make me cry here, girlfriend.

SP: You're going to make me cry in a minute, Patti.

SP: Do you have a favorite Elvis song?

PP: I like "I'll Remember You" and I like "Just Pretend." I go to sleep every night listening to Elvis, I can't sleep without Elvis, I like listening to "I'll Remember You." I used to be like his little sister, but I'm his big sister now. I love his voice. I lived Elvis; I lived ate and breathed Elvis for 17 years, you can't change that, and I still do.

SP: I want to finish this interview on a happier note.

PP: Thank God!

SP: She's a cheeky mare, isn't she?

SP: Elvis had a really distinctive laugh and when he cracked up it was extremely infectious, so what things would make Elvis laugh, what would bring a smile to his beautiful face?

PP: Elvis would laugh at everything. You've heard the story about his chimpanzee Scatter, right?

SP Oh, yeah, I heard he had a chimpanzee.

PP: He had a chimp named Scatter, and Scatter was crazy. Scatter would go around drinking all the drinks that everyone had left, then he would go after the girls and would lift their dresses up and bite them, and he would steal their jewelry. So, anyway, I walked into the den one day, and Scatter comes running at me, and he puts his hands up in the air and screams, he comes towards me and I thought, right... I gave him a right hook.

SP: You did not!

PP: I did, and he flew back, and then Elvis laughed for half an hour, half an hour!! But that monkey never came near me again.

PP: Then in Las Vegas on that tape that Elvis laughs at, that's because there was a guy in the audience and Elvis was singing "Are You Lonesome Tonight?" with that line about "without any hair" and the guy had a wig on and he took it off to show his bald head... well, that was it. When Elvis laughed, Elvis really laughed.

SP: Okay, I'm going to finish this interview now, Patti.

PP: Thank God. [We both crack up laughing.]

SP: I could talk to you for hours, you really are a wonderful lady. Patti Parry, thank you, darling, for allowing me to come and sit in your home with you today and listen to your special memories of Elvis Presley. We all love you. Thank you, darling. Love and peace to you, Patti.

PP: It's my pleasure. You are very welcome, darling. I'm happy to remember and honor my friend.

Whenever I listen to this interview, I smile to myself. Patti was a force to be reckoned with. She was a tough cookie with a gentle heart and a love for Elvis that was immeasurable. I'm so grateful to have known her, as brief as it was, I'll never forget her.

TOP: Joe Moscheo, member of the Imperials, with Myrna and Patti, 2009; **ABOVE:** Patti; **LEFT:** Patti and Shelly during interview; **OPPOSITE:** Elvis.

ELVIS

REMEMBERED

"When I first heard 'Heartbreak Hotel' my whole life changed. I was completely shaken by it. I thought: 'This is it!' And I started trying to grow sideburns and all that gear."

John Lennon

"**Without Elvis, there would be no Beatles…**"
John Lennon

"Someone asked me is there anything you didn't like about Elvis, and I said, 'Yeah, the fact that he died too young'..."

ED BONJA ON ELVIS PRESLEY

Ed Bonja

Ed Bonja was Elvis's personal photographer. He is recognized as the person responsible for some of the most iconic Elvis images ever taken. He published his own book too, *Elvis: Shot by Ed Bonja* and also a DVD *Elvis, The Colonel & Me*. Ed worked for Colonel Parker all through the seventies but, he had an integral part in the Elvis family since his childhood.

OPPOSITE: A portrait of Ed reflecting, taken during the interview.

Interviewing Ed...

Thoughts of Ed Bonja leave me feeling quite emotional. I feel honored to have spent time with him, privileged to have known him, and forever grateful that he shared his images of Elvis, some of them that have never been seen before. I also have so much gratitude in my heart for the fact that he allowed me to interview him in the first place and later for his friendship, which led to us becoming very close.

TOP: Ed and Shelly during the interview; **ABOVE:** Ed checking the hold of the plane on the way to another concert.

Admittedly, I wish I had made him more aware of how much I thought of him; it isn't until the people we love pass on that we reminisce and wish we had told them more often how much they mean to us. Ed Bonja was a dear and wonderful man, and he made it quite clear how much he cared about me as his friend. Ed visited my family and myself in England. He stayed as a guest at our home in Manchester, and we also traveled to Winchester in the south of England, where he worked on a book with my brother who had his own publishing company at the time. I know that Ed did not get the recognition he deserved for his talent as an amazing photographer in the early days when shooting photos of Elvis, but this was largely due to Colonel Parker. Remembering Ed, I think of a quiet, kind man with a dry sense of humor and hidden talents. For one thing it wasn't until at the end of my interview with Patti

Parry (Presley's "little sister") that I discovered Ed could sing! When Patti informed me of Ed's singing talents at the close of her interview we pleaded with him to give us a quick song, which can actually be heard on the interview and what a sweet voice that man had.

I was blown away. He also did a great impression of J.D. Sumner. Patti Parry told me that whenever Ed called her on the phone she wouldn't let him hang up until he had sung a few lines of a song to her. Ed's sense of humor was to me another of his most endearing qualities. I recall a time when he had accompanied me and my then husband Eddie (who was an Elvis impersonator) to a special event in England where Eddie was going to be a guest performer. It was a tribute artist contest, and Ed Bonja was a judge. I think Eddie came in at third place at the time, but week's later when Ed was staying over at my brother's home in

Winchester, in conversation with Ed, Damien asked him, "So, Ed, does Eddie look anything like the real Elvis?" Ed casually replied, "Well, maybe to a blind man on a galloping horse." My brother laughed then asked, "Well, does he sound anything like the real Elvis?" Ed's reply was, "Depends on how far away you are." Ed was good to be around; he may not have been the loudest person in the room with a lot to say, but when Ed shared stories about Elvis and his life, one was captivated. He told a great story. He was genuine, kind, and not in the least bit materialistic, just a good soul.

SP: How was it for you, Ed, working with EP?

EB: Well, I was just lucky enough to go with him and be there. When Elvis would come in, I would just look at him and think to myself how could one guy have everything? The guy is just perfect.

SP: His features were just so fine, he had it all, the looks, the personality.

EB: Yeah, there was a comedian who had just seen Elvis in Vegas. He left Vegas, and he went to be on the Johnny Carson show, and Johnny said to him, "Hey, I hear you had some excitement yesterday,

you got to meet Elvis," and he replied with great enthusiasm, "Yeah, I got to meet Elvis!" So Johnny said, "Well, how was it?" and the comedian replied, "Well, he's the most handsome man I ever saw in my life. I was wishing I was a woman!"

SP: I've heard something like that from other men, they could look at Elvis and say "Yeah, he is such a beautiful man," they can just appreciate his beauty... anybody that interacted with him maybe would expect him to be vain.

EB: Not at all, that was probably the best thing about him. It was like sitting here talking to Rudy [meaning Rudy my photographer, who was a mild-mannered gentle soul]. He was down to earth, very humble.

SP: First of all, Ed, can we just talk a little bit about yourself, how you got started?

EB: How I got started?

SP: Yeah, did you always want to be a photographer?

EB: No, I was going to school to be a PE major, coach football, basketball, which I practiced in high school for a few years, and my minor was French, so I had PE and French, and in 1969 my brother Ronnie, who was in the army and was in research and development and photography... he got hooked on photography.

TOP: Ed with one of the many brilliant photographs he took during his career as Elvis's personal photographer; **ABOVE:** More of Ed's Elvis pictures.

71

ELVIS PRESLEY CONCERT

TOP: The Colonel's office at the Las Vegas Hilton was on the fourth floor. Ed was sitting at his desk in the office taking care of business when a colleague, Charles stone, snapped this photo of him; **ABOVE:** Ed's concert badge.

So for Christmas he sent me this old camera, where you press the button and the lens pops out. You had to set the footage and guess everything, and he sent me some rolls of film and cartridges with some instructions on how to roll my own film and put it into cartridges. I started doing that, and I thought, God this is really fun. So I was at the university in Los Angeles and decided I was going to take a photography class. I signed up for Photo One, and I really enjoyed it. I started taking pictures and while I was doing that Colonel Parker called me. I go back with Colonel Parker as far as 1948—he was an old family friend before he was a colonel.

SP: Really!

EB: Yeah, he called me and because he was a family friend he talked to my mum and dad all the time, you know, and he said, "We decided we are going to go out and do personal appearance tours again. Would you and your brother Ronnie be interested in coming along and acting as roadies? Just doing whatever it takes to make sure the show runs smoothly. Loading the truck, setting the stage, tearing down, whatever." So I thought for a second and said, "Yeah, when do we leave?" So he said, "I understand you're taking pictures now and you're

into photography, so if you want to bring your camera, feel free to take all the pictures you want." And that was what changed my life, my career.

SP: So at that point you hadn't met Elvis?

EB: No, I had met him as I had worked as Colonel Parker's secretary on the set at MGM studios during the making of *Girl Happy* in the summer of '64. I graduated from high school and started college in '63. I got sick and had to drop out for a few months until I got stronger, so the Colonel said here's a soft, easy job you can do. It paid 75 dollars a week, so I jumped at that. I moved to Cheviot Hills where my uncle Tom Diskin was the Colonel's right-hand man; he had an apartment there, so I stayed with him and worked at MGM every day and that's where I first met Elvis.

SP: Fantastic! So what was it like for you meeting Elvis Presley for the first time?

EB: It happened so quickly, and it was so casual it hardly made an impact. Elvis was throwing a surprise birthday party for the Colonel. Our offices were in the set next door, which was a huge room. So we all went over for the party, and the Colonel was supposed to act surprised, you know, but everyone knew what was going on anyway. I was walking

"So, here I am, 24 years old, very quiet, strictly raised Catholic kid. Never taken pictures of anybody in his life, and here I am taking pictures of Elvis Presley on tour and on this airplane. So when he stopped, and he turned like this to face me, I'm thinking to myself, 'Oh, God, I shouldn't be doing this, I'm imposing on him, I'm interfering on his private time,' something which was always on my mind..." ED BONJA ON HIS FIRST TIME SNAPPING ELVIS

around and the Colonel introduced me to Elvis and said, "This is my nephew, Eddie." Everybody always called me Eddie. I went years without having a last name, it was always Eddie, not Ed Bonja or whatever. We shook hands and that was it. Several weeks later when the movie was over I had gone to Palm Springs for ten days with the Colonel, who was unwinding after working so hard on the movie, and he had put on an awful lot of weight and he strained his back. It went out on him, so we drove back to LA, and he went into the hospital, the Good Samaritan Hospital in Los Angeles, and he was in there about a week. When he got out and went back to his apartment on Wilshire Boulevard in West LA—he had a three-bedroom apartment—he had to be in traction for three more weeks so the plan was I moved in there and stayed in the extra room to... do everything that needed to be done. He was there with my quote "Pseudo Aunt" Marie, as we

called her [his wife]. About the third day I was there, after dinner the Colonel said to me, "Tonight about midnight Elvis and Joe are coming over [Joe Esposito]." He said when they get here just send Elvis back to the room—he had this separate room set up for traction—and he said I'll talk to him first, and then I'll talk to Joe. So at midnight there was a knock on the door, and I opened the door, and there was Elvis. Anyway, I was 19 years old, and I tried to act so cool, and Joe said, "Oh, Eddie... Elvis you met Eddie, didn't you? Tom Diskin's cousin." Elvis said, "Oh, yeah, yeah." Whether he did or not, I don't know, but he was very gracious. He was always like that, and that was so nice about him.

SP: You must have been in awe.

EB: No. He was in awe of me [laughing]. No, anyway I said the Colonel is in the back bedroom and he wanted to talk to you first, Elvis. So Elvis went back there, and Joe and I sat down, and we talked a while, and about twenty minutes later Elvis comes out and said, "Joe, the Colonel wants to see you." So Elvis sat down where you are right now and for the next 15 or 18 minutes we just talked about football and sports and what was going on, you know. It was one-on-one with Elvis, and it was amazing.

SP: I bet it was! And he just made you feel totally, totally relaxed and at ease.

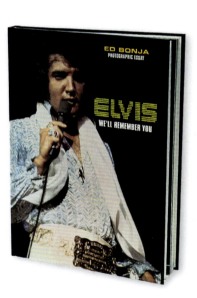

TOP LEFT: Ed's personal favorite out of all the pictures he took of Elvis; **ABOVE:** Cover of Ed's book.

ABOVE: Ed surrounded by many of the brilliant Elvis pictures he took.

EB: Yeah.

SP: Okay, so you know you must get asked this question so many times regarding that famous picture of Elvis on the plane in that cream suit?

EB: Yes, I have it here.

SP: He looks like he is in mid conversation, can you remember what was going on at that time when that picture was taken?

EB: I can, but I can't tell you otherwise I would have to kill you.

SP: [Laughing] Really, I mean what was the mood like?

EB: Let me show you a picture. [Ed starts looking through his images of Elvis.] We had just completed the first tour that Elvis had done in ten years. We finished the tour and the last date was in Mobile, Alabama, and for that tour, this is before Elvis had the Lisa Marie [his plane], he had chartered a British-made BAC One-Eleven jet, and it was gorgeous. I had never been on a customized plane like this before. For some reason, there was my Uncle Tom, one of the Sweets [Sweet Inspirations], one of the guys in the band, and Elvis and Joe. There weren't that many people on the plane.

Ed showed me an image of the plane in Mobile, Alabama, on the tarmac and explained that he was up inside that plane shooting pictures down below.

EB: That was September 15, 1970, and I was shooting pictures of him as he was signing autographs and kissing some of the fans, and I'm shooting as he's coming up the stairs. He walked by me and sat down, and I went to the back of the plane, and it was a really nice set up. There was a couch on one side, there was a door that led to the bathroom and on either side of the bathroom door there were separate chairs but all together. I went in and sat down, so I was sat there, my uncle was there, one of the Sweets. Elvis came by me and said, "I have to go into the bathroom and dry myself off. It's really hot out there." He was perspiring. So he went into the restroom and he washed his face and toweled himself off and when he came out he closed the door, and he started to take a step forward to go back to the front, and he saw me sitting there. So I got up and lifted my camera. So, here I am, 24 years old, very quiet, strictly raised Catholic kid. Never taken pictures of anybody in his life, and here I am taking pictures of Elvis Presley on tour and on this airplane. So when he stopped, and he turned like this to face me, I'm thinking to myself, "Oh, God, I shouldn't be doing this, I'm imposing on him, I'm interfering on his private time," something which was always on my mind. I should have not let this bother me but I did. So I said, "That's okay, Elvis, you don't have to pose," and once again gracious but taking the edge off it making a joke, he said, "C'mon, what do you want me to do, hold my dick in my hand?" I took the picture, and I never hesitated taking a picture of Elvis again, and that is my favorite Elvis picture.

SP: That is hilarious. Actually that is mine too. We have that one hanging over the fireplace, I love it.

EB: Someone told me in Europe that was voted the best Elvis picture.

SP: I can believe it, and when I have looked at that picture I've often wondered what was he thinking or talking about, and now I know. What was the most bizarre thing you ever witnessed at one of Elvis Presley's shows? Anything that sticks out in your mind?

EB: I don't know about bizarre, here was someone just having fun, fooling around. I have a great picture of Elvis that I never released. He's wearing the navy blue silver phoenix [jumpsuit], I call it the blue phoenix but a lot of people call it the silver phoenix.

SP: Because of the silver studs?

EB: Yeah, anyway I had this great shot of him... he's got a police cap on, he's walking towards me, he's moving in on me. I didn't shoot with a flash except on a very rare occasion in the dressing room before a show, and he's coming towards me and he's smiling because he's moving, its slightly soft and because of the lights he's got this incredible aura around him. It's really a neat picture, some day I may release it.

SP: You should do it, it sounds amazing, and I'd love to see it !

EB: Yeah, but then the next day there would be 50 million copies being sold all over the world by everybody but me. you know.

SP: Are they allowed to do that?

EB: Of course not, but they don't care.

SP: Well, actually that was one of my questions: who owns and controls all the pictures you took during the '70s? In other words, did you have to turn over the rights to RCA or EPE, etc.? Or are they yours to use as you wish?

EB: They are mine to use as I wish. I am licensed by Graceland; I signed a contract with Graceland years ago to pay a royalty. So I can sell them, but I have to pay them a percentage. Unfortunately, when I left the Elvis show in April of 1977, I was sick with pneumonia, I was depressed, I was losing tons of money—roulette with the Colonel. He would go, "You make lots of money, sit down and play it, it goes with the job." He would lose two million dollars sitting there one day. The night I walked out I lost $12,000. Twelve thousand dollars for me? I'd have cut my heart out for that!

SP: Oh, my God, I knew that he gambled, but my God, that's a lot of money!

EB: Plus I was losing three or four thousand dollars each time we sat down. We played roulette day and night. That's why we went to Vegas, we would only leave to have meals. I was making a lot of money but it was all going back to the Hilton.

SP: So you got that gambler's remorse. It must hit you hard, and you're just lining the pockets of the casino.

EB: So with that in mind, and the fact that I was so run down and so sick all the time... and my girlfriend of seven years just told me she was

TOP, LEFT AND RIGHT: Elvis in concert; **ABOVE:** Elvis with the Colonel. The Colonel often gave gag gifts to Elvis; he saw this stuffed monkey in the Hilton gift shop and brought it down to the dressing room to present it to Elvis.

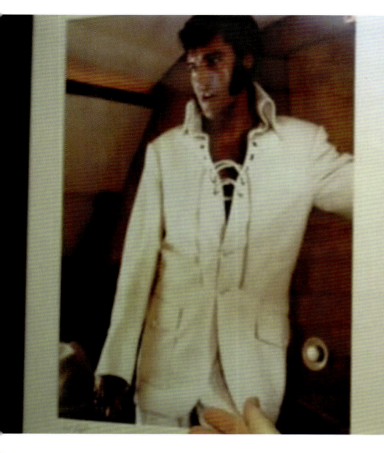

TOP: Ed with the iconic photo he took of Elvis on the airplane; **ABOVE:** Ed with the King's guitar; **OPPOSITE:** Elvis performing.

marrying a minister of her church, which didn't sit too well with me.

SP: So that really got you down.

EB: I guess she gave up after seven years. I came home from a tour and on the tour—when she hadn't already told me about this—I thought I'm going to have a heart-to-heart with her and tell her I'm going to work one more year, I'm not going to spend any money, I'm going to save the money, which was a considerable amount at that time. We will get engaged, and we will get married in one year. It was one of those things where she would stay at my house when I was out of town, and so I got home and I said I have something I want talk to you about, and she said "Well, actually I have something I need to talk to you about." And she told me she's engaged, and, well, that didn't sit too well, didn't make my day at all. Anyway, so those things were going on, and then I lost the twelve thousand, and it's six o'clock in the morning, and the Colonel and I are walking upstairs, and he's rubbing his hands together saying, "Well, we had a pretty good day," rubbing his hands just like that, and I'm thinking "I didn't have such a good day."

SP: That's so sad. Did she not go on tour with you, your girlfriend?

EB: No.

SP: That's the thing about being on tour, it must have been hard for Priscilla, too, with Elvis. I mean, it's very hard to keep a relationship going.

EB: Oh, I would call her several times a night and I could never reach her, she was always out doing something.

SP: Well, what can I say? She must have been mad. I mean look at this picture of you then, you were a good-looking boy and you still are, Ed.

EB: I like this girl! What was your name again?

SP: Yeah, and you know what, Ed, I look at this picture, and I said to my daughter, Victoria, "He looks like that actor Woody Harrelson from *Cheers*!" Has anyone ever told you that you have a look of him?

EB: No.

SP: Well, you're better looking.

EB: You already have the interview.

SP: Well, I'm sat here in the company of Ed Bonja. So did you get a commission from any of the images of yours that they used for the album sales or CD sales?

"My whole life was the Elvis Presley show, so I thought to myself 'I gotta get away before I die here.' So I grabbed my briefcase, that's the only thing I took with me. I left all my clothes, I left everything else there. I walked down the hall, put my key on the desk where the guard was, and I said tell the Colonel I said goodbye."

ED BONJA ON ELVIS'S SUPPRESSED ACTING TALENT

ABOVE AND THROUGHOUT THIS CHAPTER: Many of the dynamic photos Ed took of Elvis performing onstage.

EB: No. You know I say I'm licensed by Graceland because I proved to them that I owned those pictures. I showed them letters that say RCA had bought some of these pictures, MGM had bought pictures from me that they used for the on-tour publicity, even the Colonel. I had several checks and letters showing that he was purchasing X amount of pictures or he was giving me so much money for the use of these pictures for photo albums and other things. So when Graceland saw this stuff they said, "Okay, this whole story is intertwined." The night I left, well the morning I left, 6 o'clock in the morning, I went upstairs with the Colonel. You know we used to have the whole wing on the fourth floor and we had a desk at the front where a guard would sit so no one could go in there. So the Colonel said, "Well, let's wash up, put a clean shirt on, and I'll meet you downstairs in an hour for breakfast. So I went into my room, and I sat down. I had a bench at the foot of my bed, this was my room year round. We never checked in or out of a hotel. The Colonel's office was there, the Sweets were there, my room was there, we had all these rooms so I had clothes that would stay there year round. I was so depressed, I was feeling very bad. I thought, "What am I doing here? I'm making a lot of money, I'm giving it right back. I'm back where I started from, I'm miserable, I have no life, I don't know what's going on in the world." My whole life was the Elvis Presley show, so I thought to myself "I gotta get away before I die here." So I grabbed my briefcase, that's the only thing I took with me. I left all my clothes, I left everything else there. I walked down the hall, put my key on the desk where the guard was, and I said tell the Colonel I said goodbye.

SP: Oh, my goodness, and that was it!

EB: That was it. I took a cab to the airport, got on a plane, and went home.

SP: Do you think that's the best decision you made, looking back?

EB: I think I'd be six feet under if I had stayed.

SP: Even though you had a great life on the road?

EB: It was only great on the outside looking in.

SP: Obviously. It's not a normal lifestyle, is it?

EB: Not at all, not at all.

SP: Did you not have any contact with the Colonel after that?

EB: Well, I had three phones at home. One was a public phone, the second was a private phone that my girlfriend and I used. The third phone was the one the Colonel had me get for when the Colonel called with business. It was a red phone without a dial so I couldn't call out. I went home, and I pulled two of the phones out of the wall, and I don't know how but that son of a... but one of those phones started ringing again. He must have called the phone company and pretended to be me or something. Whatever it was I was amazed that this phone was ringing. So I literally pulled it out of the wall.

SP: So he wanted you back, didn't he?

EB: Oh, yeah. He sent letters, he sent people, he had my mum come over, all kinds of things.

SP: But you had just made your mind up.

EB: I wouldn't respond to anything. I completely isolated myself and about four months later my mother came to see me. She said, "Tom Diskin [her brother] is having a birthday party. He wants you to come, for the sake of the family, come back and make amends. The Colonel is not going to be there,

he will be in Palm Springs so you're not going to see him." Tom thought that would help. Well, for my mother I agreed to go, and I go, and I get there and my uncle's there and he greets me with open arms because he was back doing all the things that I used to be doing. He was in charge of everything again. Little did I know, I hadn't even sat down—and we have a big family so there must have been forty or fifty of us there at the party—and Tom left, he got in the station wagon, he drove to Palm Springs, picked up the Colonel, drove him back. So I'm sitting here at a long table where I can see the front door and the front door opens and I look up and there was the Colonel. I thought "Oh, God, this is gonna be fun." So everybody was surprised to see him because they knew he was in the Springs. He came in and everyone got up to say hello and he just said, "I need to talk to Eddie."

SP: Wow. He was on a mission, wasn't he?

EB: Walked over, sat down right across from me, he never once said, "What was wrong, why did you leave?" I knew the Colonel for thirty-five years at least, that's a long time, anyway. I knew he couldn't stand to have someone angry with him and especially if he didn't know why, so he just talked casually about what I was doing, how's everything, what they were doing, for an hour. Never once mentioned about me leaving or coming back or anything and once he was convinced that I was no longer angry with him he got up and said, "Well, I gotta get back to the Springs.

Aunt Marie is waiting for me. Tom, let's go!" And Tom drove him back to Palm Springs.

SP: Oh my goodness, so it was more just for himself, like you say, he couldn't stand for anyone to not like him?

EB: Yeah, exactly.

SP: And he didn't even want to know why you had left? That's terrible. I suppose that left you feeling really bitter, did it?

EB: No, not bitter. I knew how the Colonel was, you know. I knew the Colonel in a lot of ways. Other people had no idea, they only knew the Colonel through business association. You know

TOP: Shelly and Ed share a joke during the interview;
ABOVE: More of Ed's pictures of Elvis in concert.

"When, during a recent interview, Shelly Powers asked me why I hadn't written a book about Elvis, I replied that everything's already been said. What else was there to write about one of the most scrutinized and written-about men of the twentieth century? She persisted: 'Of course, most of the books written about Elvis have been written by people who didn't know him. If you were to write a book, it would be from the standpoint of someone who actually knew Elvis, who was there on the tours and in Vegas and Lake Tahoe with him, who saw him perform hundreds of times in concert, who served as the Tour Manager and Official Photographer for the Elvis Presley Show, and who knew the Colonel most of his life. Who is qualified to write a book on Elvis if not you?' Well, I hate to admit it, but she made some good points. I said, 'All right, all right! I'll do it, Shelly!' And so here, from one fan to another, are a few of my memories of Elvis, the King of Rock'n'Roll..."

ED BONJA ON BEING COERCED INTO WRITING HIS BOOK ON ELVIS

TOP RIGHT: Elvis circa 1960; **RIGHT:** Elvis in concert.

we called him Uncle Tom for the first years that we knew him, and then he got the colonel designation and we were told you have to call him Uncle Colonel. I could have been 13 years old before I knew he wasn't my blood uncle. It was always Uncle Tom and Aunt Marie. A lot of times he was almost like a father figure, and of course he was your employer too.

SP: What was your overall opinion of Colonel Tom Parker? There has been much controversy about him being bad for Elvis, good for Elvis. In general, would you say he was a good person?

EB: You know I try and look at someone and see, I don't want to look at the bad parts. I look at what's good in them and that's what I want to concentrate on. Even to this day. The Colonel had an awful lot of good in him, and people didn't know him. For years after we moved from Chicago to California, they were in town normally on a Sunday afternoon, and the Colonel and my Uncle Tom would come for dinner. The Colonel and my "Aunt" Marie, his wife, would come for Sunday dinner and before they would come to the house they would go to a supermarket near us and they had a station wagon full of food. We had ten kids in our family, so we weren't exactly rich. So

when the Colonel came in his car, the wheels would be down on the ground because they would be so loaded with all the weight of the food. You know it was a big event. We loved to see the Colonel, and he loved to play with the kids. Other people that know of the Colonel or have read about him had no idea about this other side of the Colonel.

EB: When I first went to Las Vegas in 1970, Elvis was performing at the International. Well, it was the Hilton at the time, and we used to eat up in the suite a lot, and after dinner the Colonel would sit back and light up a cigar and tell stories about the old days. One of my biggest regrets ever is that I didn't have a tape recorder. What fascinating stories he would tell; he was a great storyteller and he would always talk very low, and you would lean forward to hear, you know. I saw him do this in business with big executives here at the Hilton. He had a lot of power and it worked.

SP: No doubt, he was a great businessman.

EB: But he told me that the first week I was here, he said, "Eddie let me tell you something. In this town if you ever show any sign of weakness these people will eat you alive, you gotta be tough." I saw that and learnt that from what was going on over seven years at the Hilton.

SP: So did you ever get to spend any time with Elvis at Graceland, and if so, did you prefer to take pictures of him there in a more relaxed atmosphere?

EB: No, because there was the Colonel's group and Elvis's group... and because of the relationship with the Colonel business-wise, the Colonel wanted some separation. You didn't hang out socially supposedly except when we snuck away with Elvis's guys or with Elvis. He wanted to keep it a business relationship and not too much familiarity. The only time I was really at Graceland was to shoot a cover and back for a recorded live *From Elvis Presley Boulevard* album or after we had finished a tour with Elvis, when we were going to do Memphis, that was always the last stop and after the whole show was over everyone would go over to Graceland for a party.

SP: Okay, and what about Priscilla? Did you get to meet Priscilla?

EB: I met her a couple of times in '70 and '71. She was never on the tour so I never really knew her socially. The last time I saw her it was at Colonel Parker's memorial service at the Hilton, and I went

up with my uncle, Tom Diskin, and his wife, Janique, to offer condolences. She shook hands, she was very gracious. You know so many bad things I have heard about Priscilla, a lot of people don't like her.

SP: I like her.

EB: You know, that day she couldn't have been better, she was incredible. You know we shook hands and talked, and my uncle said, "You might remember Eddie, Eddie was with the Colonel," and she said, "I may, but there have been so many." Which I understand. I'm not good with names either, but one thing further about Priscilla was she gave one of the eulogies when the service started, and it was by far the best, by far.

SP: I can believe that, and I have a lot of respect for Priscilla, I do.

SP: How close were you to Vernon? Did you ever get to meet Vernon?

EB: Yeah, I knew Vernon like he was one of the guys.

SP: So he was a nice guy?

EB: Yeah, he was a nice guy, I don't want to make any disparaging remarks about anybody, he was like one of the boys. I talked to Vernon all the time, on tours and in Vegas, you know he liked to spend a lot of time playing the slot machines.

SP: So, Ed, are you planning on doing another photo book as a follow up to *Elvis, Shot by Ed Bonja*?

TOP AND BELOW: Elvis in concert; **ABOVE:** Elvis circa 1960.

EB: Yes.

SP: Have you considered a more in-depth biographical book with details of your story in terms of touring and being on the road with Elvis rather than just the pictures?

EB: Yes, I've had one in the works for about six years now, and when I was ready to do it, the guy I was going to do it with for some reason kept putting it off and putting it off for a couple of years and three years went by. I don't know if I lost interest or started doing other things and he came over when I was in Vegas and we got together and he gave me a pep talk, and I said, "Yeah, I'm ready, I'm gonna start doing it," And he told me I got this gig here at the Cannery, and then I'm going to Palm Springs for two nights and then I'll be back, and I'll start with it. That was about the time when Al Dvorin lived here. [Al Dvorin was the announcer responsible for coming up with the phrase "Elvis has left the building."] So we went to the Palm Springs gig and it was on the way back when we had the accident, and Al was killed. Well, I went into a somewhat depressed state for quite a while after that, and I really hadn't got back that interest to finish the book. I thought, well, the guy had everything ready except the narrative, I had picked out 120 pictures, everything was ready to go, but I just haven't had—

SP: —the motivation?

EB: Yeah, probably, that's what it is.

SP: Well, you should, you should, Ed.

SP: It's there, but it just wasn't the right time... that's what you're saying.

EB: There's a guy in Finland that wants me to do a book. It will probably be a lot of the same pictures over again but it will probably be a lot better quality.

SP: What in your opinion was Elvis Presley's most photogenic aspect?

EB: He was Elvis of course, he just... well, it was like taking pictures of you. No matter what angle you look at it, you look good!

SP: Stop it! [Laughing.]
Which brings me to the next question, actually. Many people have said that Elvis was so good looking that meeting him in person would leave them speechless. Did you ever see that?

EB: Many times, many times. Some fans might write to the office or call the office and say I've come from Belgium and I've got four girls and they

ABOVE: Various images of Elvis in concerts throughout the 1970s, all taken by Ed.

would want to present Elvis with something, and they would love to meet him, and every once in a while either Tom Diskin or the Colonel would say alright be at etc., etc., at such a time and Eddie will meet you there. Who's Eddie, some guy comes out of the sky and it's Eddie. [Laughing.] So I used to bring a lot of fans downstairs before the show at the Hilton to meet Elvis and more often than not, they were dumbstruck, they couldn't talk, they would just cry, it was incredible.

SP: Well, because of what you did and where you were you probably met a lot of nice woman yourself, Ed. Not to get too personal.

EB: Well, you see I had this girlfriend for all those years, and I was so in love and loyal and all those other good things.

SP: Bless you, lovely man. What in your opinion was Elvis's most endearing qualities as a man?

EB: It's going to sound strange but his humility, the fact that he didn't put on airs, the fact that he wasn't arrogant, he wasn't that guy you know—"I'm Elvis." He was just the most normal, nice person that you ever wanted to meet.

SP: Yeah, being close to Elvis in his final years, did you ever feel he was tired of touring and maybe he would have preferred to return to acting?

EB: No, I remember in '76 closing night in Vegas. Elvis would always have a party for the family—husbands, wives, and relatives would all come in for the party, and Elvis would often get up and talk. If he hadn't have been a singer he would have been a great preacher. He would get up and talk about what he felt, and he would field the questions, and I remember one lady asking "What do you do now the gig is over, what do you do with yourself?" and he said, "God, I don't know. I go home sometimes, and I don't know what to do. I want to be on my stage, I live to perform."

SP: If you ask anyone where they were the day Elvis passed away and what they were doing, nine times out of ten they would know exactly where they were and what they were doing, I know where I was that day. For me, that was the end of my holiday. We were raised on Elvis, my mother loved Elvis, my brothers. For you, Ed, can you recall where you were at that time and how it affected you?

EB: I had left the show April 1st, and he died August 16th. I still had three brothers and five or six friends who were taken on as roadies for the Elvis tours, and

I had trained several of them for different positions in case I was busy, never realizing or thinking that he had gone. One of my good friends, Ron Johnson, was gonna go and try to do some of the jobs that I used to do, but Ron Johnson said like all the rest of my friends, "You need to go on the tours, you need to go back, the Colonel wants you, the Colonel said you don't have to say anything, just come back, just show up," and I said, "No, I'm not, I'm through, and I'm never going back." He left on the first tour, and I think he lasted two days doing two or three of my jobs. He quit and he flew back, got on a plane to Chicago and said I can't take it. Well, after the tour was over, he met with the Colonel and he was telling the Colonel about all this stuff and he told him you're asking too much, it's impossible to do this, and the Colonel of course said, "Well, Eddie did it all." The next tour Ron Johnson was doing the same thing; he would call me every day and would say, "C'mon, just jump on a plane." So I had a big house and several garages and he came over he wanted to leave his car at my place while he was out on tour. So we went to dinner and all through dinner he was saying "Come on, come on back on the road." I got in the car and I was driving him to the airport, he was going to meet James Burton, a couple of the Sweet Inspirations, and they were going to fly an air jet to Memphis to pick up two of Elvis's boys to fly on to Maine. So while we are in the car he's once again asking me, and I said, "Well, I didn't bring my suitcase with me," and he's like, "You can buy your clothes in Maine." I made this statement to him, I said to him, "Ron, I'm never going back, you know. You gotta think of yourself, this is the only income you have in the world right now, and you've seen the shape Elvis has been in the last year. You could get a call at any time saying Elvis is dead! No one knows." So that shut him up, and I dropped him at the airport, got to see some of the people again, and that was kind a neat. Then I went home and went to bed. The next morning before nine o'clock my phone rang, and I picked it up and said, "Hello" and all the voice said was "How did you know?" I said, "What, what are you talking about, how did I know what?" He said, "Elvis is dead." That's how I heard.

SP: Did you attend his funeral?

EB: No, I called back there and I talked to Joe and I talked to Vernon and a couple of other people, and they said don't even try to get back here, it's a zoo, it's a mess.

SP: Do you recall your last conversation, the very last time you talked to Elvis?

EB: There weren't a lot of conversations, you know.

Ninety-nine percent of the time I was around Elvis I was working, apart from "Hi, how's it going?" You can't really qualify that as a conversation. We were always on the go. For the shows, as soon as the shows started I would call Joe, he was right on stage and right off and leaving; if you saw him he was usually running you know.

SP: What do you miss about him the most?

EB: Just the fact that he's not here, someone asked me is there anything you didn't like about Elvis, and I said, "Yeah, the fact that he died too young."

SP: So when you think of Elvis, how do you remember him?

EB: I think of him as someone who was just a really good person. I told Joe Esposito one time, "they said, well, you were the tour manager, wasn't Joe Esposito the tour manager?" I said, "No Joe was Elvis's road manager." There's a little distinction. I would have gladly traded places with Joe at any time but he wasn't willing to do so. Yeah, you can't help but think of him as the superstar that he was, you know you picture him on stage in front of thousands and thousands of fans and all the adoration coming his way, but then you think of him too like on the airplane when I shot that image as a normal down-to-earth person.

SP: Just to lighten the mood a bit, do you have a TCB necklace? *(TCB - Taking care of business)*

EB: [whispers] Not anymore.

SP: So you did have one, and was that given to you as a gift?

EB: Yeah, when I was very sick in Philadelphia, we were in Philadelphia, Boston, and Cincinnati. The show group moved from town to town, but Elvis stationed himself in Philadelphia and stayed there for three days. The first night in Philadelphia I had ordered some sandwiches for my crew, and by the time we got back apparently the mayonnaise had gone bad and I got deathly ill so I didn't make the trip to Boston the next night. I stayed in bed and then the following night after that, since the show plane had already gone to Boston and I was feeling somewhat better, I got on the Elvis plane to go back to Cincinnati and once again the graciousness of Elvis, I'm sitting halfway back on the plane and he got on board and came right back to where I was. He crouched down and asked,

TOP: Elvis souvenir catalogue;
ABOVE: Elvis singing.

83

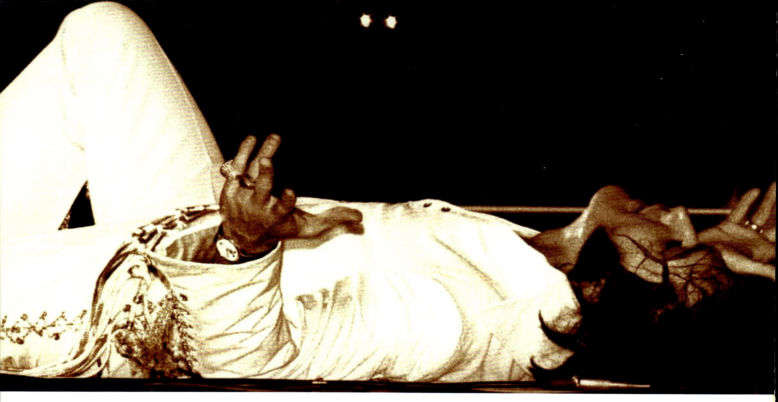

"How are ya, how are you feeling?" and that's when I got the TCB.
So gracious.

SP: Wow, that's fantastic, and how do you feel? Here's Elvis Presley crouching down next to you giving you this beautiful TCB necklace?

EB: There are no words.

SP: Do you have a favorite Elvis song?

EB: "Young and Beautiful."

SP: Perfect.

SP: What about the jumpsuits, is there one particular jumpsuit you like the best?

EB: I love the Indian figure jumpsuit. I think that is so beautiful.

SP: What do you believe is Elvis's legacy?

EB: Wow, all the music I think. It is never going to go away. He's on film everywhere, he's on video everywhere. Kids grow up and watch his movies not even knowing that he's no longer alive. They become fans at a very early age and it just continues. He's still alive, he's such a big part of so many peoples lives, young and old.

SP: Final question, Ed, this is a tough one. Would you mind if I gave you a hug and a kiss on the cheek?

EB: [Laughing.] Oh, That's a tough one with your daughter watching. Good Lord!

Ed gets up and we hug.

SP: Thank you so much, Ed.

EB: The pleasure was mine. Thank you.

Ed Bonja passed away on September 4, 2019, in a Berlin hospital, from leukemia and other medical complications. I will never forget Ed. He was the perfect gentleman, a wonderful photographer, modest and kind, a very dear man. He delivered the most beautiful, amazing images of Elvis Presley on stage and off for his fans to enjoy. It was a truly a pleasure knowing such a lovely man.

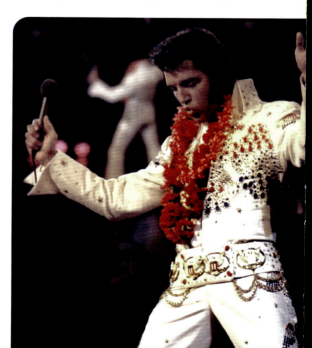

ELVIS

REMEMBERED

"He had so many girls after him that whenever he was working with us, there were always plenty left over. We had a lot of fun. We had a lot of fun in general, not just with the girls. It was nice that we could make a living at it, but every one of us would have done it for free. And you know, Elvis was so good. Every show I did with him, I never missed the chance to stand in the wings and watch. We all did. He was that charismatic."

Johnny Cash

"I was committed to taking the bullet, with a knife, with a bullet, with a chair, whatever, if someone come at him I was going to get in front of him. I wasn't gonna let him get hurt or shot or anything else..."

SONNY WEST, ELVIS'S BODYGUARD

Sonny West

Sonny West met Elvis in 1958 before Elvis left for Germany to complete his military service. Later Sonny was hired as Elvis's bodyguard, along with his cousin Red West. Sonny was not only his bodyguard but also his friend for 16 years. Sonny became a prominent figure in Elvis's entourage, known as the Memphis Mafia.

OPPOSITE: A portrait of Sonny, taken during the interview.

Interviewing Sonny...

On meeting Sonny for the first time I couldn't help but warm to him instantly. I kept an open mind always, and I feel satisfied in the knowledge that Sonny was the genuine article. I saw and heard nothing that would make me think otherwise.

TOP: Sonny and Shelly;
BELOW: Sonny (right) with Elvis and Frank Sinatra.

Before I had ever met Sonny, which was way before I set up an interview with him, I really wasn't sure what to expect as I'd heard so many different things said about him. I had watched clips of him talking about Elvis, heard plenty of negative stuff, too, mainly due to the book he assisted the Australian writer Steve Dunleavy to put together along with Red West and Dave Hebler in 1977. [Red and Dave were also former bodyguards to Elvis.] The book was a tell-all memoir regarding the personal life of his friend Elvis Presley. Whether the book was written in the heat of the moment—they had all been dismissed in July 1976 by Elvis's father Vernon Presley, who apparently cited a "cut down on expenses"—or if they were genuinely attempting to make Elvis sit up and take notice of what these drugs were doing to him, was not my incentive for the interview. I just wanted to form my own opinion of Sonny West, as a man and a friend to Elvis for 16 years, and I was determined to

not allow my judgment to be clouded by media reports. I have no doubt his love for Elvis was genuine, and my opinion is that whether or not the book was written in haste with a certain amount of bitterness and revenge as the vast majority say, I feel I sat across from a man that was sincere—he loved Elvis and had regrets about Elvis's demise at the end and especially regarding the timing of the release of the book that shook Elvis's world, as he wasn't to know that Elvis would pass away two weeks later. I met Sonny in Memphis with his lovely wife Judy at an Elvis convention. I found them to be a lovely couple. They were approachable and friendly and seemed to bounce off each other in a cute way that was endearing to witness. After chatting to them for some time I gave Sonny my contact details and asked if I could possibly interview him. We met again a couple of times after that in Vegas where I lived, and Sonny trusted that should I interview him, I would show him in a

true light to the fan club and other Elvis fans. So with that said the interview was arranged, and I hope I didn't let him down. Sonny was a sweet man, respectful to me, and courteous, a real Southern gent, and, boy, could he talk!

SP: Sonny, can you tell me how you first became friends with Elvis? Where did your friendship start?

SW: Well, I met him in 1958. A friend introduced me to him along with my three older sisters. Elvis was having a private party, it was after his mother had died and it was a short time... the end of August, part of September... before he was going to Germany for a year and a half, and Red was going with him [Red West]. Red's just getting out of the Marine Corps, you know. So he invites us out to this private skating party, it takes place after the place is closed to the public for the night, and Red introduced me and my brother-in-law to Elvis as new meat.

SP: New meat? Who said that?

SW: It was Red that said, "I want to introduce you to the new meat," and I said, "What does that mean?"

Elvis laughed and said, "I know you guys, so don't pay any attention to him." But I found out real soon what it meant, in a game they called "War."

SP: Really?

SW: Oh, yeah, it was a game where you don't hit in the face, but you can hit the guy anywhere. You can body block him, slam them, take the legs out from under them, and we watched it, and my brother-in-law got up and went back into the seats with my sister as Elvis said, "You watch it, and see how we play it, then we can take a break and you can all join in when we start back up again." So they skated over at the break, and Red said, "Where's Bill?" I said he's back up there with Barbara [Sonny's sister] and Red looked up at him and said, "Bill, c'mon." Bill said, "I'm not getting out there, man. I got a family to raise!" He was 28 or 29, he was in the Air Force, but bodies were flying all over the place and Bill was an AAU boxing champion. He went to the same school as Elvis but he was older than Elvis, about four years or so; he was a tough guy but he couldn't skate, and I couldn't skate. They had a box over there, a huge cardboard box. I had seen the guys go over there and get these elbow pads out, they would put them on their elbows and their

TOP: Elvis and Sonny;
ABOVE: Elvis was the best man at Sonny's wedding.

ABOVE: West and Presley with President Richard Nixon and Jerry Schilling at the White House on December 21, 1970.

knees, so I had done that too because I wasn't very good at all, and I knew I'd be falling. So Red looks at me and says, "What about you, Sonny?" I said, "Oh, yeah, I'll try it but I'm gonna go over to that box first." I took as many pads as I could get as high as I could get on my legs, all the way down around my ankles. I ran them up my arms and even on my hands for when I hit the ground. I looked like a hockey player, you know that game hockey?

SP: Yeah, I know hockey.

SW: I was like a goalie, I had all this stuff on, I just didn't have the mask. Now there was one girl that Elvis let join in on that game. Her name was Melinda Mullonicks, tough girl, and she could skate very good, very good and, well, of course me being the new guy on the block I was on the opposite team to Elvis, so I get over to the rail, I thought if I get to hold the rail so I don't keep falling. So Elvis's cousin, Junior, he blows the whistle, not for any penalties but when the time has come to begin, he just blows the whistle. So he blows it, and I try to start shuffling my legs to get going, and I look up and there's guess who coming towards me, the girl! Like a freight train and she's fast and when she got near me, I put my hands out in front. She hit me anyway and knocked me sprawling, boy. I got up and thought, God damn! So I look up and I start moving a little bit, and I'm

looking for someone that I could go hit, and all of a sudden someone gets me from behind my collar and smashes me down again, and it was her skating behind me! I thought, What is wrong with her? I start looking around for her now before I get up, so I get up, and I'm looking for her, and I see her and a couple of guys out there, and I start to get going, and suddenly something hits me from behind my knees, my legs fly out, and I hit the floor again... and she comes skating back.

SP: Oh, my God, she had it in for you!

SW: Yes, she did, and I got up one more time.

SP: Why was she picking on you, Sonny?

SW: She thought I was trying to hit her, and I think she might have thought because I was Red's cousin and our reputation.

SP: Did you have a reputation?

SW: Yeah.

SP: Were you always in trouble at school?

SW: Not at school but at the housing project we lived in.

SW: I was about ten years old when they started making me fight. I grew up in this gang, and the older ones taught us so we could take over when they left.

SP: Oh, no! They made you fight at ten?

SW: I'm telling ya, they were bad, they would turn your bicycle upside down, turn that wheel and put your arm against it. They were mean! So everyone fought the best they could because you didn't want to get beat up and the better you got the older the kid you had to fight. If you beat everyone your age then you moved up to eleven, twelve, or thirteen year olds. Fortunately, about six months later we moved out of the neighborhood, and that was it. I was glad because I got to thinking that they would just walk up to somebody and just hit them for no reason but the fun of it, and I grew up being so much against bullies.

SP: Was Elvis bullied in school? I heard he was.

SW: Oh, yeah, he was, and Red protected him. Red had a reputation in Humes High School, he was tough, you don't mess with him. There were some guys who were going to cut Elvis's hair one time, and Red stopped it. Another time Red was walking down the corridor, and there's Elvis leaning up against the wall there, and he wouldn't go outside. Everyone goes outside when school is over, but Elvis was just leaning against the wall, and Red asked "What are you doing?" Elvis said, "Oh, I'm just hanging out here, those guys are after me." And Red asked why and Elvis told him, "They wanna beat me up." Red said, "They do? Well, c'mon, let's go see if they can do it." So Elvis follows Red because he knew of his reputation. He walked out with him and there were these three boys out there. Red asked, "What's up, boys?" They said, "Oh, nothing we just want to talk to him." [Meaning Elvis.] Red said, "Well, start talking to him. I wanna hear it too." The guys refused to talk, and Red told them, "I know what you want, and if I hear you come after him, I'm gonna come after you. Now get out of here," and off they went.

SP: Why do you think that Red felt so protective towards Elvis?

SW: He didn't like bullies. Elvis was a quiet young man, never caused anything, never fooled around, or was loud or obnoxious, just walked around minding his own business. Elvis was very quiet, and Red didn't like that anyone could hurt someone just because they're different. And when Elvis started singing and performing years later, he ran into bullies, because there were guys out there who wanted to bully him because their girls thought Elvis was cute and sexy. So what does he do? He calls Red and says, "Red, do you wanna come out on the road with me?"

> **"When Elvis started singing and performing years later, he ran into bullies, because there were guys out there who wanted to bully him because their girls thought Elvis was cute and sexy. So what does he do? He calls Red and says, 'Red, do you wanna come out on the road with me?'..."**
>
> **SONNY ON HOW HIMSELF AND RED CAME TO WORK WITH ELVIS**

SP: And that's how it all started?

SW: That's how it all started.

SP: So where did you come into play?

SW: In '58 they were getting ready to go over to see Elvis, in Germany, and after six months Red came back, and he told me, "You know Elvis really likes you, and he said go out and see him when he gets back," and I said, "Okay." Red said, "He likes you but you say GD a lot." I used to cuss a lot.

SP: GD?

SW: I don't say it now as I'm a born-again Christian but I'd say it a lot, and Elvis didn't like that word at that time, so I said that's no problem, I can stop saying that, and I did. I stopped saying it for him: it still didn't bother me as I hadn't turned my life around yet. So I quit, and I went out to see him when he came home. The next thing you know he asked me if I'd like to go work for him. I said, "Doing what?" and he replied, "Whatever I need." So I ended up driving for him some.

SP: If you hadn't become his bodyguard, what direction would you have taken career-wise? Did you have any ideas yourself?

SW: Well, when I was in the Air Force and I saw *Rebel Without a Cause*; I was very moved by James Dean and his performance. I didn't relate to him at all. I wasn't an only child, there was six of us. So it wasn't that. I was just like a lot of other teenagers,

ABOVE: Elvis in concert.

"I think he is a creative genius. If they would have let him, it would have been unbelievable what he would have accomplished as a producer, as an actor, and all these things..."

SONNY WEST ON ELVIS'S SUPPRESSED TALENT

TOP RGHT: Sonny with Elvis;
ABOVE: Shelly with Sonny.

I just connected with him. Elvis was my idol, so to say, and so was James Dean. I was just working, fixing motors on washers, but I had a good boss, and so I told Elvis I got to give my boss notice. Elvis told me that was all right as he had to go to Florida to do a show with Frank Sinatra. Then he had to go to Nashville and then Hollywood, so I told him I'd be ready. In fact I was ready for when he went to Nashville, and I got to go and that's where he recorded "Stuck on You" and "Fame and Fortune." "Fame and Fortune" just knocked me out.

SP: Great song.

SW: I love his voice in that song.

SP: Do you have a favorite Elvis song?

SW: Well, there's three or four of them, one of them, which I got into a lot of fights over in the Air Force, but that's another story, was "I Was the One." Then another one was "The Wonder of You."

SP: Love it.

SW: Elvis dedicated that song to me and my wife one night because I told him that song was all about Judy, all about her, and like I say "Fame and Fortune" from 1960.

SP: Now there's a tremendous amount of footage for us all to enjoy. I can't get enough of it from the early days right through to the end. Seeing you go out into the audience with Elvis during a lot of his shows. You and the other guys were literally a human shield for him, weren't you?

SW: I was committed to taking the bullet, with a knife, with a bullet, with a chair, whatever, if someone come at him I was going to get in front of him. I wasn't gonna let him get hurt or shot or anything else. He knew that, he bragged on that, not just about me but Red too. He said, "I got a couple of guys that would go the route for me, they'll go the distance."

SP: So who's protecting you then when you're protecting Elvis? Did you ever get hurt?

SW: No, no. The night we went through that crowd at the Hilton Hotel I banged up my knee... I kept telling Elvis, "Keep moving, keep moving," because I knew if we stopped we wouldn't get started again. They were all crowding around us because they all wanted him, and they were pushing forward, and Colonel Parker jumped in there, too, and Joe, me, and Richard all trying to keep Elvis moving.

SP: He liked to stop sometimes.

SW: Yeah, but we were trying to make him not stop this time. He wanted to but we said, "Elvis, don't ever do that again." That's why when he got back up on stage on the other side he said, "my boy, my boy." He was so happy he had gotten through that.

SP: What lengths would the fans go to to get to Elvis?

SW: Some girls would put themselves in a box and get themselves shipped up there.

SP: Oh, my goodness!

SW: They were delivered like freight.

SP: Did they get in?

SW: Yeah, we said you earned it, so we went and told Elvis and asked him, and he said, "Yeah, they've earned it, bring them on in."

SP: How did that go?

SW: They met him and they said, "Oh, I can't believe it," and Elvis laughed and said, "I can't believe what you did!"

SP: Now Elvis got kind of lonely on tour sometimes didn't he? On tour all the time and it's been said so many times that he was a prisoner of his own fame.

SW: Well, you gotta understand something. Not just Elvis, but Bruce Springsteen and other big stars, when they're on tour they are prisoners. They have to be, they can't be accessible. When you're a star that's the way it is, and Elvis more than any other entertainer. He was so unique. You could take Barbara Streisand or Tom Jones... and you know there's an old thing that is true, if you took the Pope out of his robes or John F. Kennedy and they would walk by people might say, "Oh, he looks a bit like..." but if a Coca-Cola truck went down the street and Elvis went down the street, that's Coca-Cola and that's Elvis. So he was more so... but they're all prisoners when they're touring, they can't get out. The fans are hanging out there, a lot of them are drinking, you just don't do it. That's why he never went out when he was performing here either. [Vegas]

SP: What did he do to fill his time?

SW: He was tired, he was doing two shows a night.

Then he would stay up and visit and talk with people, maybe up to 6:30 or 7:30 in the morning, he would go to sleep and then get up around 4:30 or 5:00 in the afternoon, eat something, and then he would have to go down there for that 8 o'clock show. He was busy here, but he enjoyed visiting with the people that came up to the suite, sometimes there were celebrities. Most times they would come pay their respects at the dressing room, and then they left. Elvis wanted Ali up there [Muhammad Ali] so we had him go straight up and Elvis quickly got changed and he met him up there.

SP: What was he like?

SW: Oh, I love him, I love him to death. He's the same as Elvis, with his charisma and magnetism. He said to Elvis, "Now I know why all those women love you, because you're almost as pretty as me." Then Elvis broke down laughing, then he told Elvis, "Boy, you are somthin', You are somthin'." One of his guys, Gene Kilroy, asked if he could get a robe for Ali made like one of the suits Elvis had. So I said I'll ask Elvis. So later I told Elvis and he said he was going to get

TOP: Stylized picture of Elvis and Sonny; **ABOVE:** Elvis at Sonny's wedding.

"He said to Elvis, 'Now I know why all those women love you, because you're almost as pretty as me'…"

MUHAMMAD ALI TO ELVIS

TOP RIGHT: Elvis during the comeback special; **ABOVE:** Elvis demonstrates his martial art training to Muhammad Ali, who's wearing the robe given to him by Elvis.

one made up for him, so we did and I called Gene and said, "We have it." So Gene said Ali was going to leave a bit earlier on the way to the fight which was a week away. So they were going to come earlier as we were right next to the convention center where the fight was going to be held. So they did, and I went and got him with our security guard and brought him back over. On the way in the car Ali wanted to sit up front with me and so we get over there to give him his present and I'm stood next to Gene and Gene's grinning, he's so happy and all of a sudden Elvis appears and he brings the robe in. Ali gives Elvis some gold gloves that he had autographed, they're hanging in Graceland now. So Ali takes the robe out that Elvis gave to him. Ali says, "Whoa, man . . ." He puts it on and it's meant to say the People's Champion, but I got The People's Choice put on there, and Ali's looking at it, and Gene says, "Sonny, it's supposed to say the People's Champion." And I'm thinking, "Oh, man," and Ali's looking in that mirror and he knew it didn't say Champion, and he looks at the reflection and says, "What does that say?" And

about five guys say together. "The People's Choice." I step up and say, "I'm so sorry, Ali, that is my fault. I messed up, that's what I had them put on there." I said we will get it fixed or we will get a new one, and I looked at Elvis for confirmation, and he got that look on his face, because he was watching me just stumble around, and I felt embarrassed for him. So he indicated yeah don't worry, but I couldn't afford it, it was $5,000. So all of a sudden Ali looked at me and because I guess I stepped forward and took the blame and everything, he said, "Wait a minute, wait a minute, guys, let me think about this for a minute," and he started saying the words to himself "People's champion. People's choice. People's choice, People's champion… I like it. We gonna keep it just like it is!" So it stayed like that and it's on display at his place in Louisville, and that was me who came up with that.

SP: Wow, Sonny!

SW: Now I don't know how many he had made up, but I have a medallion with his image on it of Ali and it's got "The People's Choice" on it. He sent that to me, and I don't know how rare it is or what, but I got it and it means the world to me like the TCB I got from Elvis.

SP: Do you keep in touch with him?

SW: I sent him one of my books and signed it to him. I said I was there when the two "greatest" got together, each in their own field and I am privileged to have been there, sincerely Sonny West. I sent it up to his home in Michigan, so I'll wait and see if he gets back to me.

SP: Well, be sure to let me know.

SW: I will, everyone will know. I enclosed a letter saying I appreciate it if you would make sure Ali gets this as I know he will remember me.

SP: Floats like a butterfly, stings like a bee.

SW: Yes, ma'am.

SP: Now, Sonny, you've been married to the same woman, Judy, for… how many years is it?

SW: It'll be 37 years in December of this year.

SP: Well, I met her two years ago, and she was very sweet.

SW: It was three years, 2004.

SP: Well, you have a better memory than I do Sonny. In August it'll be three years since we met up.

Tell me a little bit about your wedding day. I want to hear all about it because Elvis was your best man, wasn't he? How did that come about?

SW: Yeah, I introduced him to her in 1969 when he was making the film *Change of Habit*. I wanted to bring her over so he could meet the girl I was going to marry and he said, "Sonny, you ain't never gonna get married, you a bachelor for life," and I said, "Well, yeah, I thought I was but thunder has struck and lightning has hit me, boss, she is it." So Elvis said, "Oh, okay then, I need to meet her." So her mum was out here too so I brought them out here and Elvis was as gracious and nice to both of them. Elvis said later, she's as sweet as her mom, and you may get hooked there Sonny, son you better be careful. I said, "I already am." So I was doing a bit of TV work myself. I was in the Beverly Hillbillies as Elly May's potential beau.

SP: I love the Beverly Hillbillies. I had a crush on Jethro!!

SW: He had a crush on my wife until he knew she was with me, and then he said, "never mind." He knew me too from playing football and everything. Yeah, in the Beverley Hillbillies I played Dr. Robert Graham, the veterinarian. The name of the episode was called "*Home Again*." Yeah, the family had been somewhere, and Granny had left her glasses, she doesn't have her glasses. So they're talking about Dr. Graham, and he's a nice-looking young man, and so she says, "I'm gonna go out there and see him." And there's a seal swimming in the pool, and she starts talking to it thinking she's talking to me. Crazy stuff. So Granny goes back in and she says,

"I saw him but I didn't think he was all that good looking, and, boy, his breath, like he's been eating fish all day." So it was funny stuff and the character Robert Graham had a little brother about eight years old or something and Graham was like in his late twenties and so they said, "Granny, did you meet his little brother? He's adorable." So Granny goes back out there and now instead of a seal there's an otter, and she says, "Boy, they sure can swim," and that's all because she doesn't have her glasses on. Anyway that was just the one show I was in, as they decided not to give the character Elly May a boyfriend. Anyway, Elvis got in touch with me and said, "Sonny, I'd like you to come back and be my chief security aide," so I did, and at that point there was only me. Red wasn't there, and it was a year later that he got the death threat. So the death threat came, and he told me to call Red to come on out. I called Red and Red came out right away, and he never left. He stayed until 1976. So we were back doing what we had done before.

SP: How serious do you think that death threat was?

SW: It was very serious, as we all know there are nuts, look at the one that shot Reagan.

SP: —and John Lennon.

SW: Exactly, Mark Chapman. So I believe John Lennon might not have been shot and killed if he had a professional bodyguard, he's gotta be armed. He can't even defend himself

TOP: Sonny West, Red West, and Elvis at the White House; **ABOVE:** Red West and Elvis sparring.

but if he has a trained bodyguard who instinctively knows… You see a fan is a fan, and they think you belong to them, and they don't call you Mr. Lennon and they don't call you Mr. Presley, they call you Elvis, they call you John. If I had been there and someone came out of the shadows and said, "Mr. Lennon," I'd have got between them. Now I might have got shot but I'd have got my gun out as quick as I could to shoot him.

SP: Were you always armed when you were with Elvis?

SW: I came out of the Air Force and I went to learn shooting. I wasn't qualified or anything but I developed a very fast draw.

SP: Did you ever have to use your gun?

SW: Never had to, and the reason I developed that fast draw, Shelly, was because I knew the only time I would have to use it was if I saw a gun in someone's hand. I don't care if they're threatening to do this or threatening to do that, if I don't see a gun, I'm not going to draw. I developed real fast because he's got the draw already, he's out and I've got to draw that gun and shoot it before he's gonna aim his gun and shoot it. I practiced, practiced. Some of the guys said to Elvis, "Sonny, he's fast on the draw." So he saw me do it and he started putting me up against policemen when we would go out on tour and we had security on the floor, on the hotel floor. They said I was like a cobra, fast. Then we had Dave Hebler—he was a black belt at karate—and Dave had this strike that he could do where it was 13 death blows in a second and a half, hit the guy and snap his neck, 13 different things he could do in two seconds and Elvis would have him show us, and then Elvis would say, "Now, Dave, show us those moves in slow motion," and Dave would do it again, and Elvis just loved it. Cops that watched it were just blown away, you know.

SP: Wow, I love that story.

SP: Can we just talk about this new book of yours? You told me in an email it took you 25 years, so what made you go ahead and write a second book, Sonny? Tell us as much as you can without giving too much away.

SW: Well, no, I'll tell you all of it. I didn't want *Elvis: What Happened* [the first book Sonny wrote] to be my legacy to Elvis. It was written out of love, it was a challenge. I would not have written that book if Elvis had died. If I was still working for him at the end, and he died. I would never had written a book like that about him.

SP: You wouldn't?

SW: No, neither would Red! We wrote that book because we put it right there in front of Elvis. "Here it is, Elvis. Here's where you're at, look at what you're doin'. You got rid of us, you fired us, it doesn't change a thing, you were killing yourself and you're hurting people's feelings around you. You're attacking people, you're being mean, you're being cruel, and he was. I mean The Sweets, he insulted them, Kathy Westmoreland, but that wasn't Elvis... drugs.

SP: What do you think made the change in him?

SW: Drugs, drugs.

SP: Didn't you say you went as far as trying to give him placebos?

SW: I didn't, we emptied stuff out, and everything, but Dr. Nick gave us something to put in there, and I flushed a whole big box of very heavy-duty pain pills away. His Aunt Delta brought a new box to me and said this is that box from Las Vegas. I opened one bottle and took out a couple and gave

them to Dr. Nick to check, and Dr Nick said these are not placebos, they are 100% the real thing. So I just knew I needed to write this book. My last book didn't look like a book of love, and it sure didn't come across as a book about love, so I said I just gotta do it again, man. So I just kept putting it, and I put it off and said some day, you see we were the only ones that wrote a book before he died; all the others books came afterwards. Jerry Hopkins had a book out but there wasn't anything to it. I just knew that I had to and all of a sudden I realized I'm getting up there. Richard died and Charlie [Charlie Hodge], and I thought, "It's time," because you never know. I'm getting up there in my twilight years. I'm 68 years old.

SP: Looking good, though!

SW: Thank you, thank you very much. I feel good. So I just thought, "I better do it." It took me four and a half years but I did it.

SP: It took you four and a half years to finish the book? You obviously put a lot of thought into this book.

SW: Oh, yeah, it had to be right. We tried to make the first book right, but we were saddled with a terrible writer, a sensationalist guy. People don't realize, we didn't get to pick our author out, we didn't pick the writer, he was assigned. We signed a deal with World News. World News hired him to do it, we had no choice on who they had to write the book. So he made everything sensational.

SP: When that first book came out did you immediately regret it?

SW: I never regretted it, I can't regret it, if I regret it that means I was wrong in doing it. I don't believe I was wrong in what we were trying to do. I wasn't trying to hurt Elvis, we were trying to wake him up! And he woke up and he got mad, he was threatening to kill us and everything and that's good, that's good, and in the front of the book, Shelly, it says, "Just maybe it'll do some good." He's gonna get mad. He knows every word's the truth, and just maybe it'll do some good, that's where we were at. I've had people say, "God if you could have written it a year earlier." I said, "A year earlier we were working for him and we were telling him it was wrong. That's why he fired us! That's the only reason that book was written, the ONLY reason."

SP: It wasn't like a retaliation?

SW: Not at all. Let me tell you something, Shelly, in

TOP: Sonny in his role in the movie *Hellcats*; **ABOVE:** Promotional poster for *The Hellcats*; **OPPOSITE:** Elvis at Sonny's wedding.

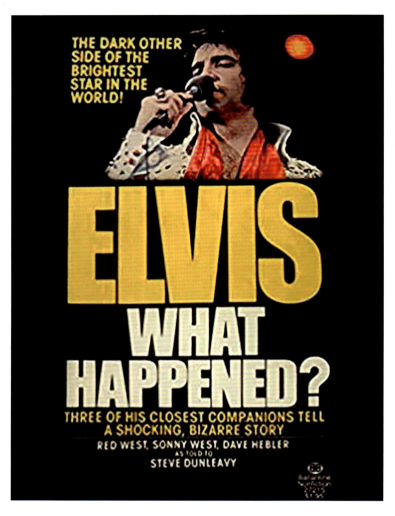

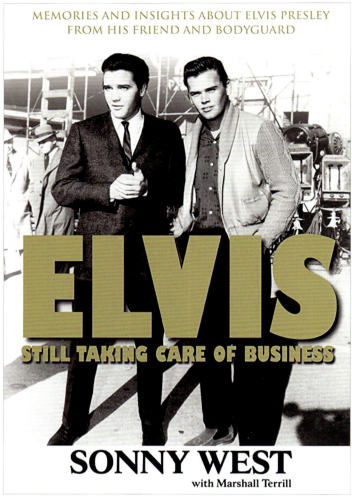

ABOVE: Sonny wrote two books about his life with Elvis. The first, *Elvis: What Happened?* caused great controversy, and was said to have caused an unfixable rift between Sonny and Elvis.

1961 Elvis hit me, with his fist, and knocked me out. He was drinking, and it was over Tuesday Weld and a girl that she brought up. He was dating Tuesday, and we had just come back from Hawaii as he was making *Blue Hawaii* so were shooting the interiors on the sound stage of Paramount and this was one of those nights when Tuesday came up there and she brought a girlfriend. So Elvis sat with Tuesday, and I was talking to the girl at the bar, and we were just talking and having a drink, then all of a sudden Elvis gets up to go to his room but he comes over to the bar, and he leans in between us, and he says, "Damn, you're cute," and he gives her a little peck.

SP: The girl that you were talking to?

SW: Yeah, and she just blushed and walked away and I just kind of smiled at her and said, "Oh, you're getting a little red there." She said, "Oh my goodness," so she went off, then she came back. Then three minutes later Elvis came back and he leaned in there again. He stared at her for a minute, then he started really kissing her, now he's leaning in between us,

he shuffled right in between us, and all of a sudden I see her arms come up around his neck and head and I just thought, "Wup, that's it." I knew she was gone. So I slid off the stool, I walked away, sat down next to Elvis's cousin Gene and Tuesday, who were watching and giggling—she was a wild thing! It wasn't even bothering her, she's just giggling, and she said, "Oh, my gosh, look at him." So I went over and I sat down next to Gene and as I walked over Gene said, "Burnt."

SP: What does burnt mean?

SW: Meaning shot down, down in flames, baby.

SP: Okay, you mean the girl.

SW: Yeah, and I said, "To a crisp." So I leaned over and said, "Gene, let me ask you something. If you had your choice between Tuesday and that girl, who would you take?" He said, "Tuesday." I said, "Me too, me too, man." I see Elvis straighten up and he hollers all the way across the bar and says, "What did you say, Sonny?"

SP: So he heard what you said?

SW: No, he thought I was saying something bad about him because he saw me whispering to Gene. Now I couldn't say what I'd said in front of Tuesday and that girl, so I said nothing. I just wanted to ask him something and he said, "GD [God damn], you're going to tell me what you said or I'm going to break a bottle over your head." He had a Pepsi bottle there with him, and all of a sudden a rage came up in me, because he's talking like that to me, and I stood up and I said, "You're not going to hit me with any bottle, you're not going to hit me with anything. You just stop, you SOB," and I said, "You have changed so much this year from the time I went to work for you, what you were. You have changed Elvis, you're mean, you're mean!"

SP: What year was this, Sonny?

SW: 1961, and so I said, "I'm outta here. I quit," and he said, "You can't quit, you're fired." I said, "Whatever, I'm outta here." He came around to stop me from leaving, stood right in front of me, he started hollering at me again. I hollered right back at him. [Then Sonny made a fist and demonstrated a punch to indicate what had happened.] All of a sudden... punch!... he hit me, and I just turned around and looked at him, and tears came into my eyes. I said, "I never thought you could do that." And I walked, and he let me go! Then Tuesday came in there with Alan, crying saying, "What is wrong with him? What did he hit you for? You did nothin'. What's he doing?" I said, "He's drinkin'." I didn't want to explain to her—she was kind of young, and when she drank she got a little sillier—so Elvis sometimes had a couple of drinks and he would get a bit silly too, so it wasn't too bad, but I couldn't tell her what I'd said. So while I was in there with Tuesday, Alan said, "I don't know what's wrong with him, man." I said, "I don't know either, Alan. He has changed, you know it. Maybe he's tired or something." Then I told them I was going to get some stuff and leave. I called a cab.

SP: You must have been really upset.

SW: I was. I was very crushed. Al said, "Where are you going?" I told him I called a girl, and I told her I'd like to come up and stay for a couple of days... I had an argument with Elvis and I want to think things out and she said, "Come on over." So he came in there and asked Tuesday and Alan to leave, and he went over to Gene and said, "Gene tell me what he said," and Gene quietly told him. He said, "What else did he say" and Gene said, "He said nothing, Elvis, he just asked me that, and I told him Tuesday... and that was "that." So Elvis felt

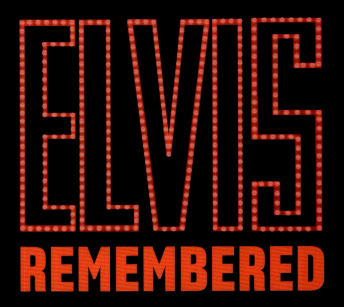

ELVIS REMEMBERED

"I can't honestly say that 'Heartbreak Hotel' is Elvis's best record. I love Elvis so much that for me to choose a favorite would be like singling out one of Picasso's paintings. What I will say is that it's Elvis's most alarming performance. When I hear it, I always get this image in my head ... Elvis driving his Lincoln down the interstate on a clear night in Tennessee. The stars are twinkling. The air is balmy. They're on their way to a show, Bill Black and Scotty Moore in the back, with Bill's double-bass strapped to the car roof. And now that bass belongs to me. It's my link to 'Heartbreak Hotel.'"

Paul McCartney

On "HEARTBREAK HOTEL"

ELVIS
REMEMBERED

"Early on somebody told me that Elvis was black. And I said, 'No, he's white but he's down-home.' And that is what it's all about. Not being black or white it's being 'down-home' and which part of down-home you come from'... I have a respect for Elvis and my friendship. It ain't my business what he did in private. The only thing I want to know is, 'Was he my friend?' 'Did I enjoy him as a performer?' 'Did he give the world of entertainment something?'—and the answer is YES on all accounts.

The other jazz just don't matter... On a scale of one to ten, I would rate Elvis eleven."

Sammy Davis Jr

bad because he knew I had not said anything but he couldn't say he was sorry. It was a perfect time, after he had told Tuesday and Alan to leave, and it was just the two of us. He could have said "Sonny, I made a mistake, I thought you were putting me down, and I'm sorry for hitting you like that." But he couldn't do it. That's why I knew after that time, or anytime, he was never going to say he was sorry to anybody because he wouldn't say it at that time, and he knew he was wrong.

SP: So Elvis had a problem saying he was sorry?

SW: I never heard him say it, he has to have a problem. He would do other things like, "Maybe I shouldn't have done this," but never saying "I'm sorry. I was wrong."

SP: Well, how did it go then when he came back into the room with you?

SW: Well, he just asked me what was I doing and this and that, and I said I'm leaving. I said, "You've changed, Elvis." I'm quieter now, and he says, "No, I haven't." I said, "Oh, yes you have, you're different." Here's the thing, the reason I say this is it wasn't just that–we used to light Elvis's cigars! He didn't carry anything on him, money or nothing, and when he would light up one of those cigars whoever was around would give him a light. I remember an instance there where we were sitting and I'd gone back and I'll tell you when I think this all started, Elvis being this way. Remember *Jailhouse Rock*?

SP: Yes, I remember *Jailhouse Rock*.

SW: He was the king that night, well, he thought he was hot stuff. He would say, "Go walk the dog, and do this, and he kind of got like that, and I'll tell you why. So one night, we're all sitting there

ALL IMAGES: Elvis with Sammy Davis Jr.

105

TOP: Sonny and Elvis; **ABOVE:** Elvis photographed by Memphis photographer William Speer at his Blue Light Studio in 1954.

starts getting him multiple picture deals, three pictures a year with Paramount, three pictures a year! One with Paramount, one with MGM, and one with Fox. Another with Paramount, with MGM, and with United Artists. So for the next three or fours years he had about 9 to 12 movies signed up to do. So he was secure, and of course he received money, they did well, all of them did. Then *Blue Hawaii* came along, and that really made him some money but he was like this before we had finished. He was like this before the contracts were signed because he knew that he was going to be around for some time with these contracts, with these pictures.

SP: So you think that changed him? That's strange because everyone I have spoken to, everyone I have interviewed have all said how humble he was, how giving he was.

SW: Exactly, exactly. I told you this was a short period of time, this happened right there in '61, but then it was gone, it was gone, and I think maybe the night he hit me he realized something is wrong here—I just hit Sonny, I just hit my friend, and he didn't do anything. That could have done it, or it may not have done it, I don't know. All of a sudden things were good, nine days after it happened we walked on the set, and we laughed about it. He said I was crazy, I said, "I'm not crazy, you crazy, you're the one that did the hitting, boy." He was very humble, very giving, and he never got like that again. He never, the rest of the time I was with him, he never did. It just happened there. Guess what my nickname was?

SP: What was your nickname?

SW: Hunk, he didn't mean it like a hunk guy, he just meant it like Hunk, that character in *Jailhouse Rock* was Hunk. They got into a fight, and when Hunk hit the guy [Elvis's character]—and remember he hit him in the throat and he thought he had lost his voice—and remember how bad Hunk felt, but in this case it was turned around.

SP: And I suppose you can get lost in the character sometimes, you know?

SW: Well, that wasn't it, he wasn't even hinting about *Jailhouse Rock* in 1961 when we did this, we were making the movie *Blue Hawaii* and *Jailhouse Rock* was years earlier in '56 you know. He just changed, he was young, you gotta remember that. Young, multi-millionaire, and the pressure on him and the stress, and he thought, "Man, I'm bigger than I thought, and I'm gonna be fine."

SP: Perhaps you're right, maybe that was a little

watching the television, he's got his feet up on the coffee table and he's leant back. So he puts them down and he leans over, and he gets a cigar. He's got this little case of German cigars, so he picked one of them out, leaned back, and right next to the box is a cigarette lighter, a table cigarette lighter. He didn't pick it up, though. He sat back, put the cigar in his mouth, and waited, and we're watching television, we're not paying attention. He said, "Am I going to sit and puff on this dry cigar all night, or is someone gonna light it for me?" A couple hands went out, and someone grabbed that lighter, it was Red, and Elvis puffed on his cigar and he didn't say nothin'. So these little things... I thought what is wrong with him? What has happened?

SP: And he was never like that before?

SW: No, Never! And the only thing I can figure out is Elvis admitted he was hearing a lot about a shooting star, a flash in the pan, he won't last, and he was hearing all that just before he was about to go out to Germany. He got to thinking what if that did actually did happen while he was in Germany. What if him being there made his fans follow some other people? Jerry Lee Lewis, and other guys kinda took his place. So when he came back, they released songs... he didn't do anything while he was in there except be in the service, so they released some songs he had recorded before he went in. When he came back all of a sudden Colonel Parker said Elvis is wondering if they're gonna want him, if the studios are gonna want him, and Colonel Parker

awakening for him when he gave out that punch.

SW: I think it was, because he knew after he had talked to Gene that it was something that shouldn't have happened, he knew, but he just could not say, "I'm sorry. I should not have hit you, man, I was wrong." He didn't say it, and I knew then I didn't think I would hear him say it to anybody, and I never did. I don't care how many of the other guys said that he said sorry to me, he didn't, he just didn't do it. I heard Marty [Marty Lacker]. I love Marty, and we were talking, and Marty said something about Elvis, about the only time he ever heard Elvis say, "I'm sorry," and Marty was saying Elvis said it to him. I love Marty, but its hard for me to accept that. Things that Elvis did sometimes, times that he could have said that he was sorry. I don't even know if he told Priscilla... if he did it wasn't in our presence.

SP: Yeah, I think I heard somewhere or read somewhere that he would never actually say he was sorry, but he would do things.

SW: Oh, yeah! Exactly, he would do things. It was like when he gave me that first car, shortly after he gave me that motorcycle, and he gave me a car, it was a Cadillac convertible. I didn't want to take it, and I walked away, would not accept the keys for it. I went back, got in the Rolls Royce that I'd driven him there in, I got back in the driver's seat. He came over and got into the back, and he says, "What's wrong with you?" I said, "Elvis, nothing's wrong with me. It's just weird, you always seem to be giving, and we always seem to be taking," and I said, "and I just don't like that." He said, "Sonny, you guys have given, I know I have put a lot on ya, but you guys handle it, and you just keep on goin' and this is just my way of saying thank you." I said, "Well, I can understand that." He said, "You can't tell me that when you were a little kid you wouldn't sit on that curb and watch Cadillac convertibles go by and say, 'I'm gonna have one of those.'" I said, "Of course, everybody does." He said, "I know, I did," then he said, "Well, you got yours. Now let's go get mine." That's why we were over there in the first place, for a baby blue Cadillac for him, a baby blue Cadillac convertible. In fact it was me, Marty and Billy, his cousin, and we had just come from looking at the bus that George Barris was customizing for him, and we were riding back up to the Bel-Air in Los Angeles. It was a beautiful night in May, and he said, "Man, this is a baby blue Caddy night," and then he said, "Sonny, turn around, and let's go to that Cadillac place." As we're going over I said,

"Elvis, are you sure about a blue car?" because he always said he liked white and black. You kinda get tired of colors because after a while, colors wear on you, that's why most of his cars were black or white. So as we're going over there I say, "Elvis, are you sure you want a baby blue one?" He says, "Yeah, yeah." So we get over there, go inside, and on the floor there's a black one, with the mahogany wood trim, and I said, "Elvis are you sure? Look at that!" And he says, "That thing is pretty, boy," but he went in there for a baby blue one. The sales guy said, "No, I don't have one, but I'll find you one." So Elvis said, "All right. Marty, you stay here with him while he does that. Sonny, you come with me and Billy." And so we walk across the street, and we went through their used car lot. I think he's looking for a baby blue one, maybe two or three years old, you know, and so there's not one over there, and Elvis says, "I don't see what I'm looking for here. Where's

ABOVE: Elvis Presley with Las Vegas entertainment columnist Forest Duke at the opening of Johnny Ray's show at the Dunes Hotel. Sonny West is behind them: January, 26, 1962.

ABOVE: Elvis on the Ed Sullivan show, 1956.

that other Cadillac place?" So I told him, and he said, "Let's go down there. Billy, tell Marty we'll be back." We jump in the car and head down there and we pull into the lot, and I let Elvis and Billy out at the entrance. I park the car across the lot there out of the way. This is early evening, around 7 o'clock or something, and by the time I park it and walk back over there, here comes Billy and the salesman. Then Elvis comes out. I say, "Well?" and Elvis turned to me and said, "Hey, Sonny, is that what you're talking about right there?" And right there is this '63 Eldorado black on black Cadillac convertible with the black leather and the lights, you know how they shine at night, and I thought, "Wow!" I said, "Yeah, look at that, Elvis! I mean, the black on black!" He said, "Here, it's yours." So I said, "No, it's not," and I turned and walked away, and that's what happened.

SP: Well that's one of the questions I have from our president of the fan club, Jason Edge. He heard that you loved cars and helped look after Elvis's fleet of cars, and he wanted to ask you what were your favorite cars that Elvis owned?

SW: Okay, yeah, you know what car I really loved? It was that 1970/71 Lincoln, the Mark 3. Elvis liked it too. He went to Palm Springs in that, and you didn't know it but you were doing 90 miles an hour in that... you don't realize it. That car was like a cloud, it was almost like it ran above the road... if you came to any dips or anything it just floated off them. He said, "This is the best damn ride I've ever had." I said, "It is, Elvis, it really is." It was a wonderful car. One of our favorites. Another one was the Stutz he had, and I liked the Pantera. You know what the Ford Pantera was? It looked like a Ferrari; they were made in '72, '73. It was yellow, and it looked like this Ferrari. It was fast, oh, man. Elvis used to take that thing out and do about 145 an hour on the Interstate 55. I was in there a couple of times, and I'd say, "Hey, man, were getting ready to take off." I felt like we were going to leave the ground. I was with him when he shot it one time. We were going for a ride, and it wouldn't start, the battery was dead, he didn't use it often. We were out in the front, and I said let's go get it jump started, but he says, "No," and he starts to get out, and I look over and I see him getting his gun, and I'm like, "Whoa." I open my door and I get out because he's pulling that gun out, then all of a sudden when he gets out he goes bang. [Sonny makes this shooting noise and poses like he's holding a gun.] Then he shoots at the dashboard and says, "Now you are dead, you son of a bitch." I'm ducking and I say, "Elvis, it's just the

battery," and he says, "It's dead now." Well, I got them to fix it, and it started up, and it was fine. We didn't go riding that day but the next time we went out I told them, I said, "Please make sure that that battery is ready all the time, because the next time it might be a stick of dynamite he throws in." So they always kept that battery charged. Another time the tires blew out on a car we were driving back to Vegas, and Elvis then wanted to trade it in, he said it's no good. I said Elvis it's not the car, it's the tires. He said, "Man, when you get something new, everything should work!" His philosophy on things sometimes was just so naive, and it was just beautiful, like a child. We said, "No, no, it's the tires. It's got nothing to do with the car." Then we went to get the spare tire out. Back then those big white walls had a blue film over them to protect the white wall until you use it, and then it wears it off. We bring that tire out, and he says, "What the hell did they give us a blue tire for?" We said, "It's not blue, Elvis, it's a film on it that washes off." He said, "Well, get it off. We can't go into Vegas with it like that." So we cleaned it off, then all of a sudden he notices that the hub cap has gone. I said, "I saw it pass us and go over the fence as Elvis was bringing the car to a stop when the tire blew." And that thing just kept on going and they had floods at that time going on in the desert so it had hopped up over the wall there. So I told him, and he said, "Well, go get it," and I thought, "Oh, man, me and my big mouth." So I went over there, and I looked over, and sure enough there it is in some tall green grass, and it's got some water around it, and it's just laying on its side, and there's the water and I'm thinking, "Snakes, there's gonna be a thousand snakes down there in that stuff." So I went down there, and I went down to the end of the dry part, I took my shoes and socks off, rolled my pants up to my knees and I counted to three and I was gonna get in there and outta there as fast as I could because I was afraid to tiptoe out there slowly. If I was going too slow, a snake might strike me, so I thought if I run I might be okay, by the time he strikes I'm gone.

SP: Poisonous snakes?

SW: Probably, rattlesnakes, there's a whole bunch of them out in the desert. I ran out there, got the thing, and got back and, boy, I didn't get bit. I took my pants and I rolled them down, put my shoes and socks back on and ran back and said, "There ya go," and we put it on and went on to Vegas.

SP: You must have had a lot of good times with Elvis.

SW: Ninety-nine percent of the time.

SP: What would you consider your best memory of just you and Elvis? Was there ever a time when it was just you and Elvis?

SW: Yeah, a couple of them. One of them was down there in Palm Springs, and I had made something, and I came out and I had heard Elvis in the kitchen, something like that, so I came out and I asked him, "Is there anything I can get you, boss?" and he just looked at me and said, "I love you, Sonny." I said, "I love you too, Elvis." He said, "You're always there." So I went on to say, "I was just looking to see what we got, and I'll make you something," and that was it, that was very touching, and when he was my best man at my wedding, it was very touching.

SP: How was that day with Elvis as your best man?

SW: He kept me loose, he kept that grin on his face the whole time.

SP: Because you were nervous?

SW: Not nervous, but knowing that here it is, it's over. I'm not going to be a bachelor in a few minutes, I'm gonna be a married man, and that word used to worry

me until I met her. That was very warm... and the time he helped that black lady in the wheelchair. She had no legs, and Marty read about it in the paper, and he said, "Elvis, look at this." It was one of those appeal stories that a columnist had done to raise money for this little black lady who had no wheelchair. She would get around on those boards nailed together with metal roller skates, and she had these special handles that she got along on like that. So we took that chair to her, and we cried, and she cried. She was so grateful, and when we left I said, "Elvis, I don't think she even knew who you were," and he said, "It doesn't matter so long as she knew someone cared." I remember one time we used some grass when me and Red and him were watching some fights, and we were stoned and Elvis and Red and I laughed at each other and we went to bed; and then Red and I were hungry, I had a taste for a BLT. I got the bacon, lettuce, tomatoes, and mayonnaise and everything out, and Red gets ham and cheese out and makes him a sandwich, and I'm waiting for my bacon to cook and he's already got a sandwich eaten, so the bacon is not cooking, its sizzling but it's not getting brown and

ABOVE: Priscilla poses with the Lincoln Mark II; **BELOW:** Red and Elvis.

TOP: Elvis and Sonny, with Linda Thompson in the background; **ABOVE:** Elvis circa 1955.

I'm stoned on grass and I'm like, "C'mon!" Finally it does cook, and I put it together. Red's eaten two sandwiches, Red's gone to bed, and just as I've got that thing finished, Elvis's head appears round the corner. "Sonny, what ya doin'?" I said I just made a BLT. He says, "Yeah, I know. I smell it. Will you make me one?" I said, "Have you had your medicine yet?" He replied, "Oh, yeah, I took it about ten minutes ago." I knew he would never make it, so I said, "Here, Elvis, you take this one." He said, "Really?" I said, "Go ahead...okay." And he left and goes on back to his room. So I get the stuff back out, and I start making some more, and that bacon was cooking, and I started panicking. I thought his head is gonna come round that corner, and he's gonna want this one too. I knew because he eats a lot and I'm watching that doorway, and I'm cooking that bacon, and finally when it's ready I didn't take my time with it. I thought if I get one bite he's not gonna want it. So I got that bite... he never showed up, though. I'm shoving this thing down, and he never even came out. No, but the time he told me that—and that's the only time he did that—but I knew it, I felt it from him, and he felt it from us guys, he knew that we loved him. Like me and my brother, we fought, we fought physical. He's twenty-two months younger than me, but we loved each other.

SP: What's Red up to these days?

SW: Red's my cousin, my brother committed suicide over gambling, so I know what it is to lose someone besides Elvis to addiction. Lost Elvis to the drugs, lost my brother to the gambling. He was a gambling addict.

SP: Was that recently?

SW: Yeah, 2004.

SP: I am so sorry.

SW: I couldn't believe it when they told me, poor Billy... he shot himself in the head through gambling, and my son stopped breathing, overdosing on OxyContin and alcohol a few years ago. I've been there; I've been down the pipe for more than just what happened with Elvis, you know.

SP: That's tragic. You know, can I tell you something? I think that maybe some fans haven't really got a clue about you, and what you're really about, Sonny. I mean, I didn't even read that first book, okay, but every time I have met you I've found you to be a lovely, warm, caring person. That's my opinion. I think you're a good guy.

SW: Thank you. Well, if you read this one here, everyone says the love is there. It's on the page. In fact one guy that reviewed the book says, "You know what? It's such a nice thing to read a book that didn't say how much Elvis loved him." He said, "The love that Elvis had for Sonny is so evident in every page. He's not constantly reminding people how close he was to Elvis."

SW: I don't. I talk about what I do, what I was ready to do, and what he needed whenever he needs it. If I could change something the one thing that I would change when I was with Elvis—or if I could do it over again—the one thing I would do is not put him in front of my wife and child.

SP: How do you mean? In what way?

SW: Well, we had come to the end of a tour, Joe would take off and come back to LA and Jerry, when he was with us, he would come back to LA, and Red was there and he would be home with his family. But Elvis would say, "Sonny, I need you to stay round just a little bit longer if you could. I'd like you to stay around just a little bit longer so I can settle back in." So I'd say, "Okay," so I'd stay another week to ten days. I could have been out there with my wife and son.

SP: I see.

SW: Infant son; he was born in '72. And I wouldn't do that today. I would say, "Elvis, I'll stay a couple of days but then I'm going home to my family. I'll be here when you need me or something." That's all I would do. I feel I did everything I could do at the right time. I couldn't have written a book earlier because we were still with him. I only wrote the book because we were fired. We couldn't get to him anymore. We couldn't tell him, "Elvis, what are ya doin'?" The Sweet Inspirations, he just hurt their feelings bad, they just left the stage... he didn't want to hear it. We were just his subconscious telling him, and he didn't want to be reminded of it.

SP: He knew.

SW: Yeah, but he wouldn't admit it. He was in a great great state of denial, but users are. Alcohol, drugs, gambling. Billy kept saying, "I'm off the load, I'll hit it." My dad, 93 years old, was in a nursing home. He wasn't sick, he was just worn out. He did three jobs for a lot of years. Well, my brother Billy and Daddy were very close. I was gone with Elvis, and I was out in California after Elvis, so when I came back Daddy said, "You know, son, What's wrong with your brother?" Daddy said he used to

ELVIS
REMEMBERED

"Elvis was my close personal friend. He came to my Deer Lake training camp about two years before he died. He told us he didn't want nobody to bother us. He wanted peace and quiet and I gave him a cabin in my camp and nobody even knew it. When the cameras started watching me train, he was up on the hill sleeping in the cabin. Elvis had a robe made for me. I don't admire nobody, but Elvis Presley was the sweetest, most humble and nicest man you'd want to know."

Muhammad Ali

Elvis Presley presented Muhammad Ali with an "Elvis Style" robe emblazoned with the words, "People's Choice" on the back in rhinestones and jewels. The wording was a mistake as Ali was known as the "The People's Champion." Elvis was very upset about this but it was too late. Ali thanked Elvis for the robe then went directly to the Las Vegas Convention Center for his fight that night against Joe Bugner, where he wore Elvis's robe for the first time. Ali won by unanimous decision.

ABOVE: Sonny West; **BELOW:** Elvis at the Shrine auditorium, 1956.

call me four or five times a week over here. He said, "I haven't seen him for a year. He don't come round anymore." I said Daddy, "Billy's got a problem." He said, "What's wrong with him?" and I said, "He's hooked on gambling, Daddy." Daddy's like, "Ohhh, no." I told him, "Yes, he's hooked on gambling. He had to give up his home, he's behind weeks at a time with payroll. They love him but they're scrambling around trying to get food for their families. It's cost him everything." Daddy said, "You gotta talk to him and get him out of that." Daddy didn't realize how bad it was. "I mean it, you gotta talk to him."

SP: It's hard to help someone when they are in total denial. You've got to be able to admit to yourself that you have a problem.

SW: I said, "Okay, I will" and I did. But he was in denial. He said "Sonny, I'm okay." But how can you protect a man against himself? You can't. I could protect him against guns and knives or whatever, from anything physical coming at him, but I couldn't protect him from himself. Not with anybody, you can try, you can get in there and they block you out! It's a brick wall you're constantly picking at it. Makes me think of that movie, *Village of the Damned*, where those kids look at you and they think, and you try to put up a brick wall, then they would just keep going, and they would start tearing that wall down, remember that movie?

SP: Yeah.

SW: Oh, Elvis loved that movie, we saw it several times. He absolutely loved it, he would say, "Watch 'em, here they go, here they go, watch 'em!!" You would see this guy trying to concentrate, then all of a sudden it would show a picture of what's going on in his mind, and there's a wall there, and it's starting to crumble, then Elvis would say, "He can't stop 'em, he just can't stop 'em." He would talk to that screen, that's why he rented the movies, he would talk to the character and holler at that screen, "I hate you, you son of a bitch!" You couldn't watch it because he would literally talk through the movie to that screen and cuss those people out: "Boy, if I could get up outta this chair!" [Laughing.]

SP: Have you ever seen that film, Rudy? [to our photographer]

RUDY: I don't think so, what is it called?

SW: *The Village of the Damned*, it's about a bunch of kids, they've all got the blonde hair and the blue eyes. They did a remake in the '80s, because the original was made in the '60s. It was made in England, it's an English movie. It's about all these kids, and they stand together and they all look alike. I can't remember if they were meant to be aliens or if they were from the devil but *Village of the Damned* makes me think that somehow some evil spirit impregnated all these women and they had the babies real fast, it didn't take nine months. Oh, it was a great movie, boy, we saw it so many times! Elvis loved it. He would say, "Watch 'em tear that damn wall down, watch it!"

SP: He loved the British stuff didn't he? The British humor. Monty Python.

SW: Oh, yeah, he loved Python. I love Monty Python too, to an extent. It got to a point where, oh man, I would just close my eyes. I had it memorized, we all did. I would just close my eyes and listen as he watched it for the third time that night. He could do every scene, he knew the lines, the whole thing. He would watch that thing three or four times a night. He did that with Patton, he memorized Patton's speech in the movie, *General Patton*. Remember that movie with George C. Scott, when he walks out in front of that big flag? The movie was called Patton, he helped to win World War II, whipped Germany's butt. Patton was the one that said, "You know what? Now that we've done this we oughta go on over there and whip those Russky's ass, we have to do it someday because they're gonna come after us." And they did rise up after we helped defeat Germany

for them, the Russians started, they got powerful and they started being against us and for communism. But he forced all that, he said they're gonna do it, so while we got the equipment over there and the men, let's just go over across the border with Russia and whip them... and Elvis loved it.

SP: Did Elvis have a favorite actor that he really looked up to?

SW: He had several of them, in the guys he really liked Gene Hackman, and I did too. Gene never gave a bad performance. The movie may not be as good as you want it to be, but Gene Hackman was as good as you wanted him to be; in *The French Connection* he was so good. He liked George C. Scott who played General Patton, he liked Steve McQueen and Brando, James Dean. A lot of people don't know, but that movie *King Creole*, Paramount bought that for James Dean, they wanted him because the guy back then, the author, his name was Harold Robbins and you know how hot that John Grisham is today. The guy that does all those great movie, *The Firm, A Time to Kill*. Everything he turns out is a hit. Back then they had two guys, one of them was called Mickey Spillane and he wrote about Mike Hammer, all that great private detective stuff. Every time a book came out it sold big time, like Harry Potter does now. And there was a guy named Harold Robbins that wrote *A Stone for Danny Fisher, 79 Park Ave*, about a professional call girl in New York, *The Carpetbaggers*. Everything he wrote was a huge hit and made into a big movie. Well, they bought the rights to *A Stone for Danny Fisher*, that was Elvis's name in the movie *King*

Creole, they took it from the book. They bought the rights for James Dean to star in.

SP: It's like Quentin Tarantino now, everything he touches turns to gold.

SW: He's a good writer.

SP: He's brilliant.

SW: I know actors love to work for him. They say he's got a way with dialogue that is phenomenal.

SP: I have a question here from one of our Elvis International members, Steven. He asked what was your favorite movie that Elvis was in, and what was your favorite movies to work on?

SW: That Elvis was in? Well, there's a few. We really had a good time making *Girl Happy* with Shelley Fabares. We had some fight scenes where we fought with Elvis. That was fun. And then there *was Live a Little, Love a Little*, where Red and I did that fight scene where we were meant to throw him out and Elvis whipped both of us. I loved *Viva Las Vegas*, everyone loved Ann-Margret, she was so good, so funny. Such a polite lady and yet there was like this volcano seething underneath there... you just knew she was a whole lotta woman.

SP: So beautiful too.

SW: Yeah, so there was a whole lot of movies that we and Elvis had fun making.

SP: Steven adds, he knows Red wrote quite a few songs and did you, Sonny, involve yourself much in song choices?

SW: Song choices? Only when we were there and he was playing dubs, he wanted to pick out what he

TOP LEFT: Elvis with members of the Memphis Mafia encircle the Colonel; **ABOVE:** Elvis with Sonny; **BELOW:** Elvis circa 1955.

TOP: Vernon Presley, Elvis and Red, Chicago, 1972; **ABOVE:** Margit Burgin, Elvis and Red, 1958.

wanted to record. There was several of us that would be there with him, and he would have a yes, a no, and a maybe pile. He would hear it, and he would say, "Put that in the yes pile." Some we would play and he would say, "No, no, no," and that would go in the no pile. We were giving opinions like, "Are you sure, Elvis? That sounds really good." And he would say, "Okay, put that in the maybe; I'll listen to it again later." That was it. I didn't write songs but Red did. You see we all gave our opinions, all the guys were around, we loved him, and it was about the music. I remember the song that he sang "Are You Lonesome Tonight." He recorded it, but he was afraid to release it because it was so different from anything he had done, he wasn't sure the fans would like it. He liked it, and we told him the fans will like it too. Elvis said, "I don't know," so finally he released it and it went right to number one. We said, "Elvis, we told you man." He said, "Yeah, you all did."

SP: Sonny what do you miss about Elvis?

SW: Everything, everything. I swear to you everything. His humor, his voice, the fun times that we had. Little things. I'd look forward to seeing him on the drive up to the house. Couldn't wait to get there. I don't miss his temper. I shouldn't say anything but, boy, his temper was bad. Shelly, I'm talking about his anger. I'm telling you it was like a black cloud. I'd go into the house or the den where he was eating, and you could feel it, you could cut it with a knife. You knew something was wrong, and he was mad at something, and it would be, "Oh, man, I hope it's not me. I hope I didn't do anything." You would get in there and he would look at ya, then he would go back to eating, and you knew it wasn't you. But if it was you, he would let you know it was you. Let me tell ya, when it wasn't you, you were so relieved you didn't feel sorry for who it was after. You didn't have time. You felt so good. I'm sorry in a way, man, but I'm just a lot happier that it wasn't me. It wasn't the same temper that every time he got mad that he would throw or break something. I'm not talking about that. I'm talking about when he was mad, it just boiled out, it came through his eyes, his body, you knew.

SP: I wonder what made him so mad like that? Where do you think he got that from?

SW: His mother had a temper.

SP: She did?

SW: Oh, yeah, he told us. He was the one that told us, I never met his mother; she had passed before I came on to the scene. He told many stories. You know I went with him many times to his mother's graveside. We would be driving in the car, and he would say, "I wanna go see Mom." So we pull in there and I'd stand back while he went closer to her graveside. He told us a story that sticks out in my mind. His mother had a brother named Tracy that was a little bit off. He was very stocky and very strong and when he got very upset he would cry. He had a tow sack that was full of bricks and he would go out and pound those bricks, and whenever she would see him she would go out there and grab him and pin his arms to his side and hold him and rock him and say, "It's okay, it's gonna be okay," and she would calm him down. He would be crying and everything, and Elvis said, "Boy, his hands would be all bruised, but that was Mom. But then one time when he cussed her—he was goin' out the door and she was on him about something and he cussed her name—and, boy, she was ironing, and she took that iron and she flung it. He ducked and went out the door, it hit the wall there." He said she would love ya and give you everything she got, but, boy, she also gave you the other side of it.

SP: So that's where he got his temper from.

SW: Exactly.

SP: On the other side of the coin, he was very funny and he had a fantastic sense of humor and he could laugh.

SW: His laugh was so infectious. I've watched footage on him today, where he's laughing and

I'm laughing. I'm right in that room with him again and watching it and laughing. You can't go without laughing. I'm still laughing because of his infectious laugh.

SP: So how do you like to remember Elvis today when you think about him and you see the adoration, it just goes on and on and on?

SW: It's very well deserved, he deserves it, he deserves all they give him because he gave it to them. When he was bad, sick, he went out there and gave 100 percent. Many times they said they were going to cancel the show, he said no. With the death threat and we told him he didn't have to go on, he said no, there are people that have come from thousands of miles, they'll be leaving tomorrow some of them. So he deserves everything the fans give him, especially the older fans that have been with him all along; and the newer fans, he just hooked them in with his raw talent. They don't have any stories, they don't have any shows where they went to see him with their girlfriends or their dates or something, like the older ones do. These are just the ones who are appreciative of his music.

SP: Well, Sonny, it's been a real pleasure meeting you here today.

SW: Me too, Shelly, I really enjoyed it.

SP: I want to wish you every success with this new book.

SW: Yeah, thank you very much.

SP: I hope you and Judy have many many more years of happiness together. On behalf of all the wonderful members of Elvis International I want to say a huge big thank you for giving me this interview today. Bless you, Sonny.

SW: Well, thank you all, and I hope that they read it and they understand a bit more about everything because, Shelly, those people out there, they judge us hard.

Even though it was the end of the interview, I found myself still asking questions because Sonny loved to talk and he was passionate and genuine about what he felt and what he wanted to get across.

SP: Are they still judging you now?

SW: Some of them are. They just don't understand, they were "not" there! They weren't there to see what he did. We are referred to as "his hangers on." I had a job. My life was on the line every day. If some nut decided to shoot him, that was my life

ABOVE: Elvis and Sonny in a trailer on set.

BELOW: Elvis, Priscilla, and Sonny (far right) at a social function.

but I accepted it, I would have given it up for him. These people refer to me as a hanger on? Get lost, man! The secretary that you pay, is that a hanger on? The company you work for? Are you a hanger on? We had responsibilities. I was his bodyguard, another guy does this, another guy does that. We were employees, we were his friends first. If he didn't like you as a friend, you weren't an employee, that followed the friendship. Friendship was number one, we didn't collect Elvis, he collected us. He accumulated us over different times in his life. Some of them came in and left, some of us came in and stayed. These people that judge us, I say get lost. I don't want to hurt anyone's feelings, and I just move away from that.

After the interview we continued chatting for a bit. When I listen back to this interview I smile to myself as I found Sonny to be so open and warm about his love for Elvis. He didn't try to hide his true feelings, he talked about Elvis and his temper but he also said 99 percent of the time it was all great. I believe Sonny loved Elvis, genuinely loved him, but there was some frustration there, trying to help a man that couldn't be helped as his addiction worsened. Sonny's wife told me when Elvis died, she lost her husband for over a year, he was so heartbroken. Like Sonny said, not all of us were there! Later I would bump into Sonny

TOP: Elvis and Sonny, in a photo that was to become the cover for Sonny's book; ABOVE: Elvis and Red on horseback; TOP RIGHT: 1971. Elvis and Red after leaving a luncheon at the Holiday Inn Rivermont, Memphis. Photo by Dave Darnell.

at the Cannery Casino in Vegas sometimes, and he took me for dinner, just him and me, one on one, putting the world to rights. He once told me, "Shelly, I love that you're a little firecracker." I made him laugh, and I'll tell you something else, Sonny was a big old teddy bear who would literally well up when he spoke about his friend. He was big, he was tough when it came to protecting Elvis in his role as his bodyguard, but he had this sweet gentle side to him, and it was as clear as day to me. You know that saying, "Don't judge my path if you haven't walked my journey." It's easy to judge, it's more difficult to understand,

understanding requires compassion. Don't judge someone unless you've heard their story, and Sonny tells a pretty good story. I miss his presence. I'm saddened he passed away with lung cancer but I would like to think that Elvis will have forgiven him for how that book portrayed his friend, which was sensationalized by a bad writer who ran with it. Sonny's second book, *ELVIS: Still Taking Care of Business*, was described as "Arguably the most authentic, no-holds-barred depiction of the greatest entertainer that ever lived." That's the book we should be reading.

Rest in peace, dear Sonny West.

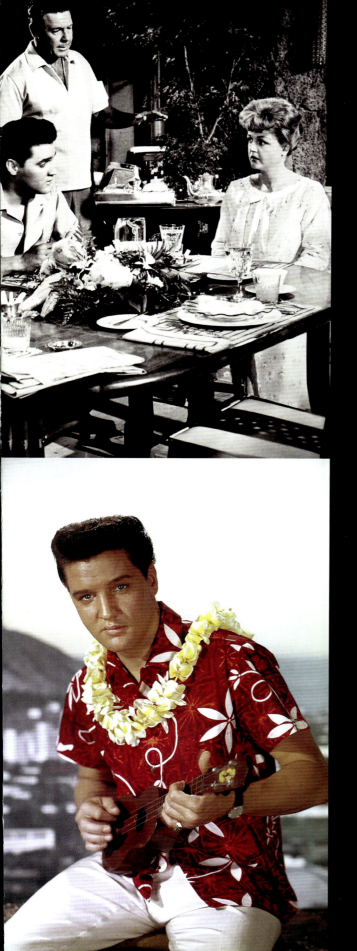

ELVIS

REMEMBERED

"Well obviously I was awed by being in the presence, but he was an awfully nice young man in those days. He always was a wonderfully nice young man, a very caring person. He had terrible problems of a very personal nature, but in those days he'd just come out of the army."

Angela Lansbury

On *Blue Hawaii*: 1961

"I used to see him round the base all the time. I never really wanted to bother him, I didn't want to disturb him, but I was very, ya know, curious about him..."

JOE ESPOSITO ON FIRST MEETING ELVIS IN THE ARMY

Joe Esposito

Joe (Diamond Joe) Esposito was Elvis Presley's right-hand man, but first and foremost he was a close friend. He met Elvis in 1958 when they were both based in Friedberg, Germany, where they were posted by the Army. I had met Joe on numerous occasions because of my connections with the Elvis International Fanclub and also because I lived in Las Vegas where Joe lived for many years, and later I would run into him when he worked in a number of casinos like the Wynn.

OPPOSITE: A portrait of Joe, taken during the interview.

Interviewing Joe...

After Elvis's death in 1977 Joe went to work for Jerry Weintraub, becoming the road manager for Michael Jackson, The Bee Gees, Karen Carpenter, and John Denver. That's the same position Joe took when he was about to come out of the Army, working for Elvis as his road manager. Whenever I met Joe he was always courteous and spoke very highly of his friend. He had a good business head on his shoulders and was a straight-talking man. I'm happy to say during the interview with Joe Esposito I managed to somehow bring out his lighter side, and we had quite a few laughs throughout the interview, because I guess I was a little cheeky (in the nicest possible way). I hope you enjoy this interview as much as I did, with the great Diamond Joe.

TOP: Joe and Shelly during the interview; **ABOVE:** Joe Esposito.

I met up with Joe at the Angel Golf Club outdoor bar in Summerlin. That was the area where I lived, and it was easy for Joe to meet me there too. It was a beautiful hot day with a warm breeze picking up as we sat down. Joe bought us each a refreshing cold drink as I prepared to find out as much as I could about his friendship with Elvis and life on the road and all that lay in between.

SP: So, Joe, I've been doing my homework, and I know that you first met Elvis when you were drafted into the Army in 1958. You were assigned to Combat Command C, and you were given the position of an office and daily report clerk.

JE: Yes.

SP: So you take it from here, Joe, and tell me how your first meeting with Elvis came about?

JE: Well, like you just said, we were stationed in Germany, Combat Command C in Friedberg Germany, and I used to see him round the base all the time. I never really wanted to bother him, I didn't want to disturb him, but I was very, ya know, curious about him.

SP: Yes, of course.

JE: So, what happened is that one of the photographers on the base was asked by the Army to take a lot of pictures of Elvis, so he became friends with Elvis. He used to play football with Elvis on the weekends. So one day Daniel, Daniel was his name, Daniel Westley, and he said, "Joe, we're short of some guys this weekend, do you wanna come and play football with us?" So I said, "Hell, yeah." That's how it started. I went to Budenheim, Germany, where he was renting

a house, and I went inside, and Elvis introduced himself to me. He said, "Hi, I'm Elvis Presley," and I said, "I'm Joe Esposito." That was strange for Elvis to come up to me and say, "I'm Elvis Presley," like I didn't know who he was. You know what I'm saying, but that's the kind of guy he was. He was very much a gentleman, he was very, very good about those kind of things. So you know, we just talked for a little bit, and then he said, "Okay, we're going to go out and play football, and you can be on my team to start with." So we went out to the field, played touch football for about two hours, came back inside the house and sat around. Had Coca-Cola and soft drinks, no booze, no wine or nothing, and we just sat and talked for a while. There was a whole bunch of us. Then he said, "Joe, anytime you want to come back on the weekends, just let me know. If you're in town we can hang out."

SP: Wasn't that so nice of him!

JE: Yeah, so that's how it started.

SP: You didn't feel intimidated at all?

JE: Well, yeah, a little bit intimidated, you know when you first meet the biggest star in the world at that time.

SP: Well, he was. Absolutely.

JE: So when you meet him of course you're intimidated, anyone who meets somebody like that.

SP: Like I am with you today.

[Joe starts laughing.]

JE: Oh, yeah. No, no but it's true, you know. Everybody's like that when they can't actually believe they're meeting someone big like that, that's what it is. So after a while, because he's such a down-to-earth person, you get used to it and...

SP: You totally relax with him?

JE: Yeah, that's it.

SP: So just tell me a bit more about life in the armed forces with him. Did he enjoy being in the Army?

JE: Well, I mean, I'm sure he would rather be out of the Army. He enjoyed it as much as he could enjoy it. You gotta remember he left when he was the biggest star in Hollywood, going from the movies to all of a sudden sleeping in the mud. You know he did a lot more work than I did in the service because they were watching him, they weren't watching me. I got away with a lot of things you know, but he had to be a real good G.I. I mean I was a good G.I. too, but I didn't have to do half the stuff he had to do.

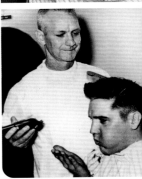

TOP: Elvis Presley is sworn into the Army with fellow recruits in Memphis, Tennessee, 1958; **ABOVE:** Army recruit, Elvis in Fort Chaffee, Arkansas, circa 1958.

121

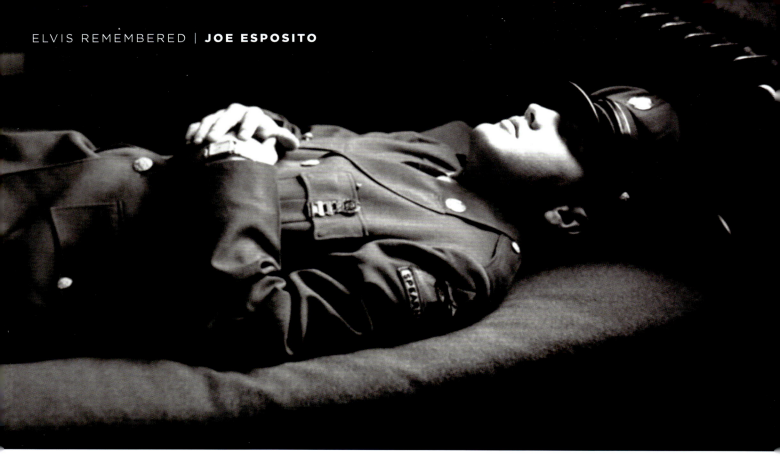

TOP: Elvis takes a break;
ABOVE: Joe and Shelly.

SP: Well, okay, I mean maybe they thought he was going to go in there with an attitude like "Hey, I'm a star."

JE: Right, right, but he didn't, and that's why all the other GIs when they met him realized he was just a really down-to-earth guy. So anybody going into the service will tell you that he was just like the rest of us.

SP: So when you left the Army you headed to Memphis but because you didn't like flying at the time it was a train trip that lasted three days? But first of all how did the job offer come about?

JE: Well, we were still in Germany at the time and before we left the service, he asked me what I was going to do when I got out of the Army, so I told him I was going to go back to Chicago, and I had my little job over there, and he said, "well, why don't you come and work for me?" That's how it started.

SP: What was this little job over in Chicago?

JE: I worked in an office, I worked as an assistant purchaser for this company, nothing exciting at all, so when he offered this to me, well, I didn't have to think too hard. That was it, and when I got out of the service—I got out a week before he did—so I went right back to Chicago, I came back by boat, and he came back by plane. A military plane from

Germany to New York, then he took the train from New York to Memphis.

SP: So you both traveled on this train?

JE: No, no. I didn't go straight to Memphis. I went to Chicago for a couple of weeks to visit my family.

SP: Oh, I see.

JE: Yeah, my friends and all that and my family. So he came back, he came back separately from me, and I had gone home for a couple of weeks, and then I went down to Memphis.

SP: So you actually met him back in Memphis?

JE: Yes, I went down to Memphis after visiting my friends and family after getting out of the Army.

SP: Okay. So now during the time he was stationed in Germany he met Priscilla?

JE: Right.

SP: Now were you actually there when he was first introduced to Priscilla?

JE: Yes, I was at the house and one of these Air Force guys, he brought Priscilla over to introduce her to Elvis, and I happened to be there that night. She came in the door, wearing this cute navy dress, a navy dress with white stripes. She was very beautiful, and Elvis walked over and introduced

"He said, 'Hi, I'm Elvis Presley,' and I said, 'I'm Joe Esposito.' That was strange for Elvis to come up to me and say, 'I'm Elvis Presley,' like I didn't know who he was. You know what I'm saying, but that's the kind of guy he was. He was very much a gentleman, he was very, very good about those kind of things..."

JOE ESPOSITO ON MEETING ELVIS

himself, same way he did to me. "Hi, I'm Elvis Presley." She was a nervous wreck naturally.

SP: Was she?

JE: Well, yeah, think about it. She was only 14 years old at the time. We didn't realize she was only 14, she certainly didn't look it. Then they just started talking and, you know, we left them alone, they were sitting over on the couch, near the piano and just talking, and that's how it all started.

SP: So would you say that it was love at first sight for Elvis?

JE: Well, I don't know if it was love at first sight, but he was definitely very interested, there's no two ways about it.

SP: So he wanted to see her again?

JE: Yes, definitely.

SP: Now Priscilla was very young, very beautiful, so pretty like a little doll wasn't she? And she still is today.

JE: Yes.

SP: Did Elvis ever confide in you with any concerns that he may have had with the fact that she was only 14 years old?

JE: No, he didn't. I was surprised but he never brought up it up, never talked about it.

SP: Golly!

JE: Well, because they weren't that close yet.

LEFT: A Hagstrom Viking guitar owned by Elvis Presley, serial number 680961. The guitar, played by both Presley and John Lennon, was purchased by Presley in Los Angeles in the mid-1960s. When the Beatles met Presley at his Bel Air home, he suggested they jam together. Lennon grabbed this guitar to play while Paul McCartney and Presley played bass. Presley gifted the guitar to Don Edwards, a friend who played football with Elvis and the Memphis Mafia; **ABOVE:** Joe Esposito.

123

ABOVE: Joe at an Elvis convention, Munich, 1998

SP: So it was just very innocent.

JE: Right, they were friends at the beginning, that's basically what it was.

SP: Now Elvis has a bit of a tricky situation on his hands because here he is leaving this little girl behind, she's fallen madly in love with him.

JE: Yes.

SP: So, he's become very attached to Priscilla but he has Anita Wood waiting to greet him in Memphis and carry on from where they left off, and I imagine she still believes that she's the only one. So did he ever discuss this with you after you arrived in Memphis about what he was going to do about Anita?

JE: I don't think he really knew what he was going to do. I mean, yes, we all knew that Anita Wood was back at home, his girlfriend at the time who he left behind when he went into the Army. But he didn't want to talk about it, I don't think. He didn't really

say anything about it. In other words, he didn't know how far it was going to go with Priscilla, so when he got back he dated Anita, yes.

SP: Carried on from where they left off.

JE: Yeah, absolutely, she hung around. I mean Anita naturally asked him about her because you know Priscilla was in the newspapers.

SP: The "girl he left behind."

JE: Yes, the girl he left behind and all that. He explained she was a friend that had been introduced through a Navy Air Force guy and, as we know, things got better and better between Elvis and Priscilla, so then Anita and Elvis split up.

SP: His homecoming was a huge celebration… it must have meant an awful lot to Elvis, yet I'm sure it must have been tinged with sadness because he's going home, and his mother is not there to greet him. Those who knew Elvis very well said that Elvis was never the same person

after he lost his mother. What do you think about that, Joe?

JE: Well, like I say, I didn't know him before, when he was with his mother, but all his other friends told me he was not the same since his mother passed, and I can understand that. They were very, very, very close. You gotta remember he had a twin brother that passed away at birth.

SP: Yeah, I know. That's sad.

JE: His mother could never have kids after that, so that was her only son. So she watched over him, they were very close, and Elvis was the only kid she would ever have.

SP: She was very protective of him.

JE: Very protective of him, yes. So they were very close.

SP: Okay, I'd like to talk to you a little bit about the movie years.

JE: Yes . . .

SP: I know you have some, shall we say, cameo appearances. [Joe laughs.]

JE: Not a cameo, just somebody in the background, something like that.

SP: You're too modest! Along with the other boys . . . and that's nice. So did you get the star treatment also like Elvis?

JE: Well, you know when you're connected with Elvis naturally they treat us very well because we're close to Elvis, so they wanted to make sure they treated us nice. It's always like that in the business when someone's a big celebrity and you're with that celebrity, they treat you nice . . . and when you're not working for him they don't know who you are. [Joe laughs again.]

SP: So how about fan mail and girls? I bet you were spoilt for choice where the girls were concerned! I mean you were a good-looking man.

JE: Well, I used to be, I guess. But, yes . . . being around Elvis, naturally you have a lot of girls around that you can meet that you normally would not meet. So, we took advantage of that naturally, but we didn't pull that, "Do you wanna spend the night with me and meet Elvis tomorrow?" We never did any of that.

SP: Like "I can get you to see Elvis if you, ya know, pay me in kind," sort of thing?

JE: Right, yeah, that kind of stuff. People say we

always did that but we did not do that.

SP: You're too much of a gentleman.

JE: Well, come on, I mean that's a bit tough.

SP: You probably didn't have to do that anyway.

JE: [Laughs.]

SP: So which film would you say Elvis had the most fun filming?

JE: The most fun? Hmm, there's a few of them. *Viva Las Vegas* he had a lot of fun with Ann-Margret. They sort of clicked together so it was a very good, fun movie. It was a hard-working movie, but if you see the movie there's this little twinkle in both their eyes, they were connected in a certain way. That was fun, we had a lot of fun with the movies though. *Follow That Dream* we shot down in Florida, so we had a great time on location with that. You know, different other girls. *Blue Hawaii* with Joan Blackman . . . he and Joan were very close. That was a lot of fun; first time I ever went to Hawaii. We were there for three or four weeks. It was amazing! The atmosphere made it wonderful, so that was good, but I think the best one that he ever made, personally, I think was *King Creole* as far as a good movie, and a good story, but otherwise they were all fun. I'll put it that way.

TOP: Elvis Presley, Charlie Hodge, Joe Esposito, Nancy Sinatra, & Frank Sinatra; **ABOVE:** Elvis Presley is on the way to his accommodation in the U.S. barracks in Friedberg on the 2nd of October in 1958.

125

TOP: Elvis in 1960, flanked by his parents and holding a guitar that says, "Welcome Home."; **ABOVE:** Elvis with his beloved mother, Gladys; **OPPOSITE:** The King.

SP: Can we talk a little bit about Elvis and Ann-Margret? Do you think that he really fell in love with Ann-Margret?

JE: Well, I cannot say that, only he can say that, but I know they were very, very close. I mean they spent a lot of time together and a lot of time just the two of them. Most of the time with other girls, all the guys would be around, too. They spent a lot of close time together just the two of them, and they had a great sense of humor. She has a great sense of humor and so did Elvis, as you know, and he loved that kind of stuff. So it just really was a good, good relationship. As far as deeply in love? I'm sure at one point they were very strong together.

SP: Yeah, because some people suggest, yeah, they were in love, and I think it's actually questionable because neither one of them wanted to jeopardize their careers, you know?

JE: Well, no, of course not.

SP: There was also Priscilla there, so I think despite his philandering with other women, I think he really did love Priscilla.

JE: Oh, I think so too. No, he loved Priscilla, there were no two ways about it, but Ann-Margret was a big star too, like Elvis, and he would not marry another big star because he wanted her to be at home, raise the kids, he wanted the wife at home.

SP: He was an old-fashioned Southern boy.

JE: Right, and that's why he would never do that. Ann-Margret was very strong.

> "He was in the Army at the time. I think it destroyed him for a long time. You see pictures of him. Elvis was very, very emotional person. He was devastated. In fact he hardly talked about her after she passed away…"

JOE ESPOSITO ON ELVIS WHEN HIS MOTHER, GLADYS DIED

ELVIS
REMEMBERED

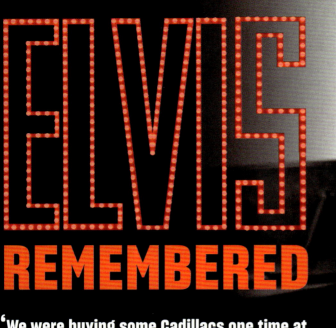

"We were buying some Cadillacs one time at the Cadillac dealership in Memphis. We were standing inside the dealership and Elvis looks outside and there's this elderly black lady looking in the window at this yellow two-door Coupe de Ville. Elvis sees her, and she's looking at it and looking at it. He goes outside and starts talking to her. He says, 'You like that car, huh?' 'Oh, yes, yes, that beautiful car.' He says, 'Would you like to have one of those?' 'Oh I could never afford one of those cars.' He said, 'Just a minute.' He goes back inside the dealership, goes to the sales manager and says, 'Give me the keys to that car.' Gives him the keys, he goes out and says, 'Ma'am, the car is yours.' She just couldn't believe that Elvis just gave her that car. She was just in awe. Just couldn't believe it. He said, 'It's yours, enjoy it.' That's the kind of guy he was. He liked to give people things he knew they couldn't afford on their own."

Joe Esposito
On Elvis's generosity

"He tipped a guy once, a limo driver, a limo. He tipped him a limo…"

Larry King
On Elvis's generosity

SP: A bit like the female version of Elvis?

JE: Right. She's not going to give her career up for that. So he understood that, but they were always friends, they were friends until he passed away.

SP: Lovely. Well regarding the movies, my two favorite Elvis movies are *Love Me Tender,* which was his first, and *Change of Habit,* which was his last.

JE: Yeah, and I'd have to say mine were *Viva Las Vegas* and *Follow That Dream.* There were a lot of favorites but it was about the fun we had while making those movies and things I remember about certain movies.

SP: Okay, Joe, me being a woman and a very inquisitive one at that—

JE: —Oh, we're in trouble now. [Joe starts laughing.]

SP: I have to ask you this . . . at times the boys were a little bit naughty?

JE: Ohhh, the boys were never naughty. [Laughing.] Depends on how you look at it, it depends what you call naughty.

SP: [Laughing.] Yes they were!

SP: I understand it must have been quite hard.

[Joe cracks up laughing.]

SP: Well, let me rephrase that.

[Both Joe and I are really laughing now, and it was lovely to see the lighter side of Joe.]

SP: It wasn't easy, okay, with all these beautiful women at your disposal for your entertainment. No disrespect to you, Joe, knowing what you know about Elvis and the other women, your loyalties obviously were first and foremost with Elvis, but then here's poor Priscilla, and she's at home like the good little wife. Did you ever feel kind of a little bit torn between the two of them, a bit like piggy in the middle?

JE: Well, you know, we didn't because we were all doing the same thing to our own wives at the time, you understand.

SP: Well, that's big of you to admit, Joe.

TOP: Elvis, Ginger Alden, and Joe; **ABOVE:** Elvis and Joe.

OPPOSITE: Elvis relaxes while in uniform.

OPPOSITE INSET: Elvis's check, which he used to pay for the yacht that he donated to St. Jude's Hospital.

129

"Being around Elvis, naturally you have a lot of girls around that you can meet that you normally would not meet. So, we took advantage of that naturally, but we didn't pull that, 'Do you wanna spend the night with me and meet Elvis tomorrow?' We never did any of that..."

JOE ESPOSITO

TOP RIGHT: Elvis Presley during his Army years in the late 1950s; **ABOVE:** Elvis Presley in a car, meets with his fans, circa 1956.

JE: We were not good boys at all. After things went astray, I got divorced, Elvis got divorced, then I really felt guilty, really. We were just too wild, we were just having too much fun, and our wives were at home taking care of our families, and not one guy was loyal to his wife, which is pretty bad, but most of them later on in life understood. That's the way things were in those days. I'm still very close to my ex-wife. I go for dinner with her and her husband when they're both in town because why not? We were friends.

SP: That's lovely, my dad was the same. He loved my mum but he was not loyal either but they're better friends now than when they were married.

Back then, it was there, he would take it, still loved Mum, though, and that's what some guys were like, especially back then.

JE: It's tough. That's why so many men in Europe have mistresses, you know. Wife is at home taking care of the kids, preparing the dinner and all that, and they're out fooling around. Us men are animals! [Laughing.]

SP: Priscilla still says to this day that Elvis was very good to her, and he was, wasn't he, Joe?

JE: Oh, yes, definitely very good to her, yes.

SP: She didn't want for anything really, she just wanted her husband to be at home and to do the normal things husbands and wives do, and cook for him, etc. So it must have been hard for her having the boys around all the time.

JE: Well, it is, definitely. That was a big thing, and I understand that, you know, because we were always there, and you know I don't want everyone in my house when I'm with my wife and my kids. We want to be able to spend time, intimate time, together, talk about different things without other people in the same conversation. That never happened with the two of them, only when they were upstairs in bed maybe watching TV.

SP: He wanted his boys around all the time?

JE: Yeah, he wanted the guys around, yeah, he did.

SP: You along with Marty Lacker were best men at Elvis and Priscilla's wedding, weren't you?

JE: Yes.

SP: Okay, did Elvis approach you himself and ask you to be best man or did the Colonel take care of that?

JE: No, no, no. Elvis asked me to be co-best man for him, and I was very very surprised because I didn't want to hurt a lot of other people's feelings . . . like Red West, because you gotta remember Red West knew Elvis since high school.

SP: What about Jerry?

JE: Not Jerry, because Jerry wasn't around that long. Jerry was only around three years. So the idea is that you know George Klein, Red West. I think it hurt Red West the most, and I understand it.

SP: He must have thought a lot of you to ask you to be best man.

JE: I'm hoping so, yes. I was very honored, and to this day I cannot believe I was one of Elvis Presley's best men.

SP: I know! Pretty amazing, isn't it?

JE: Oh, it is, yes.

SP: Didn't they look fab on their wedding day?

JE: Oh, absolutely, gorgeous, and you know he was not nervous. I thought he would be more nervous than Priscilla, but she was more nervous than he was.

SP: Really?

JE: We thought he would be a nervous wreck because he was getting married for the first time, and life changes after you get married.

SP: Yeah, so they say, well it's supposed to!

JE: Yeah, it's supposed too, and it did for a little while, for a little while.

SP: It was all meant to be kept rather hush-hush. Did you know exactly when the wedding was going to take place earlier on or was it a last-minute announcement?

JE: No, no, we knew way ahead of time. Colonel Parker, Marty Lacker, and myself would go sit down and go over a lot of things. We organized different transportation to get to Vegas and who was going to be there, where they were going to stay, how the wedding was going to be. We had it all organized way before it happened.

SP: So who decided what Elvis and Priscilla would wear on their special day?

JE: Oh, the two of them, they decided.

SP: They picked their own wedding outfits?

JE: Yes, he had that tuxedo made, and Priscilla picked out her own dress.

SP: At what point did Elvis see his bride in her wedding dress?

JE: The first time was at the wedding just before the ceremony.

SP: The wedding took place here in Vegas at The Aladdin Hotel, and after the ceremony there was a press conference, where Priscilla showed her wedding ring off to the world. How did all that go? Were you there at this press conference?

JE: Yes, I was sitting right next to them. Yeah, Colonel Parker set it all up because he figured why drive them crazy after the wedding, have a press conference in the hotel there before the reception, and that's what happened. It was very good, and I'm glad they did it.

SP: What happened after this? Was there a party?

JE: Yes, there was a reception party, you saw the cake and the pictures. We had about a hundred people, friends and stuff like that were there, all congratulating them and, yeah, it was nice.

SP: Where did they spend their first night as husband and wife?

JE: Palm Springs. After the reception we all jumped back on a plane, went to Palm Springs at the house, and that's where they

TOP: Elvis with Frank Sinatra. His father, Vernon, is far left, and Joe Esposito is in the middle; **ABOVE:** Joe and Elvis.

ABOVE: Joe at the 25th anniversary of Elvis's death, Memphis, 2002; BELOW: Joe with Linda Thompson.

spent the first night together as husband and wife.

SP: And so . . .?

JE: [Laughing.] Oh, we were all there too!

[Both of us laughing, Joe assures me with, "We weren't in the room!"]

SP: So you all went on the honeymoon with Elvis?

JE: Yes, yes.

SP: You just had to put your ear plugs in!

[Joe laughs.]

JE: They had a soundproof room.

SP: They did? Did they really?

JE: No, but the room was far enough away from us.

SP: Joe, we have a couple of questions from the members of Elvis International. Jason the president asks, "Since you were very close to both Elvis and the Colonel and there is much speculation on what the Colonel should have done in terms of managing Elvis's career, did the Colonel ever confide in you about anything that he considered to be a bad decision or anything he wished he had done differently?"

JE: No, he never did because certain people don't like admitting mistakes, but they all know when they made mistakes, everybody does. Elvis made mistakes, I made mistakes, the Colonel made mistakes, you make mistakes. We all do, we are all human beings. Okay, but overall there has never been a better manager for Elvis Presley. He would never have been

the star he was today if it wasn't for the Colonel.

SP: Wow, that's a statement!

JE: There's no way! The way he handled him, he made him such a mystery everybody was after to get a hold of him. He didn't overdo it with the press, he didn't do all these TV shows, didn't do these TV specials. After you do that for a long time, and you see him all the time you say, "Well, I don't wanna see him that much." He kept Elvis a mystery, everybody wanted to get to him, everybody wanted to see him, because that's how he handled it.

SP: You think he had a good business head on his shoulders then?

JE: Smartest manager ever in this business. Ever!

SP: What stands out in your mind as a good career decision by the Colonel, and what stands out as a bad career decision if you think there was one?

JE: Well, a bad decision was making all those motion pictures. In those days in Hollywood you signed long-term contracts. MGM–seven movies, Paramount–five movies, Twentieth Century Fox . . . So that doesn't happen today anymore because what happens is once you're committed, you have to make those movies even though it might be a lousy movie. So that was a bad deal, but the Colonel was thinking he was smart. "Hey, listen, he's got seven movies with this company!" He thought it was a great idea. It was good and bad. A lot of them were just nice movies but nothing exciting, ya know? A lot of music, a lot of pretty girls, a lot of race cars, boats, everything. So that was a bad decision, I think, but the studios didn't think it was a bad decision; they were very happy with it. Then you have the story about *A Star Is Born* movie with Streisand. We will really never ever know if it was a good or bad decision. Barbra Streisand is a very hard person to work with. She's a great actress and a great singer, and Elvis had a big ego too. He was not easy at times.

SP: Can you imagine the two of them together?

JE: That's what I'm saying, that might not have worked.

SP: I believe Kris Kristofferson was perfect for that part actually.

JE: Oh, he did a great job, absolutely.

SP: Now Jerry Schilling said that some of his favorite memories of Elvis were the ones where it was just himself and Elvis out by the barn at night with a small fire going, just shooting the breeze and talking. Do you have a similar favorite moment with Elvis, Joe?

JE: Well, definitely, there's no two ways about it, because there was just always so many people around. The intimate moments were the two of you together just talking. That's nice, you can remember those because if you're having a conversation with other people around, this one says something, that one says something, it's those moments, just the two, one-on-one was very nice, very nice moments. That's how he asked me to go to work for him. We got in the car, took a ride in Germany, and he said what are you going to do when you get home and that. We talked, and I said I'm gonna go back to my work, and he said come to work for me. Well, I mean that was a shock to me but that was just the two of us now. If he had said it amongst the other guys, I don't know if it would have been the same.

SP: Back to the fan questions, Jason said he has met you a few times and heard you talk half a dozen times, and he finds you a smart, no-nonsense straight shooter.

[Joe laughs.]

SP: Now with that said, where do you see the Elvis's fanbase in 50 or 100 years from now, when all of us that were alive have been long gone? Do you see Graceland and the Elvis phenomenon expanding, or do you think the craze will eventually die down a bit?

JE: Well, I really do think that it eventually won't be as big as it is now.

SP: Really?

JE: After a while, yes, I mean we are still getting new fans today and young ones. I see them all the time in Vegas here. They all come up to visit me here, and they're just thrilled just to shake my hand, and I say, "Hey, I was the lucky one to be with him." So that'll go on for quite a while, but in fifty years from now? I don't know. He will never be forgotten, there's no two ways about it because his music will live forever because nobody could record the songs or sing the songs the way he did it, so that's one of those things we will never know. I won't be around that long. I have about another fifty years to go maybe. [Laughing.]

SP: Oh, absolutely.

SP: Now a final question from Jason. "Did Elvis ever talk to you about what he thought he might be doing as he got older? Did he ever mention to you where he thought he might be in his 50s or 60s?"

JE: He never mentioned like "What am I going to do when I'm 50 or 60?" but I know he wanted to start directing movies. Eventually he wanted to direct some comedies. You know he loved the English humor.

SP: He did, didn't he?

JE: Monty Python and Peter Sellers and all of those people. They're here in town at the Wynn resort, *Spamalot*.

SP: Really! Oh my goodness.

JE: Yeah, the Monty Python show. It's fabulous. I haven't seen it yet, but I'm going to see it next week. He loved that kind of humor, those were the kind of movies he wanted to do and then he liked action movies, cop movies like Clint Eastwood movies, he wanted to direct those or do something with those. He still would have done those. I think he would have been great in comedy as he was a very funny guy.

SP: I have a question from a Helen in Australia. She asks, "When did you first hear Elvis sing and what did you think?"

JE: Well, I'm from Chicago, and in those days back in the '50s you know it was Frank Sinatra and Dean Martin, Perry Como, all those were big stars, Tony Bennett, and the music was very nice, great songs,

ABOVE: Elvis after receiving his final pay and separation from active duty in the U.S. Army, at Fort Dix Separation Center.

ABOVE: Joe during interview.

beautiful music, and when we heard Elvis, this guy who was singing this wild music, it was very unusual. We didn't know if we liked it or not at first, and after a while he was on the Ed Sullivan show– we saw this guy, and we couldn't believe it. We had never heard the name Elvis Presley. What is that, what kind of a name is Elvis Presley? Nobody had ever heard that name in their lives.

SP: It was very unusual.

JE: Very unusual, very different, so we all liked him. We all had discussions about him and different stars like Frank Sinatra and Bobby Darin. So overall he was great to look at, very appealing.

SP: So when you heard him, but you hadn't seen him, did you ever think, "Is he black or white?"

JE: I didn't, but a lot of people did because they all figured it was like black music at that time and it basically was, because remember Elvis loved black music, rhythm and blues, and all that, so that's why it's like rock and roll and rhythm and blues music. Then we all saw him on TV, and we realized "Hey, he's just a nice little strange boy from the South.

[Joe cracks up laughing with me.]

SP: Did you own any of his records before you met him?

JE: No, we didn't have a lot of money, don't think we even had a phonograph player, so, no, we didn't buy too many records at that time but we heard him on the radio.

SP: So how do you feel now Joe when you hear an Elvis song come on the radio?

JE: I love it. It's amazing how often how much we hear him and it's so funny, sometimes certain things happen then all of a sudden I hear an Elvis song, and it's so strange, he's so much involved in my life today. I like to hear a certain song because I remember how much fun it was making those songs, so it's a whole different thing that I hear that other people don't understand . . . because I was there when he was singing those songs and recording them, so it's a little different for me, and they bring back great memories.

SP: This is just off the cuff, have you ever had an experience like you've felt Elvis around?

JE: Like a presence?

SP: Yeah.

JE: Yeah. Sometimes. People have asked me that before. You know there's not a day goes by that I don't think about Elvis or hear his name mentioned somewhere. I don't care if it's a newspaper or whatever, so he's still a big part of my life. So, yeah, sometimes . . . like I was at Graceland about a week ago, and I was there by the graveside, and I had a little strange feeling, you know looking at the gravesite.

SP: I'm a great believer in that.

JE: Yeah, let's face it his aura is still around. When people see him on television or younger girls see a movie or a TV special, and they see him on it they get hooked, that's the presence he had that no one else will ever have.

SP: The younger people especially don't realize he's gone, he's not dated at all.

JE: Right.

SP: He could be with one of the stars today, only he would be better.

JE: Yeah, absolutely. Young kids, they don't know, and they say, "Oh, I gotta find out about this guy," and they find out he's passed away but they still investigate him, they buy the books about him, the records, and they get hooked.

SP: That's why I believe he is going to go on and on for a long time yet.

JE: Because it's good music and that's what it boils down to.

SP: What's it like for you to visit Graceland now, Joe?

JE: Well, it's strange. There are a lot of good memories and some sad memories naturally. You know the last year or so, stuff like that, it's good and bad basically.

SP: Meeting Elvis for the first time, what was your first impression of him?

JE: Well, I didn't know what to expect as I wasn't used to being around stars and that, but when I met him it didn't take me long to realize he was so down-to-earth, very caring about people, very much so, you know. He made sure he made people happy, that they were enjoying life, and that's why he loved to be on stage because he loved to perform for all his fans in the world . . . he knew all that love in his heart came from them and that's why he sang so much with his heart, because he felt so much love for them all, all of those people. So he was just such a down-to-earth, polite human being, always "Yes, sir," and "No, sir," "Yes, ma'am," "No, ma'am." It was all that way, all the time. I've met a lot of stars in my life, a lot of them, and there's a lot of nice ones and there's a lot of egomaniacs—they will not talk to their fans, they're

too busy, not enough time for them. He would stop anytime. If he saw you were here and you wanted to talk to him, he would talk to you. Other stars they would carry on walking and be like, "Hey, I'm sorry, I can't talk right now." So he was very much just like everyone else, always just wanted to get that across. He was a human being, like you and me.

SP: Elvis had a huge repertoire of material . . . why do you think it was that he played the same set for almost six years? Do you think that he had either lost interest, and he was just going through the motions, or was it due to popular demand, saying this is what his fans wanted?

JE: I think it's both, but definitely public demand, because there are certain songs they always wanted to hear because that's what made him famous and that's how they got hooked on him. A lot of stars don't do that. You'll go to see a show and say, "Why I didn't hear that, and I didn't hear that." I mean that's what fans would say, but he understood that's what

they want to hear, and he loved singing those songs. Once in a while he would change songs periodically.

SP: Kathy from the fan club wants to ask you how did you get on with Grandma Dodger and the famous Aunt Delta?

JE: I had no problems. Dodge and I met when I was in Germany, you know, she was there with Elvis, and she was just a very nice, funny lady, a great sense of humor. I can see where Elvis got it from, and Delta I had no problems with. A lot of people say they didn't care for her, but I got along great with her, I really did. She never gave me any hassles, and I treated her very nice and everything. But Aunt Delta had a drinking problem, like his mother, so . . . but otherwise I had no problem with them at all.

SP: Now my lovely friend Marion from Scotland wants to ask you, Joe, "Do you still see the other Mafia members"?

JE: Yes, I do, certain ones. I see Sam Thompson; he lives here in Las Vegas. Linda's brother is a great

guy. I saw him today, and we hung out a little bit. I see Jerry Schilling periodically, and I see George Klein a lot. I used to talk to Charlie Hodge a lot before he passed away last year. Let's see, let me think about some of the other members.

SP: What about Sonny West?

JE: No I don't. I've only seen Sonny maybe once or twice since Elvis passed away. Red I haven't seen in

a long time, maybe a couple of times, but I haven't talked to him in a long time either. Lamar and Marty I do not see, and I don't care to see [Lamar Fike and Marty Lacker]. Those are all the main Memphis Mafia guys. Lamar and Marty, I don't care if I never see them.

SP: Well, I've heard a few things about them, and I wouldn't be interested in giving them an interview, put it that way.

JE: Don't, and if you do then don't put them near my interview.

SP: Don't you worry, I won't.

SP: What do you think of the new set up with Mr. Sillerman? [Media mogul Robert Sillerman owned the Elvis Presley estate] Do you think he has Elvis's best interests at heart?

JE: I'm sure it's at heart and business, too, but in a way. It's good and bad because he could do a lot more promotion around the world because he is a very smart businessman.

SP: When Elvis was asked on numerous occasions about touring Europe, in your opinion, why do you think he never got to do this?

JE: There are so many different rumors, here is the story I have. You gotta remember in those days there were no big arenas, only outdoor arenas. There was a 4,000-seater in England and that's a small arena. He would never play outdoors ever again after he played Canada back in the 1950s. He did not like it at all because the music just went up in the sky and the kids couldn't hear him with all the screaming and yelling, they could not hear his music.

SP: A bit like the Beatles when they played Shea Stadium.

JE: Right, same thing. Elvis told Colonel Parker after that trip, I never want to play outdoors again. So you think about it, he never did play outdoors again. So that's one of the reasons. Remember Wimbledon was being built in 75/76, 10,000-seater. There were plans to go there for a month and just doing a show every night and other people from Europe would all come to England to see him, but it never happened.

SP: Sadly. Why do you think it was that there were never any pictures taken when Elvis met the Beatles [in LA] considering the Colonel was so into publicity? You would have bought there would be one for posterity.

JE: They just wanted to be left alone, be themselves, not have someone taking pictures of them all the time. So they had to be careful in case they were picking their noses, or something like that. That's when a photographer takes a picture, and if he uses that it's gonna hit the papers! So they wanted that [meeting] to be completely private and because we thought maybe down the road they would meet again too. So the idea was this: don't let there be any pressure, just no pictures or recordings like all these rumors say there are—that there's a recording

out there, yet there never has been a recording at that session; it was strictly for them to meet each other. That was the reason this was arranged.

SP: Okay, another question. Do you think that there would have been a possibility that Elvis and Priscilla would have reunited eventually had Elvis lived?

JE: I don't know. That's a tough question. That's a real hard one, he never mentioned about going back to Priscilla.

SP: He never told you that he wanted to get back with her?

JE: No, never told me that. Maybe what he had in his heart . . . here's the thing about Elvis, and other people will tell you this. He would talk to them about their problems but he never talked about his. He never gave you what was bothering him. He just kept it all in his heart and in his head, and that's the difference. That's why I say he would do anything for you if you needed help, anything he could do

ABOVE: Elvis Presley contemplates his likeness on a German-manufactured lampshade while on duty in Grafenwoehr, Germany, 1958.

OPPOSITE: Joe Esposito with Elvis Presley around 1963 at a birthday party for Tom Parker, Presley's manager.

ABOVE & TOP: Elvis during his army days.

for any of us. He did that many times but he would never be like, "This is bothering me," and "This is bothering me." He would never do that.

SP: Now Elvis gave you the martial arts nickname The Lion. Did you ever practice karate with Elvis?

JE: No, I was a lover not a fighter. [Joe laughs.] No, I was not into that kinda stuff. No, not really.

SP: There's footage of him practicing on some of his boys.

JE: Oh, yeah.

SP: I can imagine it got a bit rough at times.

JE: Yes, he did, not to me though.

SP: I also read somewhere—it's a good book that sometime you should read it—I read somewhere that when it came to girls, it was you that arranged females for Elvis to date, so you must have had a pretty good idea of what Elvis looked for in a woman. What in your mind was his idea of the perfect woman?

JE: Well, like I say, I wasn't the only one to do that. If we met someone that we thought was right for him or we thought he would like... George Klein introduced him to a lot of girls. Anita Wood, Linda Thompson. So if I met somebody I thought he would be interested in then, yes. He liked a girl with a lot of humor, he liked a girl that was funny—you know if he kidded you and you would kid him back, he loved that. He loved naturally beautiful women, there's no two ways about it. Everyone's attracted to that, but then their personality is very important, you know if you had a great personality, and you could talk to him one-on-one, interested in different things, not just him being a star, those are the kinds of woman. So you could tell when you talked to them, and you knew then if Elvis would like them or not.

SP: Okay, so he definitely wasn't shallow minded, and it wasn't all about the way they looked; that's good to hear.

JE: Well, naturally looks are going to bring you to them right away, definitely, and you sit and talk to them, and then you could tell after a while if they were interested in a short little affair, well, that's fine, but if it were to be a long relationship there had to be more, like I said—funny and nice and caring.

SP: Linda Thompson was very good for him, wasn't she?

JE: Oh, very. She was, yes.

SP: Now, Joe, Elvis bought you a Cadillac

convertible, one for you and your then-wife Joan, and he was renowned for his generosity. Did you often witness his extraordinarily giving nature?

JE: Very extraordinary, but he didn't buy one for my wife Joan.

SP: Oh, he didn't?

JE: No, he didn't. At one time I was dating this girl Shirley for about four years; he gave her a Cadillac. Yeah, and that's a whole other story. No, but very, very giving. You must have heard those stories many times. He loved to make people happy and loved the expression on someone's face when he gave them something that they could not get. That's what he loved to see. It made him feel so good because you know he was such a poor kid, never in his life did he ever think he would be able to do stuff like that, so when he was able to do it, he would do it.

SP: So he just kind of gave everything away.

JE: Oh, yeah. Material things were not important. I don't care if we gave him a beautiful watch, or a gold watch, if somebody saw him later—two, three, four, or five months later and said, "Oh, Elvis, that's a beautiful watch," he would take it off and give it to him. That's the way he felt about material things.

SP: Amazing man!

SP: Now our U.K. manager Michael Comley wants to ask, "How did you get on with Charlie Hodge?"

JE: Charlie and I were very close, very close. Funny guy, sweet man, funny all the time, always there for Elvis. There was one problem, he was a drinker.

SP: Really? I didn't know that about Charlie.

JE: Charlie drank way too much, and that was pretty bad, and he smoked too much too. Yeah, that was a bad thing but overall Charlie was great.

SP: What about Priscilla? She still has to take a lot of stick from people even now. How do you feel about Priscilla today?

JE: Priscilla and I are still friends.

SP: Good.

JE: Oh, yeah, we talk all the time. You know when I think about it, I've known her for forty-eight years.

SP: Golly, that's a long time.

JE: That's a long damn time.

SP: And she looks great, doesn't she?

JE: I know it, she looks very good.

SP: Just nipping back to the Army days, Joe, I

"Material things were not important. I don't care if we gave him a beautiful watch, or a gold watch, if somebody saw him later—two, three, four, or five months later and said, 'Oh, Elvis, that's a beautiful watch,' he would take it off and give it to him. That's the way he felt about material things..."

JOE ESPOSITO

heard that you, Elvis, and Lamar went into Paris a few times, had a bit of fun with the showgirls. Could you shed a bit of light on that?

JE: Well, I only went one time. Elvis went over there earlier one time, way before I went with him. I went with him when it was Lamar, Cliff Gleaves, his karate instructor, George from Germany, and Elvis and myself. We went to Paris on purpose because he wanted to go and take some karate lessons from this Korean gentleman over there, and that was the purpose of the trip. So while we were there during the day we were out sightseeing but then in the evenings naturally we went to all those big shows with the showgirls, you know Crazy Horse and all those. Just so happens we met a lot of those young ladies, so after the shows we would go out clubbing and partying, having a good time and then in those days a lot of those girls had to be back to their dorm after the second show, back by 12 midnight, otherwise they would have been locked out. So it just so happens that it was good for us, because then they had to stay at the hotel where we all were at the time.

SP: Oh la la! [Laughing.]

JE: We were very nice, we are making sure that they were well taken care of, so we had a lot of great times and, errr, it was very, very interesting.

SP: I bet it was!

JE: First time for me to be that way.

SP: Well now, moving on . . . That was something, wasn't it, the '68 Comeback! Is it a fact that Elvis was so nervous he actually threw up before going on stage?

JE: No, that's not true, that ain't true.

SP: So many have said that.

JE: Who? Were they there? That's the difference.

No, he did not. They don't know what they are talking about, and they were not there. I'd like to know where that originated from. No, he did not throw up. He was very nervous, a nervous wreck but he did not get sick. I never remember Elvis ever getting sick with having anything to do with going on stage.

SP: Okay. Well, that's good to hear.

SP: Now here's this brilliant man that just oozes sex appeal, talking about his sex appeal okay, here's the question—Molly, I'm going to ask your question, darling.

[Joe starts laughing.]

SP: A lot of curious women are interested to hear the answer to this question, Joe, and you're pretty broad minded.

JE: Yes, I love broads!

[This is what I mean about the lighter side of Joe: quick witted and game for a laugh.]

SP: Yeah, we know [Laughing.] Okay, it's a bit naughty, Joe.

JE: Okay, okay.

SP: Not to beat around the bush, during the '68 Special it's been said that Elvis became very visibly aroused, excited. It's been said he had a climatic experience so to speak, do you get my drift?

JE: Another story!

SP: Oh, I said—

JE: —Another made up story.

SP: I'm just the messenger.

JE: I know. No. There was one time that we were making a movie.

SP: *Girls, Girls, Girls*?

ABOVE: Joe at an Elvis convention.

139

JE: *Girls, Girls, Girls* . . . there was one little dancing scene with his co-star, he did get excited during that scene, you can see it.

SP: Did his co-star notice?

JE: I never asked her. [Laughing.]

JE: You have to remember, people are going to make up stories that they've never heard. You see, "I know this story." That's the secret, that's why they do that.

SP: Did you ever think to yourself when you were with Elvis, and he was a star . . . did you ever stop and think, "Wow, this guy is so wonderful, and I'm here because we became friends in the Army?" It's life changing.

JE: We all knew Elvis was a great star, but you didn't realize after a while, after spending 16 or 17 years with him it becomes just everyday work for us. But when I first went to work for him, I was at Miami Beach when he was doing the *Frank Sinatra Special*, and I was sitting on the patio at this beautiful Fontainebleau Hotel just having a little drink. I'm sitting there, and I think to myself, "Here I am with Elvis Presley, the biggest star in the world in Miami Beach at the Fontainebleau Hotel," which was the best hotel in the United States at the time, and on the other tower over there was Frank Sinatra, Sammy Davis Jr, and Joey Bishop, and I was thinking, "How did I get here?" When I think about it, I was very, very lucky, that was an amazing feeling, that I got to be there with all those people!

SP: When you think back now you can hardly believe it, right?

JE: Yes, when I think back. People would die to be there, you know what I'm saying?

SP: I know!

JE: Here's the most important thing, and I realize when Elvis passed away and we see fifty or sixty thousand people show up to Memphis at that gate, crying, upset, just could not believe he was gone. We did not expect it would be that big of a deal because we're on the inside, we don't see from the outside. Not realizing how many people all over the world it affected in his life . . . and look at us. Over thirty years he's been gone. The guy grossed 50 million dollars last year, and he's been gone thirty years. Now tell me about another star, another human being who has had that kind of effect on the public like he did? Nobody, nobody will have that ever again.

SP: I totally agree.

SP: I want to talk to you about the *Elvis on Tour*

ABOVE: Joe during the interview with Shelly; **OPPOSITE:** Elvis looking pensive in uniform.

video. It's got some great footage on it, and it really demonstrates your constant support for Elvis. I mean you were there at his side continually throughout everything, and I can recall a clip where Elvis is about to walk out on stage and he's waiting for his cue and you have this look on your face as you wait by his side, kind of pensive. What would be going through your mind at that moment? Did you have the same adrenaline rush that Elvis had when he walked out on stage to a multitude of fans?

JE: Well, yeah, definitely I had the rush. When you walk out on stage in front of twenty or thirty thousand people and they're all screaming and yelling, that rush of excitement goes right to the star. So the feeling is amazing, yes. I have a great feeling because I have a great feeling for him. What he's got to be feeling up there! Yes, my mind was always making sure everything was right, making note of where the wires are, telling him watch when you walk over here or walk over there because every stage was different that time on the road. All I cared about was making sure he got on stage good.

SP: So that's what that look was, concentration.

JE: Right.

SP: When Elvis was whisked off the stage, you did a lot of running in those days didn't you?

JE: Yes.

SP: I imagine the fans could still get a little crazy, even though he had all his bodyguards around him. Did Elvis ever get hurt trying to leave the arena?

JE: No, never. I mean once in a while fingernails would scratch accidentally when he was shaking somebody's hand, when he runs down there, but otherwise getting hurt bad? No.

SP: What in your opinion Joe was Elvis Presley's finest hour?

JE: There's not one finest hour, there was way way too many of them. The Aloha, the '68 Comeback Special. There's not one, there's a lot of highlights in his life that are amazing to us and to him.

SP: The birth of Lisa Marie?

JE: Very true, the birth of Lisa Marie. He was just unbelievably happy, he couldn't be happier. To see that smile on his face when he came out and told us "It's a girl!" There's too many great great moments.

SP: Just being there at that moment when his little girl is born is something else!

"Over thirty years he's been gone. The guy grossed 50 million dollars last year, and he's been gone thirty years. Now tell me about another star, another human being who has had that kind of effect on the public like he did? Nobody, nobody will have that ever again..."

JOE ESPOSITO

TOP: Elvis in one of his signature leather outfits;

ABOVE: Joe at the 25th anniversary of Elvis's death, Memphis, 2002. Patti Parry is at his left.

JE: Yes, yes.

SP: Just a few final questions, Joe. His actual death has been rehashed and rehashed, and I don't really want to go to that dark place, and I don't think you do either. You're Joe Esposito and you can call the shots.

JE: Last time I looked at my driver's licence.

SP: What I would like to talk about is the funeral. Is it true the entire yard of Graceland was filled with flowers from all over the country?

JE: Not the entire yard, but a lot. I mean it had to cover an acre at least. There are 14 acres so that's a big estate. Yes, there's a film of that stuff, the amount of flowers that came from around the world! The whole city ran out of flowers. They had to go to different cities like Nashville to bring flowers into Memphis to fill out the orders.

SP: Is it true what they say about the Presley family decided to hand them out to all the fans that hung around?

JE: They did give a lot of them away, and they took a lot of them to the cemetery, and they gave a lot of those flowers away too. Why let them go to waste?

SP: I know the family, the guys, and yourself wanted to give him a really good send off, and at Graceland there was singing and no doubt a lot of tears.

JE: Yes.

SP: What do you remember about that day when you said your final farewell to the King. Joe, what sticks out in your mind about that day?

JE: Well, I know we were so overwhelmed with what was going on. There were certain things we had to get done, no two ways about it. That was the most important thing, because that was Elvis's final appearance, and we all made sure that everything was right for him, so it was very tough. We were so busy we really didn't realize until later that night—because of all the things that went on, because we all went out to dinner together—that he was not going to be back again. That was it, he's gone, and that was very emotional for all of us. We all hugged, and we couldn't believe that had happened but we said let's all think of the great times. Focus on that, and that's what we did. It was just so amazing to see all those people show up and to drive down to Elvis Presley Boulevard and see all those people on both sides crying. Officers saluting him as we drove down . . . it was just amazing, the respect that people gave him, and still do today.

SP: Joe, do you have a favorite Elvis song?

JE: No, there's too many, different times and different places. I just remember all of those things. Too many songs to have one favorite.

SP: Well, Joe Esposito, you are indeed a diamond. It's been a complete pleasure for me today to sit here with you and talk about Elvis. Can I just say on behalf of all the members of the Elvis International Fan Club and our president Jason and all the Elvis fans that listen to this, thank you from the bottom of our hearts. Love and peace to you, Joe.

JE: You are most welcome. I have no problem ever talking about my friend, and it's been a pleasure.

SP: Bless you, you're lovely. Thanks, Joe.

Joe was a delight to chat with, he had a great sense of humor. He was respectful and patient answering all the questions I had for him. I saw Joe a few times after this interview around Las Vegas and on the Elvis Cruises hosted by Jerry Schilling. I was deeply saddened to hear of Joe's passing on November 23, 2016, a year after I returned to the United Kingdom. I will always remember Joe as Elvis Presley's best man, and

ABOVE: Elvis with Joe on a film set,
It Happened at the World's Fair.
RIGHT: Joe and Shelly.

when I think of him, I recall his wonderful dry wit and his kindness in always giving the fans time with him for pictures and chats about him and his friend Elvis.

" **…the birth of Lisa Marie. He was just unbelievably happy, he couldn't be happier. To see that smile on his face when he came out and told us 'It's a girl!'** "

JOE ESPOSITO

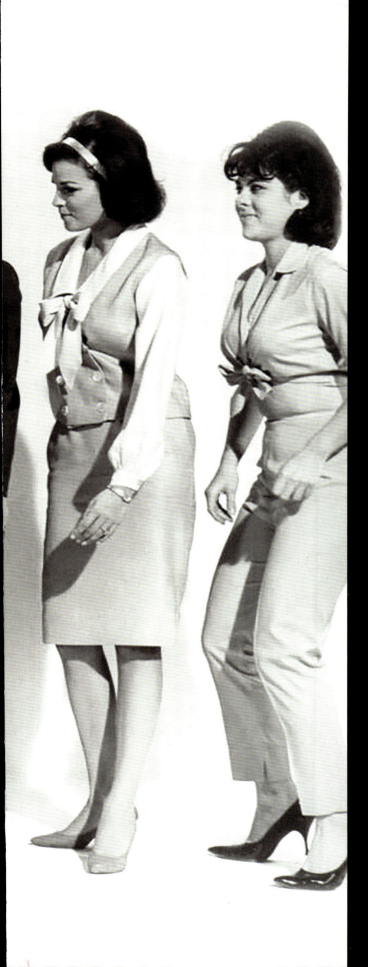

ELVIS
REMEMBERED

"When Elvis came around, I suddenly understood what sex is all about. Roustabout in 1964 was my very first film in Hollywood. I was a bit player in the opening moments. Like many adolescents of the '50s, I had been completely gaga over Elvis. I saw him live in San Diego in one of his early shows. It was my first rock 'n' roll music concert ever. That was the first time that I ever conjured up what a sexy guy could be..."

Raquel Welch

On Elvis Presley movie, *Roustabout*

"Whenever I would go up to the suite we danced. I danced with Elvis one time, and he was just shaking, he was so nervous..."

MYRNA SMITH ON HER RELATIONSHIP WITH ELVIS

INTERVIEW **SEVEN**

Myrna Smith

Myrna was an American singer and songwriter, and a member of the Sweet Inspirations soul group, Elvis's backing vocalists from 1969–1977.

OPPOSITE: A portrait of Myrna, taken during the interview.

Interviewing Myrna...

Myrna Smith was an American singer/songwriter, born in New Jersey on May 28, 1941. She began singing at the tender age of five when she sang "Jesus Loves Me" with her father's gospel group on the *Sons of Harmony* radio show. She worked as a high school English teacher in the 1960s, while still pursuing her musical career. Later Myrna became the lead singer of the Sweet Inspirations soul group. The group chose the name after their first hit single "Sweet Inspiration." The group was originally founded by Cissy Houston (aka Emily Drinkard), mother of Whitney Houston and sister of Lee Warwick (herself the mother of Dee Dee and the well-known Dionne Warwick).

TOP, LEFT TO RIGHT: Myrna Smith welcomes Ed Bonja and Shelly Powers; **ABOVE:** Myrna (right), onstage.

The group sang backup for a number of stars, including Wilson Pickett. Solomon Burke, Esther Phillips and the wonderful Aretha Franklin. Dee Dee left the group in 1965 and that is when Myrna Smith stepped in and took her place with Estelle Brown soon afterwards and then the line-up was complete. That song itself, "Sweet Inspiration," caught the attention of Elvis, whereupon he signed the group to provide the backing vocals and become the opening act for his record-breaking 1969 Las Vegas engagement, and that is where her eight-year association with Elvis began.

The Sweets met Elvis for the first time when they arrived for the rehearsals for the '69 Las Vegas engagement and so her life took off, with national concert tours and recordings from 1969 to Elvis Presley's death in 1977. Myrna also backed Elvis up at the Graceland recordings during 1976. On the day I interviewed Myrna I also did two other interviews previously that same day with Patti Parry and Jerry Schilling. Patti especially was very much on my mind so when I arrived at Myrna's—I called her Patti! She saw the funny side of it, and we both laughed. The interview took place in Myrna's bedroom, on her bed of all places, with Ed Bonja present, sitting in the room in an armchair by the window! Ed had very kindly driven me to Patti's and Myrna's places in LA.

MS: Patti, she was the belle of the ball today, right?

SP: Oh, she was so funny.

SP: Anyway here we go—"Hi, Patti."

MS: No, I'm Myrna. [We both crack up laughing.]

SP: Please forgive me, three interviews in one day! I've still got Patti on the brain.

MS: Oh, she'll be there a while.

SP: Start again. Hi, Myrna!

MS: Hi, how are you?

SP: I am absolutely fine, and you look gorgeous! Thank you so much for taking part in this interview, especially for the members of our Elvis Fan Club.

MS: Thank you.

SP: Myrna, can we start by you telling me how you became a member of the Sweet Inspirations?

MS: Well, I was recording. I was doing my own album back then, and I was also doing backup for the Sweet Inspirations, we were doing records and backup for other people. An agent from Atlantic Records approached me and asked if we would like to record, and I said, "You know I have a deal with another guy," and he said, "Well, just break it." So I said okay, but I was a little nervous because I was like 17 in high school. I had already been in the studio and recorded a song and all, so I went to him and said, "I'm gonna have to break my deal." Of course he was like, "Why?" and I explained because Jerry Webster wants me to sing with the girls for Atlantic Records. We did all the

background for everybody, we did backing for Wilson Pickett, Aretha Franklin, Dionne Warwick. Well, I did the background for Dionne Warwick and lots and lots of people. They paid us every time but the business was getting a little mysterious and they just wanted to have us there at Atlantic, so they wanted to sign us to a record deal so that they would know they had us there. So we signed for a record deal, and I left my old guy, and I went with Atlantic, and we became the Sweet Inspirations. Well, we originally became the Inspirations but we had to change our name because Inspirations was already used for a gospel group, so we had to put something in front of it, and Jerry came up with Sweet.

SP: Which is perfect, isn't it? How long had you been a part of the Sweet Inspirations before you met Elvis Presley?

MS: Two or three years.

SP: So tell me about your first encounter with Elvis… how did that go?

MS: Well, you know it was very normal. We were sitting on stage at the International Hotel.

MS: [Turns to Ed Bonja.] "What was the hotel called before the International?"

EB: It was called the International, and then it changed to the Hilton.

TOP: Shelly and Myrna;
ABOVE: Myrna photographed during Shelly's interview.

149

TOP: Myrna and Elvis during a concert at The International in Las Vegas; **ABOVE**: The Inspirations in the 1960s, with Cissy Houston at top, Myrna at bottom of the picture.

"Cissy Houston was with us at the time—her daughter is Whitney Houston. Cissy was only with us for the opening that month, and then she left..."

MYRNA SMITH ON "LIVE IN FABULOUS LAS VEGAS," JULY 1969

MS: We were sitting on stage waiting for him to come down, and then all of a sudden we heard a lot of clamor, and it was Elvis and his guys. He came in, and he didn't have on a shirt, but he had on this suit jacket.

SP: Hmmm, really? I bet he looked sexy!

MS: [Laughs.] Yeah. He did.

MS: So he came over, and he kissed each of us, so we were one right there and then.

SP: Now, Myrna, I have to tell you there are a lot of women in this fan club, and they have a lot of questions. I don't think I have met a woman today that doesn't find Elvis Presley attractive. I mean he was a beautiful-looking man. You got to spend so much time with him along with the other

Sweets and because of the tours and spending all that time with him, did you ever consider dating him yourself?

MS: Well, he had plans for that, but I didn't have any.

SP: He did?

MS: Yeah, he had some plans for us to have a little relationship, but I wasn't going to be a part of it because I knew what Elvis was into, and I didn't happen to be into that, you know. I was married when I met Elvis.

SP: So had you not been married, maybe?

MS: No, I knew too much about Elvis from what I

had heard. I knew he was not a one-woman man, and I was a one-man woman. [She laughs.] But when I split up from my husband I started dating Jerry Schilling.

SP: I was going to ask you about that. He's gorgeous, isn't he?

MS: Yeah, and Elvis told Jerry that he couldn't date me because he was having me fly down to his pad in Palm Springs, but he hadn't told me all this stuff! [Myrna laughs again.] He didn't want Jerry dating me I suppose because I worked for him, and if there was going to be anything it had to be with him. So they were both competing for me.

SP: Well, I bet you had more than Elvis and Jerry after you. You were a beautiful woman and still are.

MS: Yeah, but I wasn't the type to go after guys.

SP: You were a good girl.

MS: I was a good girl. [Myrna bursts into laughter.]

SP: I can tell you were a good girl. So it didn't amount to anything?

MS: Well, it amounted to us just playing around, not like you would think. We played around but we were very innocent, you know.

SP: Yeah, I get it.

MS: Whenever I would go up to the suite we danced. I danced with Elvis one time, and he was just shaking, he was so nervous.

SP: [Gasps.] Really?

MS: He wasn't used to dancing with women, and he was just shaking, and I was like, "What is wrong with this superstar?"

SP: He wasn't used to dancing with you!

MS: He wasn't used to dancing at all! But he asked me to dance so I said yes, but I should have said no because he was a nervous wreck. But we danced to one song, and he didn't dance with anybody else, that was enough for him that night.

SP: Okay, bless him.

MS: He was very nice. I just saw the shy side of Elvis because most of the guys didn't see that side of him.

SP: They saw the macho man.

MS: Yeah, macho, but he let me see the soft side of him. So we remained friends on those terms. He was a softie to me.

SP: Can you describe to me what it was like on July 31st, 1969, when the king hit the stage for the first time, "Live in Fabulous Las Vegas?"

MS: Well, it wasn't a big thing to me. It was in so far as all the different people that were coming in, all the movie stars and all the bigwigs that came in. I didn't expect that kind of reaction to Elvis. I knew he was a big star; he wasn't big in my music world.

SP: Okay.

TOP LEFT: The Sweet Inspirations' first album release on Atlantic Records, 1967; **TOP RIGHT:** The Inspirations around the time they began singing with Elvis; **ABOVE:** Myrna in the 1990s.

MS: The black music world. He surprised me, and he surprised me for thirty days after that because every night the same amount of crowds came. It was spectacular; you can't even explain it, it was incredible.

SP: We've all seen plenty of footage with Elvis and the Sweet Inspirations during rehearsals, would you say Elvis was a perfectionist? And how long would those rehearsals last?

MS: I couldn't say how long they were, but it seemed very fast to me. I've been in longer rehearsals for performers that weren't as big as Elvis.

SP: Would you say he was a perfectionist?

MS: Yes, I would. He let us come up with our own backgrounds. We received a lot of material to learn, which we didn't because we knew we could get the background, and we had heard Elvis songs, and we were very fast. Cissy Houston was with us at the time—her daughter is Whitney Houston. Cissy was only with us for the opening that month and then she left, and we had other problems, it wasn't Elvis, but other problems.

SP: Oh, really? Okay, apart from that you all got on really well?

MS: Yes, we were getting along fine. Cissy left because we fired her husband, and he was our road manager. After we fired him, she left.

SP: Well, you must have had good reason. But moving on, what was the most memorable concert that comes to mind?

MS: They were all memorable, it's hard to single out one because he was so amazing. Even when he didn't feel good, even when his voice wasn't at its top, he was still phenomenal.

SP: I have some questions from the members of our fan club. The first one comes from Jason and asks, "Many consider Elvis a uniting force in terms of bringing black and white music together while others look at what Elvis did as simply copying black musicians. What, Myrna, is your take on Elvis as an innovator and musician?"

MS: I think neither one of those statements is true, that black people look upon Elvis as a contributor to the sound that black people have. That's what the writers are putting in the magazines and the newspapers. Elvis was just a star! I know that he did get some of his music from black singers and whatever, but I don't believe that he did as much as they would like you to believe.

SP: Jason also says he's a big fan of both you and Jerry Schilling, and you were both once married. Jason says that he read that Elvis was supportive of your relationship. Is this true and can you all elaborate?

MS: We were going together when Elvis was alive, so Elvis knew about our relationship and he approved, and we stayed at his house up on Monovale. He had no problem with our relationship. After we did get together he calmed down on his quest, you know, and he was happy for us.

SP: Glad to hear that. Last question from Jason, "What was the happiest you saw Elvis and what was the saddest?" Let's start with the happiest.

MS: The happiest I saw Elvis? Well, Elvis was always laughing, he was either laughing, or he was sad. There were a lot of happy times, when he would be around all of us he would be happy. And when he would be with you by yourself maybe then that's when a little sadness would come out, but I would like people to know that basically he was a happy person.

SP: What is the one unique thing about Elvis that you will always remember?

MS: His laugh, his laugh was wonderful. When he laughed, you laughed. It was very contagious, and you knew when he was faking the laugh, and you knew when he was serious, and he did a lot of faking the laugh.

SP: He did?

MS: [Myrna laughs.] Oh, yeah, yes he did. He had to with all those guys around him.

SP: A few questions from my friend Marion in the U.K. She asks, "Where do you think the *Elvis: The Concert* is going as there was talk of replacing the TCB band with some younger musicians? Did you hear about that?"

MS: Yes, I heard about that, and I guess it's up to them, they're going to do what they want to do. If they want to try it then good for them.

SP: When you are performing at *Elvis: The Concert* and you have the band and then Elvis as large as life, in your mind does it ever feel like you're up there singing with Elvis again in person?

MS: Yes, it does, if you let your mind go it does feel like you are singing with him alive. It's very weird but I feel that.

SP: Yeah? I haven't actually been to one before, but I'm going to my first in Memphis soon.

SP: Of all the songs that you have performed with Elvis, which would you say is your favorite song to sing that you personally enjoyed, and which song did you love to hear Elvis sing?

MS: I loved to hear Elvis sing all of them. [Myrna laughs.] I'd mostly like to sing "Can't Help Falling in Love" because that was the last one. It wasn't like you were glad the show was over, but there's just something about that song.

SP: Yeah, I get it, and all the fans know this is the last song they will hear before he walks off stage, so the atmosphere is brilliant. Looking at all the concert footage we have today, there are some really funny incidents with Elvis goofing around. Do you have anything to share with the fans that can relate to that?

MS: Well, I wasn't messing around personally too much but we used to mess around a little bit with water guns. [Myrna cracks up.] But Elvis started it! He would bring his water gun and start shooting. He had sessions of mischief. Every once in a while he would do that, and we had fun, but he would stop

TOP: The Sweet Inspirations (Elvis's backing singers from 1969 to 1977). Recording at Ocean Way Recording Studios, 10/18/2003; **ABOVE:** Elvis on stage with the Sweet Inspirations.

153

TOP: Myrna holds forth during Shelly's interview; **CENTER:** The Sweet Inspirations 1979 album, *Hot Butterfly*; **ABOVE:** *Estelle, Myrna and Sylvia*, on Stax Records from 1973; **OPPOSITE:** The Sweet Inspirations in the 1960s.

doing it if you shot back at him; he wanted to be the one that was doing all the shooting! [Myrna starts laughing again as she relays this story to me.]

SP: Now, Myrna, you were and still are extremely beautiful.

MS: Well, thank you.

SP: What were the guys like around you, all of Elvis's guys? Were they perfect gentlemen, or did they try hitting on you?

MS: [Laughs.] I'm not telling.

SP: Really?

[At this point we are both giggling away on her bed like two teenage girls. It was really sweet.]

MS: I'd say they were mostly very nice, nobody would get into trouble for what they did, it was just harmless play.

SP: Yes, boys will be boys.

MS: Always.

EB: Always a gentleman.

SP: I believe that about you, Ed.

SP: So you didn't have to pull a fast karate chop on them then?

MS: I was just learning karate then.

SP: Did you enjoy being on the road, traveling from one place to the next?

MS: Very, very much. Elvis made it very easy for us, and I have to admit the Colonel did too. We didn't have anything to do with luggage and all that stuff, all the guys had to do that. We had a very nice easy time, just get on the bus and go.

SP: Towards the end, Myrna, during that final concert did you ever stop and think to yourself, "This is it… he's not going to be going out on the road after this?"

MS: No, no. We had seen him sick before or overweight before. All those things didn't matter. Elvis was like, lose the weight and then put a bit on, so you never thought this was going to be the last time. Never thought that.

SP: Now our U.K. manager of the fan club says, "Myrna, I've been lucky enough to meet you twice, and I have some wonderful memories of our brief encounters but the one that sticks out in my mind is where you, Estelle, and Portia sang a cappella to the Lord's Prayer." He goes on to say, "It was beautiful, and it brought tears to my eyes." He wants to know have you ever recorded this as he would love to hear this again in CD quality?

MS: Emmm, I'm thinking do we have that on CD? I don't think so but let me see. [Myrna gets off her bed and goes over to a set of drawers.]

154

TOP: Myrna, left, with Ed Bonja and the author; **ABOVE:** Myrna photographed during the interview; **BELOW:** Myrna, right, with Elvis.

"After you've been with somebody like Elvis, to come up with what *you* could be doing to help the world, it's hard..."

MYRNA SMITH ON ELVIS'S GENEROUS NATURE

MS: I have a CD, I should know but I don't. [Myrna starts searching.] Yeah, it's on a CD.

SP: What's that CD called?

MS: It's called *The Sweet Inspirations In the Right Place*. We will be bringing it to England with us. And that's for you. [Myrna hands me the CD.]

SP: Thank you so much!

MS: You're welcome.

SP: That's beautiful! Look at you there, you look gorgeous. [I'm referring to the album cover.] Aww, thank you, Myrna. I'm going to play that when I get home.

SP: Michael adds, "We hear that dear Sylvia has been ill for quite a while; do you still see her and how is she?"

MS: Yes, I still see her. Sylvia lives around the corner from us. She gets around in a wheelchair, she's had a stroke and she's paralyzed on her right side but she can walk slowly and she's on that CD so you'll hear her singing.

SP: But she's doing okay?

MS: She's doing fair, she's not great. She has gained a lot of weight, and she's not Sylvia anymore. She still knows everybody, and we wanted to bring her to Memphis, but she's not up to that. Her daughters are taking care of her.

SP: I'd like to talk about the spiritual side of Elvis. Freda, our U.S. manager asks about his Christianity, as some of his entourage said some things that were quite negative regarding his faith. What are your thoughts on Elvis and his Christianity?

MS: There is a fraction of people out there that will listen to what they have to say, especially if it's different and whether it's true or not it's nobody's business. All I can say as far as I am concerned Elvis was a believer in God. He read into all different kinds of things. He did believe, and that's all it takes for me.

SP: It's common knowledge what a good, kind-hearted man Elvis was, can you give me an example of Elvis's kind heart and his generosity towards others?

MS: He gave me plenty of gifts, he gave me more gifts than I can think of. He gave me, all of us diamonds, rings, necklaces, and whatever. But Elvis was the type of person that if he did something to hurt your feelings he wouldn't say I'm sorry, he would rather just give you a gift and that was his way of saying I'm sorry, but it was hard for him to say I'm sorry, he couldn't say it.

SP: It's funny that, isn't it?

MS: Yeah.

SP: Myrna, what do you miss about Elvis the most?

MS: I just miss him being around, you know. Sometimes I just sit here in my room, and I'm not doing anything at all, and I'm thinking what could I be doing that would be helpful to the world? You know Elvis did a lot of things that were helpful to a lot of people in the world, and I just try to think, "What could I be doing for somebody rather than just sitting here thinking," "Oh, I gotta go to work" or "I gotta do this, and it's really hard!" After you've been with somebody like Elvis, to come up with what *you*

could be doing to help the world… it's hard. I have to come to the conclusion that what I did, I did already, and maybe that was my mission, maybe that's all I can do, what I did with him, that's all I can do.

SP: What are the plans for the future now, do you have anything planned?

MS: Yeah, we're selling that CD, and we're thinking about making another one and we're doing a lot regarding Elvis. you know, singing backup for Elvis impersonators… Elvis lookalikes they should be called.

SP: Elvis tribute artists.

MS: Yes, tribute artists, but as far as the Sweet Inspirations, we are going to be doing another album soon. That's all we can do right now is music.

SP: One day at a time.

MS: One day at a time.

SP: Well, I'd just like to say, Myrna, it's been a real pleasure, and thank you for giving me the opportunity to talk about Elvis Presley. And on behalf of all the members of our great fan club and fans around the world, our president Jason and myself, Shelly Powers, I'd like to wish you love and peace and happiness for the future.

MS: That's okay, sweetie. Thank you.

Myna Smith was such a sweet, fun lady, full of life. I have never conducted an interview on someone's bed before! She was so laid back. She was so sincere and on all accounts a very good woman with a big heart. Sadly, Myrna passed away on Christmas Eve [December 24, 2010] from kidney failure. While performing on *Elvis: The Concert European tour* in March 2010 Myrna developed pneumonia, which eventually led to kidney failure and a stroke. She passed away in Canoga Park, California, at the age of 69. I'd like to imagine she got to spend Christmas Day with Elvis that year.

TOP LEFT: Poster for the Elvis Summer Festival at the International Hotel, Las Vegas. The Sweet Inspirations are also on the bill; **ABOVE:** Elvis onstage with the Sweet Inspirations; **BELOW:** Myrna, snapped before Shelly's interview.

ELVIS
REMEMBERED

"'Let me tell you the definitive truth about Elvis Presley and racism,' the King of the Blues, B.B. King, said in 2010. 'With Elvis, there was not a single drop of racism in that man. And when I say that, believe me I should know'..."

B.B. KING

On "Racist Accusations"

"...when my agent told me they were interviewing, and I said I wanted to go out and get this interview, he started laughing, because I can't sing or dance!"

DARLENE TOMPKINS ON HER AUDITION FOR *BLUE HAWAII*

INTERVIEW **EIGHT**

Darlene Tompkins

Darlene was an American actress who worked with Elvis on the movie *Blue Hawaii* in 1961. She remained close with Elvis up until his passing. She herself died in 2019.

OPPOSITE: The beautiful, charming and charismatic Darlene Tompkins during the interview.

Interviewing Darlene...

Darlene Tompkins was an American actress born November 16, 1940, in Chicago, Illinois. She died July 18, 2019, aged 78. Her birth name was Darlene Perfect, and after meeting her on numerous occasions in Las Vegas I would say her name was absolutely fitting as she was a perfect lady—beautiful, charming, and charismatic. Her first acting role was in *Beyond the Time Barrier* in 1960. Before this she had won many beauty pageants and had appeared in numerous commercials. In 1961 she co-starred opposite Elvis Presley in *Blue Hawaii*. She had a role in *My Six Loves* in 1963 and played parts in several television shows. Darlene also had a part in another Elvis Presley movie, *Fun in Acapulco*.

TOP: Shelly (left) and Darlene share a joke during the interview at Shelly's Summerlin home; **ABOVE:** The young Darlene Tompkins in *Beyond the Time Barrier*, 1960.

After *Fun in Acapulco*, her career was put on hold after she married and gave birth to two sons. By that time Darlene was in her thirties, and landing roles wasn't easy. Her final film role was portraying the part of a bosomy blonde in the movie *A Guide for the Married Man*. Since further roles were hard to come by, Darlene decided to work as a stand-in and a stuntwoman instead, and she also remarried. I was honored and privileged to interview Darlene at my home in Summerlin, Las Vegas. When she arrived I presented her with a beautiful Hawaiian lei, which she wore throughout the entire interview. Darlene was a sweet lady, she laughed easily, was genuinely warm, kind and extremely graceful. Following the interview we met frequently at social gatherings, Elvis Conventions, and shows.

I was deeply saddened to hear of her passing while I was back in England.

SP: Aloha, Darlene.

DT: And aloha to you.

SP: Before we talk about your role in *Blue Hawaii* let's chat a little bit about how you first started out. You came from a show business family, so tell me a little bit about that.

DT: Well, my aunts, great aunts, they were in vaudeville, and I started out as a stand-in for Lora Lee Michels in the movie, *The Snake Pit*, starring Olivia de Havilland, when I was a little girl.

SP: How old were you?

DT: Probably around eight.

SP: So how did you land the role in *Blue Hawaii*?

DT: Well, naturally I was a fan of Elvis, loved his music, loved him and everything about him, and I had done a lot of drama but I had never done a musical. I heard they were interviewing at Paramount Studios, so what I decided to do was I would go over there, and I would meet Elvis and get to see him and be all excited and everything and then, er, leave. Because when my agent told me they were interviewing, and I said I wanted to go out and get this interview, he started laughing… because I can't sing or dance! I can't carry a tune or anything, but I would do anything to see Elvis. So I went there, went on the interview, and there were about four hundred girls they had at the interview. It was huge, huge, very large. So they did the interview, and I didn't get to see Elvis because at that time he was in Hawaii, and he wasn't there. He was probably doing some other stuff so he wasn't there. So I came home quite disappointed that I didn't get to see Elvis… and the next day my agent called and said I had gotten the part.

SP: Wow, that's wonderful!

DT: You see what happens, which I later found out, is if you go on an interview for a musical they assume that you can sing and dance, so nobody ever asked me if I could sing or dance. I would have told them, but now I had a chance to go to Hawaii, so I thought, "Oh, my gosh what am I gonna do? But I get to fly to Hawaii, and I'll get to meet Elvis. So like anybody else—"

SP: —you didn't care. You thought at the very least, "I'll get to meet Elvis!"

DT: I wasn't going to miss out on that, would you?

SP: Absolutely not!!

DT: They didn't ask, so you know I thought I'm going to go and meet Elvis!

SP: So what happened?

DT: Well, I got there, and I was very, very lucky because in all of the Elvis movies that he did, there were about seven ladies they allowed to use their own voice, and I was very, very lucky in this movie because some of the other ladies were known for singing and dancing and had recordings and were professional singers like Pamela Austen—she was a beautiful singer, beautiful dancer, and had the prettiest legs in show business. Some of the others sang—Joan Blackman sang—but they never used their voices. By sheer luck because everything was

TOP: Elvis and collected girls in a publicity still for *Blue Hawaii*, 1961. Darlene is second right; **ABOVE:** Darlene in 1961.

163

"He used to say, 'My gosh, here I am, and I should be a truck driver, but here I am,' and he would get the giggles..."

DARLENE TOMPKINS ON THE DOWN-TO-EARTH ELVIS

TOP: Darlene, close-up, photographed during the interview; **ABOVE:** A hug for Darlene from Elvis.

lip-synced I could just fake that little sucker, and so when we did the "Moonlight Swim" number I never uttered a word, nobody did, not one person. None of our voices are on that, none.

SP: So whose voices did they use then?

DT: Professional singers, and I don't know why they didn't use their voices but I was so glad. The others were kind of sad because they were good singers, their voices were beautiful and prettier than the ones there, but I got lucky.

SP: Very lucky!

DT: I think so.

SP: But you're just so beautiful, we don't care if you can't sing or dance.

DT: Bless you, thank you.

SP: Now I am imagining what it would be like for me to meet Elvis for the first time face to face, I would be like jelly I'm sure. So what was it like for you when you very first set eyes on Elvis Presley in person?

DT: Well, the first reaction I had was I couldn't believe anyone was that beautiful. He was beautiful! He had to be. You can't even call him handsome; he was too beautiful to be called handsome. And

the second thing that was so strange about him was his stature. [Don't forget he was one of the top stars at that particular time and he only got bigger afterwards.] But at that time he was still the highest-paid actor there. He was so gentle and unassuming that he never made anyone feel that he was a star. You knew he was but you never felt it because it was always like he was your friend. Everybody that I have talked to, that met Elvis, felt the same way, he made everybody comfortable, and he treated everybody the same. Didn't matter what you did, what color, height, shape you were, whatever. There wasn't a prejudiced bone in his body, and he was always with a sense of humor, always.

SP: I have heard people talk about how humble he was, how modest.

DT: He really, really was. He used to say, "My gosh, here I am, and I should be a truck driver, here I am," and he would get the giggles.

SP: He laughed a lot didn't he? On some of his recordings you can hear him laughing and cracking up.

DT: Also if you close your eyes, his laughter would rise above a crowd.

ブルー・ハワイ

"When we were doing 'Slicin' Sand,' there he was. He was built like a swimmer, lean and athletic, and he used to show me his hands because at that time one of his passions was karate…"

DARLENE TOMPKINS ON ELVIS'S PHYSIQUE

SP: He had a very distinctive laugh.

DT: Absolutely, absolutely.

SP: I love to hear Elvis laugh, it makes you feel so good.

DT: It was really a deep, deep laugh, just fabulous.

SP: What a location too for filming a movie, Darlene! "Do you want to come to Hawaii and appear in a film with Elvis?" "Yes, please!"

[Darlene laughs.]

SP: Had you ever been to Hawaii before this movie?

DT: No, never, and I haven't had a chance to go back either with things happening. This year is too busy, but I'm hoping to go back next year.

SP: I was watching *Blue Hawaii* the other night because I wanted to brush up on everything for this interview, Darlene. I was sitting there in my recliner with my bowl of popcorn drooling over Elvis in his skimpy shorts.

DT: He had fabulous legs!

SP: Didn't he just? He really did!

SP: Was it the same for you when you got to see him all tanned and beautiful running around, did you get to see him running around in those little skimpy shorts?

DT: Oh, yeah, yes we did. When we were doing "Slicin' Sand," there he was. He was built like a

swimmer, lean and athletic, and he used to show me his hands because at that time one of his passions was karate and when he showed me his hand from his little finger to his wrist was all heavy, heavy muscular, like a callous on his hand. I know that right before he shot *Blue Hawaii* they did the soundtrack, and the night before he was doing the soundtrack I believe he said he was chopping boards, and he broke a little bone in his hand. He went out and got his hand taped, and I believe at that time Jimmy Velvet—he was a good friend of ours, and he loved Elvis totally—and I believe Jimmy still has a picture of that.

SP: Really? I will have to ask him if I can take a look at that. We love Jimmy.

DT: Jimmy is a great man.

SP: You know, talking about Elvis and his hands. He had very distinctive hands, didn't he? You instantly recognize Elvis's hands.

DT: He had artist's hands.

SP: Yeah, beautiful hands, everything about him was beautiful.

SP: *Blue Hawaii* is such an upbeat movie, it makes you want to go and grab a grass skirt and do the hula. It's such a happy movie… so what was the atmosphere like on set in such a fab place?

TOP LEFT: Elvis in shorts! The poster for the Japanese release of *Blue Hawaii*; **ABOVE:** Darlene describing her time with Elvis during the making of *Blue Hawaii*, 1961.

TOP RIGHT: Elvis still, snapped during the making of *Blue Hawaii*; **TOP LEFT:** Patti Page in 1959; **CENTER:** Joan Blackman; **ABOVE:** Elvis and co-star Joan Blackman take direction from Norman Taurog on the set of *Blue Hawaii*.

DT: Well, it was absolutely beautiful. Everybody was upbeat, it was fun. A lot of celebrities came over at that time to say hi to Elvis and one of them I remember was Patti Page.

SP: Is she a lovely woman?

DT: Oh, absolutely.

SP: What did Elvis think of Hawaii, do you know?

DT: He loved it. I think that his three favorite places were his home in Memphis, Hawaii, and Las Vegas.

SP: We were just saying the same thing, that he loved Las Vegas.

DT: He did, he always wanted to go home. His home he always felt was Tennessee but those other places he absolutely loved.

SP: Do you think he got to enjoy his surroundings much while on location or was it a case of work, work, work?

DT: No, he absolutely enjoyed his time there but he couldn't go out. He wanted to go to the theater, and he wanted to go into town. When you're here in Vegas or California you work five days a week, whereas when you're on location you work six days a week, so the only day off he had was Sunday, and he would have liked to be able to do that, but the whole town was completely surrounded with fans. It was amazing. A couple of young girls around thirteen years old went to great lengths to meet

Elvis. He was in the penthouse about twelve stories high and he had a guard up on that penthouse floor so you couldn't get up there by the elevators. So what these girls did, they found a way to get up there to his room, and they swung down because Elvis had this patio to walk out onto with sliding glass doors... and they swung back and forth to get in onto the patio. Twelve or thirteen years old! If they would have dropped they would have gone down twelve or thirteen floors. They didn't give it a second thought, they would do anything, anything, to see Elvis.

SP: The lengths that fans would go to try and get to Elvis amazes me!

SP: Now can you try and tell me a little bit about Roland Winters who played the part as Elvis's daddy in the movie *Blue Hawaii*, the character Fred Gates, I believe?

DT: Yes, that is correct. Now one thing to make clear—Angela Lansbury was one of my favorite actresses but I never had the occasion to work with her on that movie. I worked with her on *Murder She Wrote* but I didn't have the chance to do it on *Blue Hawaii* as the sets were different. So whatever the sets are, the interiors were shot at Paramount Studio, so we had different sets and different dates. So they would shoot our interiors on Monday and Angela Lansbury and all the interiors from his mansion on the other dates. But I know how wonderful she is. She is one of the most gracious, wonderful women ever! The most talented singer, dancer, comedian. She does everything, and I always wanted to but I didn't have the chance on that movie. Roland Winters—the thing is, I wanted to meet him but I never got the chance either because it was the same situation. But I tried my best, however the work conflict didn't make it possible. But what had happened is I grew up in the 1940s and in the 1940s I used to watch one of my favorite shows, which was the *Charlie Chan* movies. They did nineteen *Charlie Chan* movies but when they did those movies they always had a Caucasian play Charlie Chan, not an Asian actor. Well, about seven of them were done by Roland Winters. He plays Charlie Chan, and because I was such a fan of the *Charlie Chan* movies I wanted his autograph. So I didn't get that in *Blue Hawaii*, which I was sad about, but I also understand he was such a wonderful, gracious man, which made me want to meet him even more.

SP: Well, you can see that, with Angela Lansbury especially. They're such amazing people, they can take on any role and be brilliant. I've heard a lot of things about the character role she played in *Blue Hawaii*, that later on in life she was almost embarrassed about that. I thought she was great for that part, so what is your take on that, Darlene?

DT: Well, also the other thing about her is nobody ever doubted in the movie that she was his mother and looked old enough to play his mother, but if you look at her age she was only 15 years older than him but she could make herself older for that part.

SP: The thing is with Angela Lansbury, even when she was young she looked the same as she does now.

DT: Yes, that's true, even in *Gaslight*, a fabulous movie. Also *The Manchurian Candidate* because it shows her range... *Bedknobs and Broomsticks*, you know the range of that woman!

SP: Now, Darlene, poor you... I mean you had to go horseback riding with Elvis, sailing with Elvis, riding around in the car with Elvis... must have been tough for you.

[Darlene is laughing and giggling away here, and it's lovely to see.]

SP: What was it like having to do all these fun activities with this adorable man and get paid for it at the same time? Did you ever stop and think to yourself, "I'm here sitting in a car with Elvis Presley"?

DT: It was utterly amazing and the horseback riding thing, one thing I thought was that it was a little scary. They put Elvis on a stallion, they put the rest of us on mares and geldings. My roommate was Pamela Austin, just a delightful girl, and she was a very good friend, sweet lady. Well we used to ride horses you know every once in a while, next to each other, so Pamela was on the left side, and we were riding together, and Elvis is on this black stallion behind us. Well, at this particular time Pamela starts screaming. I was so close to Pamela I could touch her knee and what had happened is the mare had come in season. The stallion that Elvis was on tried to get on top of her horse. Pamela fell forward, grabbed the mane, she was holding on to the neck of her mare. My mare was jumping up and down, and all I could see over my left shoulder was this huge black shadow with his legs coming down, and because Elvis was such a strong man—a wonderful horseman—I don't think people know how well this man could ride—he stood up. Now this is a huge stallion he's mounted on. He stood up in the saddle,

TOP, LEFT AND RIGHT: Roland Winters played Fred Gates, Elvis's father in *Blue Hawaii*, and Angela Lansbury, Sarah Lee Gates, Elvis's mom. During his career Roland played Charlie Chan in several movies starring the Asian detective; **ABOVE:** Pamela Austin, who played Selena "Sandy" Emerson in *Blue Hawaii*.

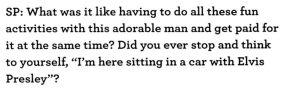

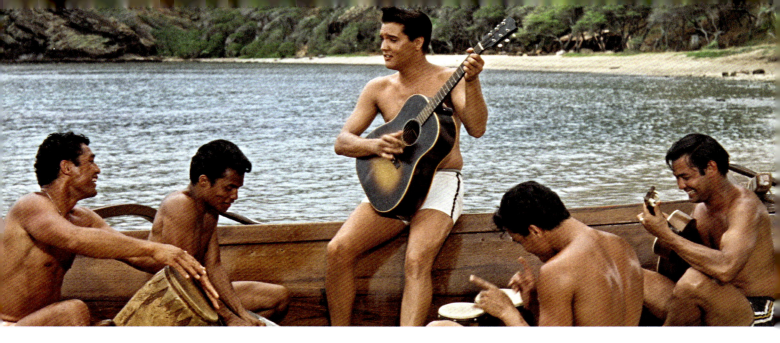

"Now this is a huge stallion he's mounted on. He stood up in the saddle, pulled the reins up and physically pulled the horse's head over backwards and risked the horse falling on him..."

DARLENE TOMPKINS ON ELVIS'S HORSEMANSHIP

TOP: A still from the 4K UltraHD Blu-ray release of *Blue Hawaii* (Paramount); **CENTER:** Elvis on Horseback in 1960's *Flaming Star*, directed by Don Siegel; **ABOVE:** Elvis and Steve Forrest out on the range in West Texas in another scene from *Flaming Star*; **OPPOSITE:** Main U.S. release movie poster for *Blue Hawaii*.

pulled the reins up and physically pulled the horse's head over backwards and risked the horse falling on him! Then Pamela's mare who was so frightened she bolted forward. Elvis had control of that stallion by the time, he brought that horse back down. That was a very scary moment. It was amazing the strength of the man and the steadiness of him.

SP: Wow, what a story! I owned a horse, and they are powerful creatures, but I imagine his adrenaline kicked in. Also, so he assessed the situation pretty quickly by the sound of things and took control... what a hero!

SP: What do you remember the most about working with Elvis? What sticks out in your mind the most?

DT: I think the main thing is I never met anybody that enjoyed people so much. I've always been a little more shy than others but he could see that and would always come over to say hi. He was a very sociable person and a very intelligent man. He could read something... and I believe he had a photographic memory because he would read something, look at it, and that was it.

SP: I have heard that before, that he could memorize his script quite quickly and everybody else's.

DT: Right, right he could, all the lines. Well, I think one of the things, one of the reasons that sharpened that gift he had was that he was so poor when he was growing up. He couldn't buy a record. He would just listen to the radio and he would hear a song one time and memorize it so later on they were amazed at Sun Studios because he knew so much—from everything he had ever heard—and they were just amazed at his range. He would hear it once, and he would know it.

SP: So, were there any funny incidents? It looked like you guys had such a lot of fun during the movie. Was there anything in particular that you can recall?

DT: Well, for me there was a funny one. For me when it came to the time to shoot "Slicin' Sand" I wanted to be sure that I was in the background. I didn't want anyone to see me or nothing because I didn't get the dance thing at all, and I was quite frightened. So I thought, "Well, I'll just wear something quiet that blends in with the sand." Edith

ECSTATIC ROMANCE...EXOTIC DANCES...EXCITING MUSIC
IN THE WORLD'S LUSHEST PARADISE OF SONG!

ELVIS PRESLEY
RIDES THE CREST OF THE WAVE IN

BLUE HAWAII

A HAL WALLIS PRODUCTION

TECHNICOLOR® AND IN PANAVISION®

14 TERRIFIC SONGS!

CO-STARRING
JOAN BLACKMAN   ANGELA LANSBURY   NANCY WALTERS   DIRECTED BY NORMAN TAUROG   SCREENPLAY BY HAL KANTER
A PARAMOUNT RELEASE

"...to tell Edith Head you don't want to wear what she has picked out is like telling Picasso what to paint. I mean, you just don't do it..."

DARLENE TOMPKINS ON *BLUE HAWAII*'S COSTUME DESIGNER

CENTER: The Academy Award-winning Edith Head, costume designer on *Blue Hawaii*; **ABOVE:** *Blue Hawaii*'s director Norman Taurog, back in 1938, on the set of *Boys Town*, with Mickey Rooney.

Head was the costume designer and she is the epitome of all wardrobe ladies, forever! Anything that comes up, who's the best? It would be Edith Head. So I thought one thing about the camera is that immediately if you look at anything on camera that has red on it your eye goes to it immediately. So I thought, well, number one I'm not going to wear anything with red on it because I don't want anyone to see me, no way. So here comes Edith Head and she says, "I have this for you to wear," and I'm wearing shorts, right, because we are on the beach, and I thought who in the world wears a long-sleeved sweater on the beach? And it was red and white stripes, and I looked at this sweater and thought, "Oh my gosh, everyone is going to look at me in a red and white sweater." But to tell Edith Head you don't want to wear what she has picked out is like telling Picasso what to paint. I mean, you just don't do it. So anyway's, I thought, "Here we go, now I can't hide because I've got this red sweater on." So we are doing "Slicin' Sand," and Norman Taurog, the director, said, "Now, when we are doing this, Darlene, I want you to stand right in front, and I want you right next to Elvis, directly." Well, anybody would have loved to have done that.

SP: You wouldn't have had to ask me twice!

DT: Yes, if they could dance, right? But not if you can't! I was so embarrassed, I thought I was going to die. So when you see "Slicin' Sand" you will see at the very beginning, I am standing right in front with Elvis like I was told to.

SP: Yes, and I notice how you go to the back. I was watching you on film.

DT: Well, you see the thing was that Elvis was known as "one-take" Elvis. You don't have to do retakes in his movies. It's one take, very seldom two. One take, that's it, whatever, and it was fun and easy, and he didn't want to make it look like it wasn't spontaneous, especially the fun, light-hearted scenes. So anyways I had that advantage, and I knew the odds because this was a fun thing, and we probably wouldn't be doing it if we thought there were going to be more takes. So I thought, "Well, that's real easy. As soon as the music starts I'll turn around and I'll go to the back, and I will go hide." So that's what happened. You'll see me at the very front but the minute the music starts you will see me turn around and go to the back.

SP: Yep, you did, sure enough you went to the back and hid.

DT: Then when I got back there and everyone was dancing, I was bouncing up and down and everything.

SP: Then you got into it.

DT: I really did, I thought my gosh I can bounce around because tell me something, if you're singing and dancing with Elvis who in the world is gonna look at ya? [Laughing.]

SP: Well, yeah, all eyes are going to be on Elvis.

DT: Yeah, so there you go.

SP: So, Darlene, a few questions from some of the fans and members of the fan club Elvis International. One of the questions is, "Did Elvis really drive like a maniac?"

DT: Well, that I don't know because the car was either being towed or when we were being filmed it was perfect because it had to be, because we were

TOP LEFT: Jenny Maxwell and Elvis on surfboard, with back projection!; **TOP RIGHT:** Jenny Maxwell, around the time she featured in *Blue Hawaii*; **ABOVE:** Jenny in *Shotgun Wedding*, 1963.

on camera and the interiors of that car scene were on stage. It's a stationary car, and the background is moving, the scenery in the back is moving. With wind fans and all that. I have heard that he did everything full out, so I imagine that he liked driving fast motorcycles, anything. I'm sure that he was a daredevil; he always pushed it.

SP: As always, where there's an Elvis film there are lots of beautiful women. Did you make any new girlfriends on this set?

DT: Well, Pamela Austen was a girlfriend, she was really wonderful. Jenny Maxwell I liked very, very much. She was a wonderful actress. She brought her little boy on the set, she had a little boy named Brian, and I keep in contact with him. He was an only child and he's a very nice young man… and it's very sad because Jenny was an only child too, and Jenny was murdered in 1980 in Beverley Hills. She was gunned down, and they never found out who did it. There were all different rumors. Thousands of them. Everybody has an opinion but they never found out who did it, and it's also been very hard for her son, who's in his 40s now. Sweet, sweet young man. He still lives in California, and he loves talking about his mother and everything. He's got the picture of *Blue Hawaii* in his bedroom, and he

sees the picture of me and his mother on posters and stuff.

SP: Such a tragic story but I'm so happy to hear you keep in touch with him.

SP: Now, all the other woman on the set… were they all swarming around Elvis like bees round a honeypot, competing for his attention?

DT: Well, I'm not sure about competing for the attention as Elvis made sure there was enough to go around! He didn't sleep very much—he had a problem sleeping so he would get up so very, very early. He was a natural blonde as you know, so he would have to have his hair touched up. We would have to be out by the time the sun was up, in makeup, full dress, and we worked until the sun went down. It's a long schedule, but he would still have time to go to the little restaurant there, Cocoa Palms, and sing and do things with his buddies and everybody and stay out all night, and it never fazed him. He had amazing energy.

SP: Yeah, for sure. You just have to watch him on stage to see that, he's just all over the place and two shows a night in Vegas! He was incredible.

SP: How much time did you get to spend with Elvis off set?

171

"...and when she passed away, it was not only a blow to him losing his mother—losing his best friend, losing someone who believed in him so much..."

DARLENE ON ELVIS LOSING HIS MOM

TOP: Elvis with his mom, Gladys, and Teddy bear, just before his draft into the U.S. Army; **CENTER**, and **ABOVE**, on March 24, 1958.

DT: Off set? Quite a lot. We didn't date... we were very, very good friends and as I said he had a penthouse and he would invite a number of us up to have dinner at his penthouse and then he would have time to come and sit with everybody. We talked a great deal about things like his mother and my mother and at that time he told me that he missed the Army... he absolutely loved it!

SP: That's a real surprise!

DT: Oh, he absolutely loved it!

SP: I know that he didn't want to go in the Army in the beginning but he went and did everything everybody else did.

DT: The reason he didn't want to was because he loved show business so much and he loved to sing and he was afraid that everybody would forget him. He was terribly afraid and he used to cry and say, "Someone's gonna replace me," and "They'll never remember me," and the Colonel was the best thing that happened to him at that time. You see the Colonel was a carny man before he met Elvis. He would do these carnivals, and he started out making chickens dance. He had this cage with a flame underneath it and he would put the chickens in the cage with the flame underneath and he would play music and the flame shoots up, so whenever the flame shoots up the chickens danced! They danced their little feathers off, honey.

SP: Pardon, what? And they had roast chicken for dinner?

DT: Roast feet for sure!

SP: Oh, no, how mean, poor chickens.

DT: Well, he started off like that, and he knew how to merchandise, and they were doing Howdy Doody and Roy Rogers, Hopalong Cassidy. So when he got with Elvis what the Colonel did was he made sure there was a record released all the time while Elvis was in the Army. Elvis told me he used to cry himself to sleep thinking they would forget about him. He would also be on the phone all the time with his mother, and as you know his mother passed away while he was in the service, and that was very hard. He mourned that very much, and he wanted to make her a queen because she used to make his clothes for him, she did two jobs, she did everything, and he wanted to do things for her because he absolutely adored his mother. He cherished her, absolutely cherished her. So he wanted to give her every present he could possibly give. The pink Cadillac, the house, just presents.

SP: He just showered her with gifts...

DT: Yes, and when she passed away it was not only a blow to him losing his mother—losing his best friend, losing someone that believed in him so much, but also it was such a shock to him as nobody knew she was so sick, nobody knew. They thought she was tired, pale and just not feeling good, but nobody knew the seriousness of how sick she was, and it shocked everybody. Nobody knew because she was a quiet, reserved lady to begin with, and she was very protective of him. It was such a shock and before this he wanted to be sure that she had all these gifts. So he wanted to give gifts and he did that even when he was a little boy. They were very poor but he would get her a

Christmas present and after he played with his Christmas present he would go across the tracks and give his present away to the children. So even at a young age he always did that. I think he had a Teddy bear and I can't remember what the other thing was but he had two things that he kept but everything that he received as a gift he gave to somebody else. Money, everything.

SP: He was a very, very special person.

DT: Beyond imagining and in every way.

SP: That's actually very moving and quite beautiful.

SP: Moving back to the questions, this one has come up before but I want to ask you what did Elvis smell like?

[Darlene giggles.]

DT: He smelt a little bit like a clean perspiration; he really didn't have anything that you could smell if you sat next to him but a clean fresh scent. You had to put your head on his shoulder.

SP: And did you get to put your head on his shoulder?

DT: [Darlene laughs.] Yes, yes, that I did.

SP: Elvis always had his bodyguards around him and his buddies, did you get to hang out with any of them?

DT: Yes, Joe Esposito and Sonny. Joe Esposito is the one that told me about Priscilla. See, nobody knew that Priscilla was back at the ranch at Graceland nobody knew it... and Elvis was a flirt.

SP: Oh, yes, just a little!

DT: And a lot of the girls and I were becoming very fond of him, and I was starting to think very seriously about him.

SP: You were?

DT: Oh, yes, and Joe Esposito happened to be a friend, I enjoyed him very much, and he was a good man and still is. So Joe Esposito said, "Darlene, I just want you to know that Elvis has somebody back at Graceland." Well, I have always been of the type that if somebody has somebody then that's it.

SP: You're just not interested.

DT: [Darlene cracks up laughing.] I may be interested. Let's not get hysterical here, Shelly, I may be interested. Hello, Earth to Shelly. There is such a thing as off limits.

SP: [Laughing.] You're very interested but you wouldn't take it any further.

DT: Yes, yes.

SP: You're a good girl, Darlene, and I mean how could you not be not interested when it comes to Elvis.

DT: Yes, yes. The drill keeps goin', honey.

SP: So Joe told you he was off limits basically?

DT: No, Joe didn't use that term "he's off limits," no, no, but he wanted to let me know that he had someone back home in Memphis.

DT: It's like almost every single entertainer married or not married when people go to the stage they kiss and hug their fans they love and everything, there is a difference between your fans and your personal love. Like you love oranges, and you love your wife. So Elvis thought that everybody understood that, and so he could have people there and go home to your fires. Well, the thing is if you're involved it's still hard but luckily enough we talked so much and visited so much it was easy for us to stay as just friends.

SP: Well, I would rather have Elvis as a friend than nothing at all.

TOP: Priscilla Beaulieu writes to Elvis during his tour of duty in Germany, in 1960; **CENTER:** The 16 year-old Priscilla plays the latest Elvis album release; **ABOVE:** Elvis with Joe Esposito.

TOP: Shelly (left), with Darlene, at the close of the interview; **ABOVE:** Elvis co-starred with Ursula Andress in *Fun in Acapulco*, in 1963.

DT: Well, good friends stay forever, God willing and the creek don't rise. In fact a couple of years later that's how I got the part in *Fun in Acapulco*.

SP: Okay, tell me a bit about that.

DT: Well, with *Fun in Acapulco* I just went out to visit Elvis to have lunch with him, and when I went over there they were shooting that particular scene.

SP: So you and Elvis were actually very good friends?

DT: Yes, we were, and so what had happened was Elvis said put her in, so they gave me one line where I say, "Uh oh, back to the convent."

SP: So Elvis actually invited you on to the set, and you got a line in it.

DT: Yes.

SP: I think *Blue Hawaii* had one of the better soundtracks... what was your favorite song from that movie?

DT: "Can't Help Falling in Love." It's my favorite song to hear but the one to do with him was "Moonlight Swim," because I could get right up close to him, and I just adored him, and it was like he was driving his car just for me.

SP: Just a few more questions from some of the fans. So you didn't know about Priscilla back home but I presume his buddies knew. Do

you think they were asked not to disclose this information because of his fans and how it might affect them?

DT: All his buddies, the bodyguards, they all knew... but I don't think they wanted to make this public knowledge, and Elvis certainly didn't. I think the only reason Joe did is because Joe liked me, and he could see that I very much liked Elvis, and Elvis had an effect on woman.

SP: Oh, yeah, he did!

DT: He made every woman feel that you were special and the leading lady and you could easily believe this, and I naturally was one of them so I am really grateful to Joe because I can't imagine how I would have felt if I had gotten more involved with him. I can't imagine how it would have affected me when he passed. I mean it affected me so bad when I heard about it on the radio. I was driving on the freeway, and I had to find an off ramp as fast as possible. By the time I made it to the off ramp I was crying so hard and shaking so bad I could barely turn the wheel of my car. I was crying so much I just had to pull over. He affected everybody, even people that had never met him. Anybody who has ever seen him, at a show or even in a car driving by waving at them. One of the things that I have always done when I go for a meet-and-greet and a signing, I always ask the people in the audience who have actually seen Elvis in person to stand up, and they do, but there are so many people that have never seen Elvis live, and yet he has really touched so many lives through his music.

SP: While playing your part in *Blue Hawaii* did you then ever imagine how big he was going to be and for many years afterwards?

DT: The top spoken three words in the world, there are three. Do you know what they are? Pick what you think are the top three. Have a guess.

SP: Well, definitely Elvis, Jesus... and I am not comparing Elvis to Jesus to set that straight for a start... and I'm stuck for the third.

DT: Well, its my understanding that the three of them are... and not in this order, Elvis, Coca-Cola, and Mickey Mouse.

SP: Really? I was sure Jesus would be in there somewhere.

DT: Well, I am a born-again Christian so you would think.

SP: I'm going to check that out Jesus, Elvis, and Coca-Cola for sure.

DT: It's a big world, a big world.

SP: Elvis and Coca-Cola. [Laughing.]

SP: At the end of the movie *Blue Hawaii* when you and the other girls were walking on the shore do you remember what you were thinking at that time, be it about Elvis or not?

DT: I remember exactly. I was wearing a blue sun dress with spaghetti straps and I have on high heels and Elvis is going to get married on the raft and I'm walking along on this wet sand and my heels are sinking in with every step. I can't get my heels out of this muddy sand, and I wanna be on the raft, [laughing] "Put me on that raft!"

SP: Would you say that Elvis was easy to work with?

DT: Absolutely, absolutely. He wanted everybody to have as much fun as him. He told people if it's not fun then we're not going to do it, and there was one time he was with his buddies and they were horsing around and somebody said something like we have to start shooting or you better get back to work, and Elvis said well if it's not fun then we aren't doing it, and that's how it had to be. It was a passion to have fun and to live every minute and it was taking care of business... when he was on, he was on.

SP: What is your all time favorite Elvis song, Darlene?

DT: "If I Can Dream."

SP: When you think of Elvis Presley how do you like to remember him?

DT: I like to remember him as a man that made everybody comfortable and made everybody feel they were important. When he talked to you, you were the only one he was talking to. He made you feel so important, and he always listened to what you had to say, and he never ever forgot a face. I have a lot of Elvis friends from years and years and years that I met recently and they have loved Elvis from the '60s. They followed him, and they will testify to this, every single solitary one of them, when they were in the audience and Elvis would look at them one time and when they come back again, he would remember them always. He knew who they were. I could tell you story after story about that how he would remember people.

SP: Darlene, I could talk to you all day about Elvis but we have to wrap it up here so can I just say on behalf of all the Elvis fans, thank you. It's been a wonderful experience, you are a beautiful lady.

DT: Thank you so much, Shelly, you are so kind and you make everything so easy, so thank you.

TOP: Darlene and Shelly pose for a final picture together; **ABOVE:** Elvis performing "If I Can Dream," during his '68 Comeback Special.

175

"...June Carter kidded me around, but she got me backstage, and I was talking to this guitar player for close to an hour, and he said, 'Oh, by the way, my name is Elvis Presley' and I thought, what a strange name that was."

JIMMY VELVET ON FIRST MEETING THE YOUNG ELVIS PRESLEY

INTERVIEW **NINE**

Jimmy Velvet

Jimmy is an American soft rock 'n' roll vocalist from the 1960s. He was friends with all the big entertainment names of the era, and a close friend of Elvis Presley for 22 years. Jimmy was well respected by Elvis, and following Elvis's death, Jimmy opened the Elvis Memorabilia Museum, close to Graceland, which stayed open for almost 20 years.

OPPOSITE: An informal portrait of Jimmy.

Interviewing Jimmy...

Jimmy was originally from Jacksonville in Florida. Better known as Jimmy Velvet, he was an American soft rock and roll vocalist during the 1960s. A friend of Elvis for 22 years, at one time he owned the largest collection of Elvis memorabilia in the world. According to *Rolling Stone* magazine he was "the Godfather of Memorabilia."

TOP: Jimmy and Shelly, during the interview; **ABOVE:** Shelly and Jimmy, sometime in Las Vegas.

He first met Elvis at the Gator Bowl in May 1955, when he got to go backstage. He talked to Elvis for a long time. He was 15 and Elvis was 19. Jimmy was a local entertainer and playing some local shows but wasn't recording anything at the time, but when Elvis and Jimmy became friends Elvis invited him onto some shows and encouraged Jimmy to work hard on his music. Jimmy became close friends with the Presley family but never worked for Elvis, just a true friend. When Elvis died, his father Vernon Presley gave Jimmy permission to open an Elvis memorabilia museum in Memphis as he agreed it was a wonderful idea.

Jimmy opened the museum across the road from Graceland on June 1, 1978, four years before Graceland opened its doors to the public. Jimmy had received many items directly from Elvis himself during their twenty two-year friendship. It was the only museum licensed by Elvis Presley

Enterprises, Inc. When Jimmy retired he sold off a lot of his Elvis memorabilia, though today Jimmy still attends Elvis conventions and meet-and-greets to talk about his friend Elvis Presley with Elvis fans from around the world.

JV: Should I keep my glasses on or off for the photos, Shelly?

SP: Darling, you do whatever feels comfortable for you.

JV: Well, I will leave them on.

SP: You look handsome with or without them, Jimmy, so either way.

[Jimmy whistles.]

SP: Now, Jimmy, we need to hear about how it happened that you became friends with Elvis. My first question to everybody I interview is regarding that first encounter with him.

JV: Well, that's kind of a strange one. I was fifteen and my English teacher happened to be a show promoter on the side and she had a show at the Ballpark, right next to the Gator bowl. She had a show coming up with the Carter Family, and I wanted to meet June Carter.

SP: June Carter who was Johnny Cash's wife?

JV: Yes, and at the time we both lived on Dellwood Avenue, so I went down the street to her house to talk to her as I wanted to get in and get backstage, and she knew that. She sort of kidded around with me, but she got me backstage, and I was talking to this guitar player for close to an hour and he said, "Oh, by the way, my name is Elvis Presley," and I thought, what a strange name that was. [Jimmy laughs.] I had never heard that name before in my life, and I had no idea who he was, and then my English teacher walks into the room a little later and says, "Hey, Jimmy, I see you've met Elvis." I said, "Yes, ma'am," and she said, "Well, he's recording one of my songs next month." I said, "Well, that's great." I still didn't know who he was but the song was "Heartbreak Hotel" and that song was written by my English teacher—Mae Boren Axton, along with Tommy Durden. Her husband John was my coach,

and that's how I met Elvis. What a wonderful guy. I mean that night he was telling me that someday he was going to have six Cadillacs, and he was going to save up a million dollars and keep that put away for his family, and he was going to give everything else he made away. He was a dreamer, like me.

SP: That's what he said to you?

JV: Yeah, he was a dreamer like me, just talking, you know, and he was four, maybe five years older than me.

SP: So you were just fifteen years old?

JV: Yeah, I was fifteen, and he was maybe nineteen or twenty.

SP: Wow, that's fascinating.

JV: What was fascinating was when he went out on stage.

SP: How was that then… because you hadn't heard of Elvis Presley?

JV: He stole the show! Here's how it went… you see Colonel Parker had just taken over Elvis. Colonel Parker was managing Eddy Arnold and Hank Snow at the time, this was a Hank Snow show, and if you wanted Hank Snow, then you had to take Elvis, and if you wanted Eddie Arnold, you had to take Elvis.

TOP LEFT: The Gator Bowl in Jacksonville, Florida, circa late 1950s; **TOP RIGHT:** Jimmy Velvet's English teacher was Mae Boren Axton, otherwise known as "the Queen Mother of Nashville." It was Mae who introduced the 19-year-old Elvis Presley to Colonel Tom Parker, and persuaded RCA Records to sign him. With Tommy Durden, she co-wrote "Heartbreak Hotel."; **ABOVE:** June Carter, the future Mrs. Johnny Cash, circa 1950s.

179

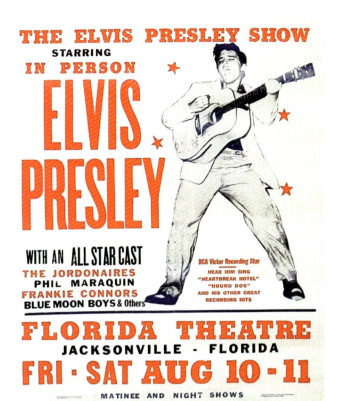

TOP LEFT: Poster advertising The Elvis Presley Show in the Florida Theatre (sic), Jacksonville, August 10–11, 1956; **TOP RIGHT:** Elvis and early superfan Ardys Bell Clawson, backstage after the Gator Bowl show in July 1955; **ABOVE**: Elvis snapped going onstage at Overton Park Shell.

So when people were booking them that was the Colonel's way of getting Elvis seen—knowing if he got seen he would steal the show—and that's how he worked it. And it worked every time.

SP: Oh my goodness!

JV: He would go into these towns where people had never heard of Elvis, they would introduce him, and he would steal the show.

SP: He would steal the show, and before you knew it Elvis was headlining!

JV: Exactly, exactly. So that's how we met.

SP: Okay, so then after the first meeting would you just go to see him perform other places?

JV: He came back to Jacksonville the following year, and by then he was a major star. And of course I knew him very well, and he invited me to his show—we kept each other's numbers and stuff—so I got to go to that show, and he was there two days— he had a matinee show and an evening show. It was fun. The first show where I met him, I didn't have a camera, never even used one, but for the second show I went out and I bought a Brownie Hawkeye camera, which took some very famous pictures ...those were the ones at the Florida Theatre in

Jacksonville. So I took those, and he invited me to go to a couple of other places on that tour with him, like Miami and New Orleans also. That was pretty much it and how it began.

SP: So what was it like in those days, the very early days?

JV: To me it was unbelievable because I was a fresh-off-the-farm kid, very poor. Maybe he saw a lot of himself in me being a poor kid, and I imagine we were a little bit poorer than him. I dunno.

SP: Did you live close to Elvis? Were you in Memphis, Jimmy?

JV: No, I lived in Jacksonville, Florida.

SP: Okay, so how did you get to actually be in Memphis... you went to Graceland, didn't you? You spent some time there?

JV: Well, that same year the following month I went to Memphis, visited Graceland and Tupelo, and his mother and father went to Tupelo also. I had that same camera again, only this time I had slides for it. I took twelve photos, and I was the only one that shot in color so any of the color photos shot at the Tupelo Fair were mine. Like I said there were twelve shots but I've only ever had eleven. I don't know

"He would go into these towns where people had never heard of Elvis, they would introduce him, and he would steal the show..."

JIMMY VELVET ON ELVIS'S EARLY SHOWS

what happened to the twelfth, but five of those were on stage and six of them were backstage with his mother and father together, and I've still got those.

SP: Now I've heard that you were very close to Gladys [Elvis's mother] and she really liked you.

JV: She did, though now you see a lot of people had made that bigger than it was. I'd like to say that she was fond of me.

SP: She was, yes, I've heard that. She didn't like having her photograph taken, did she?

JV: No, she didn't, and she didn't take photos with anyone.

SP: I have a picture of you with Gladys.

JV: Yes, there's actually four or five different ones, but I have only found two of them so far. One of us with the pink Cadillac that Elvis gave her and the same year before that picture was made, that car was with Elvis in Philadelphia when he invited me to the Arena, 1956, '57.

SP: You have a good memory.

JV: Yes, I do, and I've got good pictures of that. I took black and white and color that night. We also took pictures in front of the pink Cadillac at the hotel in Philadelphia and his band is there. Remember my foot's propped up on the bumper of the pink Cadillac and it shows the same license number as the one taken at home. That was '56 July/August, but when you were saying she was very fond of me and she liked me, well she allowed me to do something that

she never let anyone do and she told me this day in the kitchen... well, we will get to that one in a minute, but she allowed me to take pictures inside Graceland that same day and take some upstairs in the bedroom and everything and she told me, "I will let you take pictures if you promise me you will never show these pictures or sell them to a magazine because Elvis has been talking to *Life* magazine, and they have offered him $100,000 to allow them to come in and photograph the house, and he wouldn't let them."

SP: Really? Oh, wow, all that money back then!

JV: Yes, and she said, "I'm letting you do this because you've told me that you won't share them," and I never did.

SP: So nobody has ever seen those pictures.

JV: No, just like the flying saucer pictures I took. I mean I showed those ones to a to a lot of people actually but those were hard not to show until the government took those negatives from me.

SP: Are you kidding me?

JV: No, I have some great flying saucer pictures.

SP No way, really?

JV: Oh, yes, I do. Taken in '63.

SP: You have genuine flying saucer pictures?

TOP LEFT: Elvis's mom, Gladys, and Jimmy hang out by the pink Cadillac that Elvis gave her, 1957 (*see also* page 194); **ABOVE:** Elvis onstage in Tampa, Florida, August 5, 1956.

TOP AND ABOVE: Jimmy's UFO photographs might have looked something like these two well-known examples.

JV: Yes, I took rolls of shots of them flying over Albuquerque.

SP: I am so into all that kind of thing, I mean, wow.

JV: Really? Well, you got to see these, they're in my album back home.

SP: Okay, we will go back to Elvis in a minute... just tell me about these flying saucers.

JV: By the way, I took them to the museum this year and showed them to all the guys at the museum, and they were just knocked out by them.

SP: How did you come across a flying saucer? [Laughing.]

JV: Well, this has nothing to do with Elvis but we're off to another thing so I'll tell you. A friend of mine lives in Albuquerque, and I was going through town so I spent the night over there with him, and we were in his old pick up truck and we were out, he wanted to go hunting, 1963 I think. We are out where there are trees and things and like a desert area and we saw this flying saucer, and I took a picture instantly, and we were amazed.

SP: Right there in the sky?

JV: It was like a mile off and it was moving very sporadically, then stopping in mid air, then darting, doing this and doing that [Jimmy uses his hands to demonstrate] then it shot a ray down from it which lit these bushes on fire, which were probably a quarter of a mile away, and I took a picture of that. Then it came down and landed on three tripods that came down from under it and then after sitting there for a little bit—and it was way off but the pictures I got are real good—and then it took off, raising up, and when it reached yay high it dropped three smaller ones out of the belly that went this way and that in different directions, and I got pictures of that.

SP: This sounds like something from *Close Encounters of the Third Kind*. [Laughing.]

JV: When I told friends they all had to have copies so I gave some copies of the pictures to people I worked with; the government found out about them and they confiscated my negatives and took everybody's pictures, and I thought I had none at all until my mother died; we went through all of her pictures, and there was a set of my flying saucer pictures. My sister said, "I got a set of these flying saucer pictures, do you want them?" and I said, "Yes," and all of my other negatives were there too, what was left of them. That's why I passed my polygraph to the government when I had said I had turned all my copies in to the government but then here I had another set that I had given to my mother which I had forgotten about.

SP: Did you have to give those away too?

JV: No, I have them in an album, and I will show you them but I don't want to do anything with them as I don't want to get into trouble. [Jimmy starts laughing.]

SP: Amazing!

JV: Seeing is believing.

SP: Well, I believe in all that, don't you, Rudy? [Speaking to the photographer taking pictures throughout the interview.]

Rudy: Yes, I do.

SP: Did you show Elvis these pictures?

JV: Yes, I did.

SP: You showed Elvis your UFO pictures?

JV: Yes, and he loved them, and I gave him a set—which I forgot about—but he had to have them, and I gave him the set I had with me that day.

SP: Tell me about that day and how that conversation went.

JV: Well, I was giving Elvis one of these figurines that I had brought into the United States and it said Jimmy Velvet Productions under the bottom and it

was a cherub and if you pushed the button it would pee. It was a liquor decanter, and it would pee in the glass [we all start laughing] and Elvis just loved it.

SP: I remember those coming out years later.

JV: Well, years later after Elvis had died a friend gave me mine back and said that Elvis had given it to her when she was up at Graceland and it didn't work any longer but Elvis had given it to her and he told her, "Jimmy Velvet gave that to me."

SP: Oh, fantastic.

JV: Yeah, and it was on that same day when I gave him that I showed him my UFO pictures. So he had to have a set, so I just gave him my set.

SP: He believed in all that did he?

JV: Oh, yes he did, very much so.

SP: Well he was always searching wasn't he for answers.

JV: Yes, he was.

SP: So, wow... well, getting back to Gladys.

JV: She allowed me to take those pictures and none of those pictures inside the house were ever shown by me because I promised her I never would.

SP: Bless your heart.

JV: Why thank you.

SP: You're such a sweetie.

JV: I tried to keep my word anyway.

SP: Yeah, good for you, Jimmy.

JV: That was just an amazing time. She was nice to me, she was good, she didn't smile a lot but she was sweet and some people say she was always in a bad mood but she wasn't.

SP: I was going to ask you about that.

JV: She was not.

SP: I had heard and read that she had a bit of a hot temper at times.

JV: Didn't any mother have a temper if she thought that her son was being mistreated?

TOP AND ABOVE: Elvis sits between his father, Vernon, and mom, Gladys, in these two pictures, taken in the first flush of the King's success.

"...Well, then, they don't need to blame her for that because she was a normal human being who loved her son..."

JIMMY VELVET ON ELVIS'S MOM

TOP AND CENTER: Elvis and his mom Gladys in 1956. He's wearing the same plaid jacket that he wore on his first appearance on *The Ed Sullivan Show* that year; **ABOVE:** Gladys Presley, seemingly caught in a moment of melancholy thought; **OPPOSITE:** A smouldering 1956 portrait of the King, sporting his ruby ring.

SP: True, absolutely!

JV: Well, then, they don't need to blame her for that because she was a normal human being who loved her son.

SP: She loved Elvis so much.

JV: She loved him to pieces, no doubt there.

SP: You never saw that hot temper with Elvis?

JV: With Elvis? No, lord no, and remember I wasn't around her all the time. There was only those few times, and I can count them on one hand. When I went to Tupelo and when I was visiting Graceland, I would say three times.

SP: Well, during those times she liked you enough to let you in and take images of her home, and who doesn't like Jimmy?

JV: Oh, I don't know, somebody somewhere don't like me.

SP: Oh no, no, no, no. Everybody I have spoken to regarding you has only good things to say.

JV: Well, I'm sorry I got carried away and off track there with talking about the flying saucers.

SP: No, listen we will have to talk some more about that another time.

JV: I photographed everything in those days.

SW: You always had your camera around with you, did you?

JV: Well, my book got picked as the best new book in November in the radio television interview reports and they gave it the front cover and when I read this I thought, "Wow, this is cool." In big letters it says, "Before there was the paparazzi, before there was the *Rolling Stone* magazine, there was Jimmy Velvet, entertainer and photographer to the stars." I wasn't a professional photographer, I just always had my camera at the ready and it was just a Brownie Hawkeye. Now here's a photographer. [Jimmy motions to Rudy, our photographer for the interviews.] Here's somebody that knows what he's doing. I would love to spend some time with you, Rudy, and learn, maybe get to know about all the digital stuff. You amaze me, I just watched you out of the corner of my eye, and you're good.

Rudy: Thank you.

SP: He's our EI photographer, and we wouldn't use anybody else. He's really good, and we really appreciate the work he does for us.

SP: I have to tell you, Jimmy, all the female fans on EI love you to bits and the ones that haven't met you cannot wait to meet you, you are so lovely.

JV: I have met very few Elvis fans that I didn't like.

SP: I remember a little story you shared with me. I think it was when you had your Elvis memorabilia at Elvis-A-Rama and it was to do with a plaid jacket? A check jacket?

JV: Yeah, that was at the Philadelphia show we were talking about.

SP: I think it was a cold night or something, please tell us about that.

JV: Well, it was a very cold night in Philadelphia, for me anyway. Yeah, sure... so I was wearing this green jacket that he had given me with some black pants he had also given me, and there are pictures of me at the show wearing it, and when we got ready to leave he said, "Where's your overcoat?" and I said, "I don't have one." Now, I had heard his mother say, "You'll catch your death," and that's what he said, "You'll catch your death of cold."

SP: That's what my gran used to say!

JV: Really? [Jimmy laughs.] Well, that's what he said. Well, he took that plaid jacket off that he was wearing and that's why it was too big on me, and he put it right over the top of the green one, he helped to put it right on me. I said, "Well, I'll send it back to you when I get back." Elvis said, "Just keep it, I've got more." And they brought him another coat to put on.

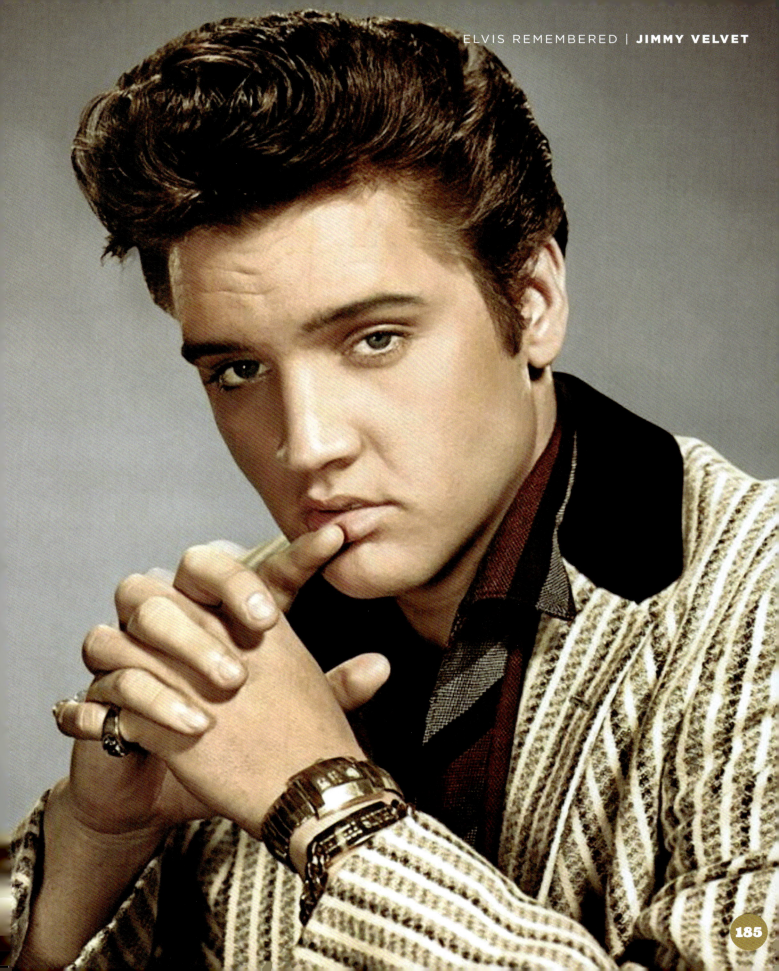

"...He did give me a TCB necklace—though I lost it a long time ago. It wasn't stolen, I think it just broke off, and I lost it...that was 1973..."

JIMMY ON ELVIS'S GENEROSITY

ABOVE: Wearing one of his familiar plaid jackets, Elvis makes his first appearance on *the Ed Sullivan Show*, September 9, 1956; **TOP RIGHT:** Elvis's mom, Gladys, sharing a joke with the photographer. Elvis was drafted into the U.S. Army in the March of 1958, and shortly before he was due to leave for Germany, received news that his mom was in the hospital, desperately ill. He was given emergency leave to see her and was flown home from Fort Hood, Texas. She died two days later on August 14, 1958, of a heart attack, brought on by acute hepatitis and cirrhosis. She was just 46.

SP: What a fantastic story, that's just an example of his generosity.

JV: Exactly, he would give you the shirt off his back... and his jacket too.

SP: So kind.

JV: He would, and he was.

SP: Did Elvis ever give you a TCB necklace?

JV: He did give me a TCB necklace—though I lost it a long time ago. It wasn't stolen, I think it just broke off, and I lost it, and I never did find it. That was 1973.

SP: 1973, tell me a bit about that? Can you remember how that came about because Elvis was very selective about who he gave a TCB necklace too?

JV: Yes, that's true, well, it was almost at the same time, not the same moment but the same time that we were both sworn in as deputy sheriffs that day and that's when he was made chief deputy and I was made captain and his father was also made captain that day, and we have pictures of it.

SP: How was that, what brought that about?

JV: Roy Nixon was the sheriff, and he invited me over for that. Roy had been over to my club in Nashville. I had the largest nightclub in Nashville at the time with a big restaurant, and we brought him over to meet the stars, in fact we had Sonny and Cher that week, but it was one of those moments, and he looked great, he looked fabulous, and the only pictures I made that day... I made some outside with the white studs but the only ones there were Sonny, Vernon, and me and Sheriff Nixon (Roy

Nixon) but we called him Skip and Red and Sonny, but inside the only pictures that were taken were with my camera and Vernon, who couldn't take a picture, shot them. When he took pictures they were always blurred. If you look in the book you can see them, and the certificate where we were sworn in. I've still got my badge, and I do have copies of the certificates signed by the sheriff of his and mine that were given to us that day.

SP: Okay, well, we are going to talk about your book towards the end of the interview. I would like to talk about that but can I talk about Sonny? Elvis was always surrounded by his guys, wasn't he? And it was probably a rare occasion to have Elvis to yourself and be alone with him. Can you remember a time when you did have a one on one with Elvis, when it was just you and him being able to chat?

JV: Apart from when we first met, I'd say Vernon and I spent a lot of time together.

SP: Tell me about that, Jimmy.

JV: I spent a bit of time over at Vernon's house.

SP: So where was Vernon living then?

JV: Well, by that time he was already living over at Dolan and Vernon and I were sitting out by the pool, and I had already been there for two weeks, and I was visiting there. Elvis had been in Hollywood a lot of the time but the limo was sitting under the carport and the hood was up the whole time he was gone. So Elvis was back from Hollywood, and he rode up and tied his horse to the gate there and came over and sat beside us.

SP: So he rode over on his horse?

JV: Yes, he did, and I didn't even know he was back in town but he had been out riding. So he came and sat down and during the conversation I said something about the car. Basically I was kind of bored because I had been sat there for two weeks so I asked was there something wrong with the car, did the car need the spark plugs looked at, or some oil or what have you, and Elvis said, "Oh, that piece of junk"—he didn't say junk, he used some other word. [We all begin to laugh at this.] He said, "Daddy, call the junkyard and tell them to come over and get that piece of … s—." I said, "Now, wait a minute, you're gonna throw that car in the junkyard?" He said, "Jimmy, it's not worth fixin'." And he was right, it wasn't worth fixing, because I took it to Mercedes, and it needed a new short block which had to come from Germany. It was $12,500 for the short block itself.

SP: My goodness.

JV: The car new back then was like twenty-two grand for a Mercedes limo.

SP: Wow.

JV: So it wasn't worth fixing, but I kept it. Then after he died I decided to go on ahead and fix it, and I'm looking at the title and on the back of it, it said Bank of America, Santa Monica. It still had a lien on it. Elvis had not taken the lien off it, and I said, "Oh my God!" So I went out to the bank, I was out in California, so I went by there and the manager of the bank said, "Mr. Presley doesn't owe us any money. He used to buy cars, and sometimes he would finance five or six at a time, and sometimes he would just come in and pay them all off." He said, "These girls would just go crazy whenever he came in and someone just forgot to sign off on it." So then they signed off on it for me there and then, and if you look at the title you can see it was then 1978, after he had passed away.

SP: Fascinating. Great story.

JV: Yeah, so, back to the original question… there wasn't a lot of alone times that we were together.

SP: He always had his entourage with him, didn't he?

TOP LEFT: A youthful Jimmy Velvet poses with Elvis's dad, Vernon, in front of the recently-purchased Graceland. Jimmy and Vernon spent a lot of time together during Jimmy's 22-year-long friendship with Elvis; **ABOVE LEFT AND ABOVE RIGHT:** Elvis bought Graceland in the spring of 1957 for $100,000. Estimates of the estate's worth today put it at $500 million. The mansion is part of the National Register of Historic Places, and still attracts over 650,000 visitors every year, making it one of the most-visited places in the U.S.

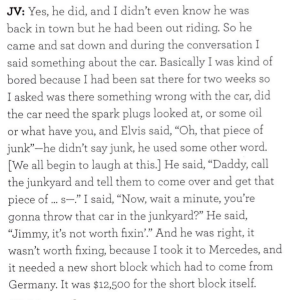

"Sonny still loves Elvis to this day and he will go to his grave loving him..."

JIMMY VELVET ON SONNY WEST

RIGHT: A signed photograph of Sonny West, with Elvis on the set of *Wild in the Country*, released 1961; **ABOVE, TOP TO BOTTOM:** Sonny West, Elvis's bodyguard and friend, from the early 1960s (top), through 1970 at the White House (center), to the mid-2000s (above).

JV: Yes, he did, there weren't many times when it was just the two of you.

SP: He had Sonny West around him a lot of the time. I'm very fond of Sonny.

JV: Me too. Yeah, Sonny lives not a mile from me. I run into Sonny once or twice a week at the post office when he's in town.

SP: You do?

JV: Yeah.

SP: Well, please give Sonny my love next time you see him. I really enjoyed interviewing Sonny. Remember we were having a little chat about Sonny on the way up to the house. I don't know but people should just—

JV: You're talking about forgiveness, people should forgive, is that what you're talking about? I do feel that way.

SP: Yes, I think Sonny has always had good intentions.

JV: Sonny has had good intentions, and Sonny has tried for years to get his story across.

SP: Bless his heart.

JV: To do it in a way that was right and classy and whatever.

SP: I know.

JV: He spoke his mind of what happened back then and probably at a moment of hurt and pain coming from it, and he deserves to be forgiven, he has tried, if there is anything to forgive then it needs to be done, and he's been asking for that basically and searching for that, his heart is good.

SP: He has a good heart, and he wears his heart on his sleeve and anybody that knows Sonny knows that his heart is genuine, he's a good man and I think Sonny thinks out loud.

JV: He does, sometimes. He's a big teddy bear, and he can be a grizzly if he needs to be. [Laughing.]

SP: I know it! And that's why he was Elvis's bodyguard and he loved him so much.

JV: Yes, yes, and he still does. Sonny still loves Elvis to this day and he will go to his grave loving him.

SP: Very good. I'm glad you said that.

JV: Sonny has had so many things thrown at him by fans through the years, and you can't blame them. But on the other hand if they just could communicate the point and then bury it.

SP: Exactly.

JV: Red too. I haven't seen Red in many years. I recall when I had my museum [the first one] in Memphis, Red had all this stuff that Elvis had given him and every piece of it he leased to me on a yearly basis. I leased it for two years, and then on the third year Red came by, and he said would you just like to just buy all of it because we are moving to California and we could use the extra money and so on. We made a deal on it, and I bought every piece of it except I didn't take the tape of the last conversation with Elvis, as I was never planning to ever use that, and there was one ring, a ruby ring, that I didn't buy at the time… but I bought all the other things. We made a deal, and I did a buy-out on it. Red's family are good people, and you know this is 30 years later, and whatever you have in your mind, speaking to the fans here, you know that if we want to be forgiven when we go, we had best not go to sleep at night with someone in mind that we haven't forgiven.

SP: Exactly, and what would Elvis want?

JV: He would want that. I know I don't go to sleep at night if there is anyone I am upset with until I have forgiven them and you would hope they have with me.

SP: You're a sweetheart.

SP: Now at what part of your life was the longest time that you didn't see Elvis?

JV: In the later years I didn't see him nearly as much as I did in the '50s and '60s because I had my own career. Even in the '60s I had records out, and I was touring a lot and working with a lot of tours, and I had some records that went to number one in some cities.

SP: Yeah, tell me about your records, we touched on that briefly earlier on.

JV: "Teen Angel," it was kind of like "Blue Velvet." I had "Blue Velvet" out in '58, and six years later Bobby Vinton had it and his was much bigger than mine, so I always give Bobby credit for the big hit. As for "Teen Angel," Mark Dinning did it in 1960, I did it in '64, and we both had hits on it. Mark Dinning and I were close friends and the Dinning sisters, his sisters. One of his sisters sang on a lot of Elvis records and on all of mine actually, along with the Jordanaires. They sang on all my earlier records. They sang on "We Belong Together,"

TOP: Elvis and Red West in the early 1960s; **ABOVE:** Red and his cousin Sonny, circa 1975.

ABOVE, LEFT: Jimmy and Elvis clicked right at the outset of their friendship; **ABOVE, CENTER:** From left, Jimmy, Jerry Lee Lewis at the piano, Don Everly, and Buddy Holly; **ABOVE, RIGHT:** From left: Phil Everly, Jimmy, Buddy Holly, and Don Everly.

BELOW: Original disc of ofJimmy's early hit—1964's "Teen Angel."

"You're Mine," "Mission Bell," and "It's Almost Tomorrow." In my book you will see pictures, Jerry Reed's wife, Chrissy, she was a good vocalist, and I used her singing with the Jordanaires.

SP: Just remind us, Jimmy, what is your new book called?

JV: It's called *Inside the Dream*.

SP: *Inside the Dream***, and we have a few copies here that I'm going to send out to a few people as little presents.**

JV: It's a great book, it's got so much history of rock and roll, and movies, and TV, because I always had my camera with me. I shot candid shots. I liked the candid shots, and there are not a lot of posed shots, though I did take some of them too. When I was taking those shots I was sending them home to my grandmother, that was the reason I was taking them because she liked to know where I was and who I was with, and she didn't know half of them anyway.

SP: Keeping her updated.

JV: Yeah, keeping her updated. And what was amazing to me was having the time to get to know the people that my grandmother loved like Bob Hope, Red Skelton, people like that.

SP: So these images of so many great people are in this book and some of these photos have never been seen before?

JV: Well, there are over a thousand photos that have never been seen before, there are actually a thousand and forty three. So it's a winner, and it has also got some radio station charts... like you will see my record "We Belong Together" in there.

SP: What did Elvis think about you having these hits?

JV: Oh, Elvis really liked it, and I'll tell you a little funny story but it wasn't funny at the time to me! [We all start laughing.] I went in and recorded a song, and I got a really good cut of it, brought in the Jordanaires, string section, and everything. Spent a fortune, and the record was great. I pressed it, and it was coming out as a single. So I happened to be spending that week with Vernon (Elvis's father) and Dee—it was his birthday. So Vernon and Dee came down to Huntsville, Alabama, to spend the week with me where I was, and Dee brought her brother Richard and after that we all came back together to their house to celebrate Vernon's birthday, so it was actually two weeks together. During that time I told them, "Oh, I got a new record coming out, my first stab at a country record." It was called "I Really Don't Want to Know," and I wanted them to hear it so I played it for Vernon and Dee. Then I saw the looks on their faces... and it wasn't that they were thinking it was bad because it really wasn't a bad record. So I'm thinking, "Well, they wouldn't do that to me anyway, they would tell me it was good even if it wasn't." [Jimmy starts laughing with us.] But I'm watching their faces as they're listening to it and thinking, "Oh, God, what's wrong?" and then Vernon said, "Jimmy, you're going to have a problem with that." So I said, "What?" Vernon said, "Elvis has just recorded that and it's coming out Friday."

SP: No! Oh my goodness!

JV: I pulled my record off, took it off the single. I pressed just a thousand copies to send to DJs. I pulled it back, and I have those thousand records still sitting on a shelf, but I put it on an album. For respect for Elvis I was not going to put it out, and also, I'd get buried alive by Elvis. [We're all laughing.]

SP: What year was that, Jimmy?

JV: That was 1968.

SP: So you were quite close to Vernon really then?

JV: I was very close to Vernon, like Sonny or anyone would tell you, "Jimmy was much closer to Vernon than he was to Elvis," and that's true.

JV: You know I think a lot of people think... [Jimmy gives a heavy sigh] well, somebody wrote in a book that I think I am probably far more important than I was to Elvis. I saw that in a book somebody wrote, and I thought, "Why would you write something like that in the first place?" and in the second place, I never thought that. I have always said I was Elvis's friend, and I am still Elvis's friend. I've written nothing bad about Elvis, never said anything bad about Elvis, and I don't intend to, never would, and besides that there was nothing but good between Elvis and I, so that's not even a valid thing. So why would someone write something like that?

SP: I don't know why these people write such things, Jimmy, like, "I knew Elvis better than you did, I was a better friend to Elvis," and so on and so forth.

JV: All of those guys were closer to Elvis than me because they worked for him, they were there night and day.

SP: Yeah, and you didn't work for Elvis.

JV: Let me ask you something, we have been friends for a while now, Shelly.

SP: Yes, we have.

JV: How many times have I come over and knocked on your door?

SP: I know.

JV: You see I wouldn't do that to Elvis either. I didn't show up at Graceland every day or every week or even every month.

SP: Right.

JV: If I was in town I would say to Vernon, because Vernon always wanted me to come over to tell him what I was doing and such things, because Vernon and I were real close. If Elvis was in town or something, then Vernon would say, "Well, let's go do such and such." You know I'll never forget this—1969, Vernon and Dee and the boys and I had gone to see the Ice Capades together here. The next day we went to church together, and Vernon said, "Jimmy, Elvis is opening at the International in Vegas, it's his first show, it's been forever. Why don't you fly out with us? Elvis said to invite you

out, and we would like you to sit at our table." I said, "I can't, I've got things I've got to do at home," and two days later I left and went back home. And I'm killing myself for missing that. All these years I've thought, "God, why did I skip that?" and I see all these pictures of Vernon and Dee with Elvis in the booth, and I should be sitting there too because I was invited by Vernon and Elvis and Dee... and I didn't go! So you see I have had opportunities like that but I didn't always go, and so people say, "You weren't as close." You're a friend or you're not. I was a friend, and I never planned to be anything else. How good a friend can you be if you never say anything bad about them? You're a good friend if you're there when your friend needs you... you're a good friend. Do I have to be the one who has been there the most, do I have to have worked for him?

SP: No, you don't.

JV: Also, why can't you be a friend and still work for him? A lot of those guys say, "Oh, I just worked for him," and people say they weren't friends. I say, "No, you're wrong. Those guys were Elvis's friends."

TOP: In July of 1969 the marquee of the International Hotel in Las Vegas advertises the upcoming Elvis shows; **ABOVE:** Elvis onstage during the July 1969 shows at the International in Las Vegas.

191

THIS PAGE: Images from Elvis's shows at the International Hotel in Las Vegas, from July 31, 1969.

SP: Did Vernon ever talk to you about handling the business? Because it's a well-known fact Vernon didn't have a good business brain.

JV: Well, there is one business venture—and really Graceland owes me a lot, for this one anyway. If nothing else it's for this one, and I'm going to tell you this story about how Vernon allowed me to open my first museum across the road from Graceland. It was a small museum, and I could probably get a dozen people in at a time. I had twenty-one items I opened with. I charged a dollar, and we had crowds out there from seven in the morning to evenings, seven days a week. I had to have some time to eat and sleep. Vernon called me one day and said, "Can you come up to the house for a minute?" I said, "Vernon, I can't. I'm so busy but how about tonight?" He said, "No, I need to see you now." I told him, "I can't get free, I've got tons of fans outside," so he said, "Okay, I'm coming down." So he drove down the hill and came across the street to see me, and we talked for a few minutes as I had other people waiting to come in. Then I happened to get a break, and he said I want to show you something. So we got in his car and we went down the street to the dry cleaners. Here, lined up, were sixty-two jumpsuits that Vernon had had cleaned, and they had plastic bags on them. So Vernon said, "Now, I want you to help me sell them." I said, "What do you want for them?" and Vernon told me. "Well, there are sixty-two and I'll take $500 a piece for them... or $25,000 for all of them."

SP: No!

JV: I said, "Vernon, you don't want to do that." I said, "Would I love to have them? Yes. But let me tell you something, what it all comes down to is Elvis is not going to go away." I said, "Graceland needs to keep those suits, they need them there. Sell something else, sell guns, anything else that you've got, badges, clothes, normal clothes, but not the jumpsuits." I convinced him not to and it wasn't much later that he passed, and those things were there, and now after all the crap that has gone on I said to myself a hundred times, "I should have bought the whole lot and given him the $25,000 because I would have had the most fantastic Elvis museum and none could have matched it because of the jumpsuits. But I felt like they belonged there, and I convinced him to keep them. He was asking

my opinion about what to do, and I felt honored at that and yet at the same time he listened to my advice and he didn't sell them off to anyone else either... and believe me, he could have.

SP: You did the right thing.

JV: I thought I did the right thing, and there's another right thing while you're doing interviews. Colonel Tom Parker called me from Hollywood and said they were going to sue all the stores over there to stop them from selling [Elvis items], including the museum. Well, we knew they couldn't because we were there before them. However the Colonel had a meeting at his office at RCA Hollywood and every store owner went out there for the meeting and we sat down and listened to the Colonel talking. I got up first and spoke, and I said, "You know, he's right. Lisa is entitled to a percentage of what we are doing, and I think we should sign. No one else agreed with me, and we left that meeting with no one agreeing but me. I agreed to sign, and after I signed, I was under their thumb from then on. And as you know how those stories go, it just made it impossible to do anything, but I came to her defense saying we should do it. I had trademarks on Elvis Presley like TCB, TLC, King of Rock 'n' Roll. I gave all of those to Graceland. They didn't earn those, I gave those to them. I think I have always been fair and honest with them... and that's another thing, I did sign the agreement and no one else did. I paid my royalties for all those years, and they audited me twice, and both times they audited me I overpaid them, both times. So I feel like Jimmy Velvet has done right with the fans, with the family, and with everything else. I don't deserve people to cut me down for anything because I've done nothing wrong.

SP: And do people do that, Jimmy, do they cut you down?

JV: Very seldom have I ever seen anything other than what was written in that book that time. I hope I haven't left that opinion with anyone because that would break my heart. I put everyone in front of me, I always have.

SP: You do, Jimmy, everybody loves you, you're a wonderful guy. Also, Jimmy, I want you to know how much I appreciate you doing this interview as I know you have had a couple of

TOP AND CENTER: Elvis in two of his famous jumpsuits, onstage during his 1972 *Elvis on Tour*. These jumpsuits were handmade by the acclaimed stage costume designer, Bill Belew; **ABOVE:** Colonel Tom Parker.

TOP: Twenty-one of Elvis's cars were acquired by Jimmy, but this 1955 pink Cadillac (*see also* page 181) is in the Graceland Museum; **CENTER AND ABOVE:** Jimmy also bought many of Elvis's stage costumes.

bad experiences with interviews in the past. Especially people that have talked you into doing phone interviews, and you have said something where they have twisted it.

JV: Yes, they have done that, they're not going to get me to say anything bad about Elvis because I don't know anything bad about Elvis, and even if I did I wouldn't tell them. But what I will tell them is that I won't tell them. [We all laugh at this.]

SP: So in the end did those jumpsuits stay at Graceland, Jimmy?

JV: Yes, they did. I have eleven of his jumpsuits but I bought them off other people. I bought them off Joe Esposito, I bought them off different fans that were given jumpsuits. I've had jumpsuits come to me from different people. One time a coffin was delivered to my museum by someone who was covered in mud and the coffin was, and he opened it up and inside there were three jumpsuits inside plastic. He wanted $2,000 for all three of them, and I wouldn't buy them. I'm not naming names but they were very, very close… and I said, "No, I'm not," because these were stolen out of Graceland and buried out back of Graceland and dug up and brought down in a Graceland truck to sell them.

SP: Oh, my God!

JV: And I didn't buy them.

SP: Good for you.

JV: I did not buy them.

SP: What happened to them, do you know?

JV: I have no idea.

SP: What in the world, wow.

JV: You know, though, I have had a great collection of Elvis's things. When you think back to some of the things I've had, I've had twenty-one of his cars, twenty-one of his guns, 240 pieces of his jewelry, eleven of his jumpsuits and thousands of other items… and all through the years of buying things that belonged to Elvis there have only ever been two items that were fake. One was bought from a fan club president and the other was bought from a family member, but what did I do with them? I destroyed them. I'll tell you another little story. Aunt Nash called me, she said, "Jimmy, can you go up to Graceland tonight about eleven o'clock?" I said, "Yes, what's up?" She told me Delta wants to talk to you. So I asked what about and she said, "Well, she's got some things that she wants to do something with and we've talked about it and you're the only person in the world that we trust." The "only one we trust," and she made that very clear. [Jimmy starts to get a little emotional, so I held his hand as he was welling up.]

SP: It's okay, Jimmy.

JV: I'm sorry. So I went up there that night, and it was sad because Delta and I went into her bedroom, sat on her bed, and she was showing me some of the things she wanted to sell me. She said, "Jimmy, I want to sell you these things as I'm not going to live much longer I've been told, and I don't want my family fighting over this stuff, so I want to sell everything I have except my clothes, which aren't worth anything anyway, and I want to leave the money for them to split. One dollar looks the same as one dollar, [that was her comment] and that's what I want to do." So she sold me a lot of stuff. I wrote her three large checks that night. I went out, down to my museum, I came back with my typewriter, sat it down. We didn't have computers then so I sat it down right in the kitchen at Graceland and typed up a certificate for every item, and she signed it, and I bought all of that stuff from her. She had some beautiful things.

She had a TCB that Elvis had given to her that was his personal one, a TLC that he gave her for herself, she sold me a big twenty-dollar gold piece with diamonds around it. She sold me a lot of beautiful

"...I got another story here, while we were looking at all the stuff she was selling. Aunt Delta had this dog up there. Can't remember the name, but he grabbed this big ring—that belonged to Elvis—in his mouth and he ran with it! We chased that dog all over the house for the ring...all the way upstairs, all the way back down, then under the bed in her room..."

JIMMY VELVET ON PURCHASING SOME OF ELVIS'S POSSESSIONS AFTER HIS DEATH

stuff, about thirty-something items. So of course the next day Jack Soden [Graceland's president and CEO of Elvis Presley Enterprises] was furious that she had me go up to the house and sell me that stuff and not him, and he wanted to know how did that happen. So I said, "Well, she trusted me."

SP: What was his answer to that?

JV: Well, he was very upset.

SP: You see, the thing is, that was her choice.

JV: That was her choice, and if it didn't live at Graceland, it had to live somewhere else, but it was her stuff to sell.

JV: I got another story here, while we were looking at all the stuff she was selling. Aunt Delta had this dog up there. Can't remember the name, but he grabbed this big ring—that belonged to Elvis—in his mouth and he ran with it! We chased that dog all over that house for the ring... all the way upstairs, [we're all laughing now] all the way back down, then under the bed in her room—with the ring in its mouth. He got right underneath the bed, and Delta is on one side, and I'm on the other to try and get that ring from that dog. In the end we got it!

SP: [Laughing.] Oh my goodness, that is something our dog would do, and once he's under that bed he's not coming out!
So Aunt Delta wanted you to have that stuff and nobody else. What a compliment to you, Jimmy.

JV: Well, yeah, I pulled up to the gates of Graceland and the guard said, "Yes, Mr. Velvet, Aunt Delta is waiting for you, and she wants you to pull around

to the back and come in the back kitchen door." She wanted it quiet, she didn't want anybody knowing, but they all got to know about it as maybe the guard or somebody told Jack the next day. They were so upset that she had done that.

SP: You did what she wanted.

JV: Yeah, and I can't help that. She told me I was the only person in the world she trusted, and she had known me a long time. You know I have photographed that family, and I have been around that family, and I have never done anything to hurt any of them. I don't know why anyone would think otherwise.

SP: Well, some people can get very jealous.

JV: Graceland don't want those that were close to Elvis to be involved with Graceland, including family. They can do whatever they want you know, that's theirs to do but I've never asked for anything and I've given, given, given.

SP: Let's just talk a little bit about Elvis's girlfriends. Did you meet many of his girlfriends? Elvis had a lot of girlfriends, did he not?

JV: They weren't all really girlfriends.

SP: Okay, so he had "girl friends."

JV: Yes, he did. He did, and you would be surprised how many times Elvis would have some girl come up to the house and he would take her up to his bedroom and read the Bible to her.

SP: Oh, I've heard that, and he just loved the company.

TOP: One of Elvis's familiar stage costumes; **ABOVE:** Graceland Director Kevin Kern poses with Elvis's gold suit—worn by Elvis on the cover of his album *50,000,000 Elvis Fans Can't Be Wrong*—at the O2 Elvis Exhibition in London, 2015.

195

"I don't have a relationship with Priscilla only because she doesn't respond. Or if I send something to her that I think she might like to have, there's never a letter back or a phone call saying thank you..."

JIMMY ON PRISCILLA

ABOVE, TOP: Elvis and Natalie Wood, 1956; **CENTER:** Natalie Wood in 1960; **ABOVE:** Natalie Wood (Maria) and Richard Beymer (Tony) in *West Side Story*, 1961. Well before Natalie Wood was invited to play Maria, Elvis had been offered the part of Tony. However, the Colonel turned down the offer to his boy.

JV: He just loved the company, and it wasn't about the sex.

SP: No.

JV: He had a good heart, and he loved to talk to people who weren't the people that were there all the time. He liked those moments.

SP: Did you ever meet the beautiful Natalie Wood?

JV: There's a picture in my book... I helped throw a big birthday party for her at her home, and we filled the pool with balloons and put all the presents on the diving board. Her father Nick and her sister Lana were there, and Tuesday Weld was there... and her sister Lana lived in the apartment above me.

SP: Did you see Natalie when she dated Elvis briefly?

JV: I did, the one time she was at Graceland when I was there. I wasn't there that long. I was there and gone.

SP: Did Elvis have a real crush on her? I mean she was very pretty, wasn't she?

JV: I don't know to be honest, but it was short lived.

SP: I must have a look through that book of yours when I get a chance.

SP: What about Priscilla? Did you have many dealings with Priscilla?

JV: I didn't have a lot of dealings with Priscilla, I had a couple. You know I had two hundred and seven Polaroid photos of Lisa growing up, and I offered them to Lisa when she was about 15, and she was like oh no, she wasn't that interested so that was the end of that. [We all laugh.]

SP: She must have been going though that teenage thing.

JV: So then I put them all in a bag and handed them to Jack Soden, and said, "I want you to give all these to Priscilla."

SP: How lovely.

JV: Yeah, and evidently she got them because I've seen them come up in all kinds of TV shows, the pictures, but you know those were mine.

SP: Did she ever approach you about those pictures?

JV: Not a word, she never said thank you or anything.

SP: Oh dear, no?

JV: But that's okay, I'm used to that.

SP: I'm sure she appreciated it though, Jimmy.

JV: Though we sat at the same table at the Colonel's birthday party.

SP: How was that?

JV: Oh we got along just fine, and she said to me, "Well, I hear you're on our side now," and I said, "I'm always on your side, I've always been on your side."

SP: What a funny thing to say.

JV: And you know what? I always have, through the years, all the tours of the museum. Every time we were in a city there were news reporters from everywhere, and there were television cameras, and I always pushed Graceland and how great a job Priscilla is doing.

SP: Well, she is!

JV: Yes, but I always said that, so I thought, "I've always been on your side."

SP: Maybe you should have asked about it.

JV: Yes, what she meant.

SP: Yes, and the thing is, Jimmy, you know how rumors can start, and people might tell the family things.

JV: Sure.

SP: I have always said that she has done so much for Elvis's memory and is still doing it. I really admire her and have a lot of respect for Priscilla. She's a wonderful lady. She has said, "I will defend him until the day I die."

JV: Well, good for her, good, and she should because he has done good for her too, and he really took good care of her, before and after.

SP: Yes, he certainly did.

JV: He went far beyond.

SP: Well, he really loved Priscilla.

JV: I have nothing at all bad to say about Priscilla. I don't have a relationship with Priscilla only because she doesn't respond. Or if I send something to her that I think she might like to have, there's never a letter back or a phone call saying thank you. There's... well, like that night wasn't bad, and we got along fine. We talked a lot and she was fine and then at the last licensing meeting we talked there and everything was fine, and that's when they introduced the jukebox that you have here in the house.

SP: Oh, really?

JV: Yeah, that was a new product that was coming out, and I took pictures of Priscilla with the jukebox and stuff.

SP: Well, Priscilla, if you're listening to this, give Jimmy a little call. He's a good guy.

JV: Yeah, I've always loved ya!

SP: Yeah, give him a call, maybe go out and have a cup of tea.

SP: I love Priscilla, and I love Jimmy... so Priscilla, let Jimmy know that you love him.

JV: I don't think anybody realizes that I did give them my trademarks, and I would never do anything to hurt them. You know my trademarks? I had two trademarks left. One I won't tell you the name of because I still have it, and the other one was Elvis-A-Rama, and I offered that to Graceland but they didn't want it, so I sold it to Chris Davidson, and Chris ended up selling it to Graceland.

SP: I know, it goes in roundabouts.

JV: I tried so hard to please them through the years.

SP: I'm sure.

SP: Did you ever meet Ginger Alden?

JV: Yes, I did.

SP: You did? What did you make of her?

JV: I liked her.

SP: You did?

JV: Ginger has never said a bad thing about Elvis, and she waited thirty years to even begin to sell the things that she has other than a few things, and they're original. Okay, I bought the last Cadillac that he had, from Ginger, and I bought one of the jumpsuits from her and the last piece of jewelry that was given to Elvis by the Las Vegas Hilton... and a few things like that. Then a few years went by, and she never did the interviews or anything because she wanted to just let it be and not be put into that corner. So I respect her for that.

THIS PAGE: Priscilla down the years—**TOP LEFT:** A young Ms. Beaulieu, already promised to Elvis, in 1965; **TOP RIGHT:** Priscilla in 2015; **CENTER:** A working actress—Priscilla in 1985; **ABOVE:** Priscillia in 2001 at event for *Harry Potter and the Sorcerer's Stone*.

TOP: Ginger Alden, sometime in 1980. Ginger found Elvis's body on August 16, 1977; **CENTER AND ABOVE:** Elvis and Linda Thompson. Linda was with Elvis for over four years from 1972, after his marriage to Priscilla had broken down.

SP: When was the last time you saw Ginger Alden?

JV: I spoke to her last night. [Jimmy whispers this.]

SP: Did she meet anyone else after Elvis?

JV: Oh, she's married now.

SP: She is? She has a family and everything? I've never heard anything about her after he passed.

JV: Well, yeah, you see that's what I mean. She could have done anything and that's my point—she didn't, and no one should be angry at her, certainly not Priscilla. Ginger came long after that.

SP: So do you think that Ginger really loved Elvis or do you think she was just riding the wave, in it for the excitement of being Elvis Presley's girlfriend and what she would get from this?

JV: I got to tell ya, my opinion—and it's different to all the guys—is yes, she did love him, but of course by saying that I leave myself wide open for all the guys to attack me.

SP: Yes, I'm sure but then, Jimmy, that is just your opinion.

JV: They have to let me have mine, and I let them have theirs.

SP: Exactly.

JV: I'm not saying it against them or that they're wrong. I'm saying my opinion through conversations with her and her family is that she loved him very much.

SP: You see, I don't really know but if somebody asked my opinion I would say that Ginger Alden may have loved Elvis in her own way, but not in the same way that Priscilla loved him or even Linda loved him.

JV: Linda loved Elvis more than anyone, and I don't want to get into that scuffle with Priscilla but, gosh, they all loved him.

SP: Who couldn't love Elvis? And I personally still believe to this day that Priscilla still does love Elvis very much. I have to tell you this, Jimmy. We went to the very last concert that was held in Memphis, and it was sold out.

JV: My wife went to that. I couldn't go because I was selling books, but let me tell you this: my wife was never an Elvis fan. She has been buying every CD since. My wife became a diehard Elvis fan after attending that concert. She's never been around him but after that she became an Elvis fan, so, hey, something worked.

SP: Wow, you know the reason why I brought this up, Jimmy, was because that night we were there at that concert [*Elvis: The Concert*], Priscilla was there not too far away from us with Lisa Marie and the family. And I think it was at the point where Elvis was on the large screen singing, "I'll Remember You," and Priscilla stood there with her son (Navarone Garibaldi Garcia), he had his arm around her and she was just swaying to the song and she looked so emotional, so moved. You could see it, and you could feel the sadness and see that she loved him and missed him. It was very emotional to watch and not to mention there is a whole auditorium of people staring at you, and there is her husband singing this song, and she looked genuinely swept away by the whole thing. I believe that was his 30th anniversary... So briefly, Jimmy, what memories do you have of the Colonel and how did you get on with him?

JV: We got along with each other just fine. We never had a set-to. The colonel called me when he wanted to sell something from his collection. He called me, and I went over to him but we were not on the same track at that point financially. What he wanted was to sell the house and the house behind that, the next house on the street. His attorney, Jack Maggots, and I. [We all start laughing at this name.]

JV: Yeah, and he was the Colonel's attorney. We all went over to meet together and he offered me the houses at two million dollars, and I offered him one million, a cash deal for it, and he didn't sell it to me. I couldn't go to two million, and that was that. What else? Mmm... funny story, I don't know if I told you about the photo of the Colonel?

SP: No, I don't believe you did.

JV: Well, at my auction I sold a lot of things. It was a big auction at the Hilton, and one item that sold was a picture of the Colonel and Elvis, and so the Colonel made some kind of little comment about it at dinner. I said, "Yeah. You know what?" I pulled the check out of my pocket, and I said, "I kind of thought you might say something about that picture, even though I owned the picture, it was my picture. So I thought... you know, eighteen hundred dollars for a picture of the Colonel and Elvis—and I had some great pictures that didn't bring half of that—so I figured this eighteen hundred should go to you." And the Colonel looked at the check, and he says, "You know, I've never accepted a check this small for anything, so I'm going to frame it and put it on my wall, but I what I want you to do is write a check for the same $1,800 to Joe [Joe Esposito], he could use it more." Joe was at the table with us—me and my wife, Joe, and the Colonel with his wife all having dinner. So I wrote a check the next day for Joe.

SP: You did?

JV: Yeah.

SP: Did the Colonel put that check on the wall?

JV: He did put that check on the wall, and he never did cash it.

JV: There were two or three other times I was with him and of course his last birthday party, and Priscilla was there, and I think I have ten of those pictures in my book. Yeah, there are pics of Hank Snow before he died, Jerry Schilling, Priscilla and the Colonel, George Hamilton. Fun party time.

SP: You must have had a wonderful time.

JV: I did, and I have hundreds of negatives.

SP: Okay, so now that we are approaching the Christmas season, let me ask you, Jimmy, were you ever at Graceland around the Christmas holidays?

JV: Because I had family things going on I never went to Graceland at Christmas. But I was invited on more than one occasion.

SP: Yeah?

JV: My ex-wife was not an Elvis fan, and we were invited to a lot of things, and she just said no, she was not interested. She grew up during swing and all that, you know, Glenn Miller, but was never into Elvis.

SP: How can you not be into Elvis? [Laughing.]

JV: Well, she didn't, she never listened to the music. So she wasn't a fan, she never really was allowed to watch or listen to stuff like that growing up, it was a totally different market.

SP: In your opinion Jimmy, what do you think made Elvis the happiest, when was he the happiest?

JV: I think Elvis was not the sad person everybody said he was all the time. I think he went through

moods and things. He was always happiest when he was giving. He loved to laugh and have fun, and he loved to give. He loved to look you in the eye and give you something because it was special, and he was like a child. You broke his bubble if you didn't accept what he was giving you. It would make him angry.

SP: Really?

JV: Yeah, right up to the end Elvis was still a big kid, he really was.

SP: You can see that, he loved to fool around, didn't he?

JV: Oh, yeah, he loved practical jokes and he was a clown, and that's what made him fun. One of the funniest things would be if you saw Elvis maybe hurt himself trying to show off or clown around, and then you would see the look on his face and he tries to hide it, but if he caught you laughing he would get real mad at ya.

SP: [Laughing.] Really?

JV: Yeah, he never caught me laughing, yeah but Elvis... to answer your question, I think he was happy most of the time. All of us have sad moments but was he happy with his life? Sometimes I think he was happiest or happier in the late, late '60s through to early '70s. I think maybe '73, maybe to '74. I think at that time he kind of lost his... I don't know how to say it.

SP: Lost some motivation?

JV: Maybe.

SP: Do you believe he was becoming bored? He wanted to travel and tour Europe, didn't he?

JV: He definitely wanted to tour Europe, and I think that would have helped. Places like Australia too. I think he would have loved that.

SP: He needed something different for sure, didn't he?

JV: Yes, and I think we all go through that. I was on the road but I was burnt out. I was making good money but I said this is my last show.

SP: Everybody needs something new in their life from time to time.

JV: Yes, that's it, and it's like that's when I opened the Elvis museum. I was burnt out on the road. I was playing a show in Memphis, and I'd done my first

TOP: Elvis meeting fans who won an essay contest hosted by a local newspaper at the Fox Theater, Detroit, Michigan, 1956; **CENTER:** Elvis and the Colonel in October 1955. Elvis has just signed the recording contract with RCA Victor; **ABOVE:** Elvis and the Colonel in discussion, 1962.

"I was burnt out on the road. I was playing a show in Memphis... and I was getting ready for my second show when it came on the news that the city of Memphis was thinking about building an Elvis museum. I thought, 'thinking about it? He's been dead 10 months, and they're just now thinking about it?'"

JIMMY VELVET ON WHY HE STARTED HIS ELVIS MUSEUM

TOP: Jimmy interviewed in his Elvis Presley Museum, circa 1982; **ABOVE:** Jimmy welcoming Linda Thompson, Elvis's former girlfriend, into the museum in more recent times.

show, and I was getting ready for my second show when it came on the news that the city of Memphis was thinking about building an Elvis museum. I thought "thinking about it? He's been dead 10 months, and they're just now thinking about it?" So I went out on the stage and I sang a song, and then I announced, "You know what? The city of Memphis is only 'just thinking' about building a museum, so this is my last show, and I'm going to open an Elvis Museum!" I went to Vernon the next day and he said, "Go ahead," and I leased a place right across from the gates of Graceland, a small room about the width of the room here, and it was two rooms about that size, and it had three showcases for the 21 items on exhibit. I called it The Elvis Mini Museum the first year, and then as I expanded I called it the Elvis Presley Museum. I was the one that opened it... I felt that somebody needed to do something, you know? So I took the initiative and did it, and it worked because all Elvis's guys started bringing me everything they had, and I started buying it.

SP: Wow.

JV: It grew, rapidly.

SP: So you were the first one to open an Elvis museum?

JV: I was the first, June 1st of 1978.

SP: So what article, Jimmy, brings the most emotion to you that you have had... obviously after his passing?

JV: A couple of things. There was a little calendar thing that Priscilla had given to Elvis. It had a ruby for January the 8th in it [his birthday]. It was something she gave him, and I thought that was

nice. Another was the tree of life pendant, that was very special. A white Bible was given to him at Christmas and because he liked that pendant so much he had it engraved in gold onto his bible. I've had a lot of great pieces through the years, some knockout pieces.

JV: You know what? I have some pieces that were taken from me, and I'm going to break this story.

SP: Okay, great.

JV: When I was at the Emperor's enthronement in Tokyo, which you will see in my book, when I had photographed the heads of state of every nation in the world... that night I met Princess Diana. I was also there delivering 108 pieces of Elvis's stuff, and there were some great pieces—the lion necklace, watches, rings, costumes, everything. I placed them with a company over there called Key Buy, it was an auction company. They sold them or kept them, but they never paid me for them, and then when I went over there to try and locate them I found out that they were owned by a company called JAM [Japan All Round Music]... they have that "Love Me Tender" shop down Beale Street, they own that also. Okay, so I go in there, and they have all my stuff on display with the certificates from the Elvis Museum signed by me... but I could not get a lawsuit in Japan against them because if you are an American it takes ten years to get to court, and it costs a fortune and you never win. Two years later they sent me a letter saying if I would just settle this thing they would send me back one of Elvis's outfits. I thought, "This is awful," so the thing is, there are beautiful pieces that I still own, and I got screwed

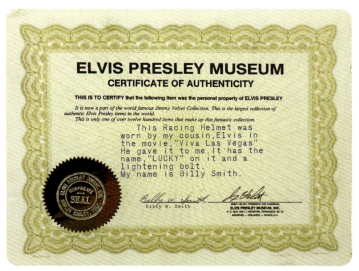

by them, and it's disgusting to me that I had to go through that.

SP: That's terrible!

JV: I tried to meet with them and they threatened our lives. I had an American interpreter with me and a Japanese lawyer with me and he said to me at one point during our meeting, "We have to leave right now, don't say one more word, not one more word, we must turn around and leave right now. If you value your life, this is what we have to do." Then they told me after we left that these guys were part of the Japanese Mafia thing.

SP: [Gasps.] Good Grief!

JV: I have friends that went over there just last year and tried to investigate it and they got beat up real bad and so I'm never gonna get that stuff back, and I think at my age now it's okay if they come after me, it doesn't matter but I wish that stuff could get to America, you know? It could go to Graceland, or I could donate it to St Jude's, or whatever. It's just that they took it from me, and it's mine. The interpreter said, "You can't prove you own it," and I said, "Yes I can. You have it on display, it's got my certificates on the items. Here's the paperwork where I took it to the auction company that you own." It's a large music company in Japan, and I just can't win, so that probably eats at me the most.

SP: That's such a terrible thing, and I don't know how some people can live with themselves! That's just theft.

JV: They'll be coming after me now.

SP: [Laughing.] God, I hope not. They won't be coming knocking on our door will they? [Laughing.] We'll set Presley on them [our dog].

JV: That'll do it!

[Everyone starts laughing and the mood is lighter. I give Jimmy a big hug.]

JV: You smell good. [More laughing.]

SP: You're such a sweetie. I love talking to you, Jimmy, could talk to you all night but we have to wrap it up soon. Just another question, Jimmy. Do you remember where you were when you heard about the passing of Elvis?

JV: I was in Pitsburg, Ohio, doing a show out there, and I heard about it. I was out in the tour bus at the time when they came out and told me. They said, "We got something to tell you," and when they told me I lost it. That night I tried to go back on stage but I couldn't because I couldn't get the words out.

SP: I'm sure everybody remembers what they were doing or where they were when Elvis died.

JV: It's like the same with Kennedy when he was assassinated. I know where I was.

SP: Yes, and the same for Princess Diana.

SP: Did you go to the funeral for Elvis?

JV: I wanted to, I wanted to real bad but there was so many thousands of people gathering around Graceland. It was August 1977 and the heat of the summer, and I had a problem with heat, my heart wasn't good at the time. So we just decided it was best that I didn't go.

TOP LEFT: Elvis in 1971, wearing the lion necklace; **TOP RIGHT:** The authentication certificate of the Elvis Presley Museum for Elvis's racing helmet in the movie *Viva Las Vegas*, 1964; **ABOVE:** The Baume & Mercier 14K gold watch, given by Elvis to Las Vegas International Hotel bandleader Bobby Morris. It's engraved "To Bobby from Squirrly EP."

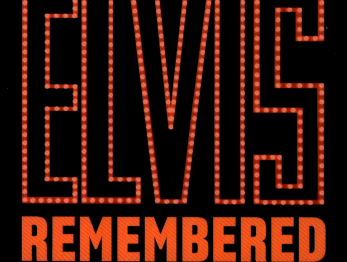

ELVIS REMEMBERED

"Elvis continued performing until the end. In my eyes, he was some kind of angel; both terribly and awfully human yet divine in his meteoric reach that touched so many hearts. He was fallible and God-like at the same time. He crucified himself on stage in Vegas, at the supper show and the late show, hundreds and hundreds of times. His latter years on Earth were as sad and lonely as any can be, but his Vegas performances were epic triumphs of human transcendence, where the angels looked down on one who had fallen so far, then looked up to where he ascended.."

Nick Cave

On Elvis's final years

203

ABOVE: Jimmy and Shelly during the interview.

SP: Did you speak to J.D. Sumner at that time, Jimmy?

JV: Not at that time but he and I spoke a lot.

SP: Well, I know J.D. was very close to Elvis.

JV: Oh, yeah.

SP: Do you have a favorite Elvis song, Jimmy?

JV: I have always had the same favorite Elvis song, "I Was the One," and it was his favorite song. I just loved that, and he did too.

SP: Can you recall one of the last conversations you had with Elvis?

JV: Yeah, it was three weeks before he died. I had just got back into Memphis, and I was going down Elvis Presley Boulevard, and it was about two in the morning. I looked over and there was a gas station, and there was Elvis putting gas in his Harley by himself. Two o'clock in the morning, and I stopped to chat but he didn't make sense. He was talking but he was rambling, and people were starting to come around.

SP: Did you ask him what he was doing on his own, I mean where were his bodyguards?

JV: No, I mean obviously I thought it was strange.

SP: So tell us a bit more... so you saw him and how did the conversation go?

JV: Well, he was nice and everything, and he was trying to show me stuff on his Harley but he was slurring his words and not making much sense. It really bothered me so the next day I went over to Vernon's house. I said, "Vernon, I saw Elvis," and I told him what happened and he said, "Well, Jimmy, we have tried everything, and he doesn't believe he has a problem." I said, "Maybe you should get all the guys together and tie him up if you have to to try and get him somewhere to get help, because he's getting worse and worse"... and I don't really like to talk about the drug thing because they were prescribed, he was seeing four different doctors. Elvis didn't realize he had a problem, he really didn't. He thought he was taking what he needed, and he would forget, and the only reason I believe that from the bottom of my heart, is because my grandmother, when I was growing up— before I met Elvis—she had to be hospitalized. She was on two prescribed drugs, and she would talk out of her head because she had lost the notes on what to take.

We could be totally still and she would shout, "Quiet, children, the Lord's talking to me!" and she was taking only two prescribed drugs. She being the Christian person that she was, my grandmother would never abuse drugs or anything else. My grandmother was the greatest. I loved her so much, but that happened to her, and if it happened to her then it can surely happen to Elvis. I'm on five prescriptions for my heart and lungs and everything and there are times I forget I have taken them. With Elvis I think I knew it was coming but I didn't. I hoped someone could do something. I'm not one of the employees there, and I didn't work for him, but I didn't want Elvis mad at me any more than the other guys did.

SP: Before you go tonight, Jimmy... when you mentioned tying Elvis up... I want to give you a copy of this brilliant book by Paul Pullen. It's fictional but it's brilliant. I don't want to tell you too much about it, but it's a group of people who are trying to save Elvis and hearing you say that it just jogged my memory about this book. They kidnap him out of Graceland but I'm not saying anything else. I'll give you Paul's book as it's the same theme as what you're talking about.

JV: Well, it's like what the other guys will tell ya, what could they do? If they did that then Elvis would hate them and fire them and all this. My opinion was, well, yes that may be true but if you saved his life and he didn't get back in it then he would probably thank them.

SP: I am convinced that it took the death of Elvis Presley for the first Betty Ford center to open as it wasn't available until after he passed. It was too late for him unfortunately.

JV: You're right, if only that had opened a couple of years earlier Elvis could have been saved, I think, but I also think he was taking those drugs for a reason. He had some serious stuff wrong with him, and I'll tell you why I'm saying that is because at one point I was sold Elvis's medical records.

SP: That's crazy.

JV: Yeah, the year he died he had applied for a two million dollar insurance policy, and it was turned down. The reason it was turned down was because of the doctors' reports and hospital reports; all of these things that were wrong with Elvis would blow your mind, and you would hope that you didn't have them. Myself, if I had all of those things I would have died. So when I saw that I realized what he went through, he took so many drugs to cover the pain and as sick as he was he was still determined to go and do that last show in Portland. He would never let his fans down no matter what, he would suffer the pain and do it and through it all he still had that magnificent voice.

SP: Golly, yeah, he did.

JV: That voice never left him.

SP: He was just amazing, amazing. He never lost that.

SP: Jimmy, what do you miss most about the King of rock 'n' roll?

JV: Lets see, I miss him, the fact that he was alive, and he was there. Going back to Graceland and realizing I'm never going to see him again. I miss his laughter.

JV: Oh, I got to tell you this. You know I'm old and things just come to me. I was in New York and they had these laughing bags, you push the button on the bag and it would start laughing.

SP: Oh, I remember those.

JV: I bought about two dozen of them, and I put them in a briefcase and I was on an airplane coming home and I was sleeping on the plane with my head on my briefcase then all of a sudden I must have pushed some of those buttons, then there was all this laughing, and everyone on the plane was laughing. Then I got to thinking, I ought to find a recording of Elvis laughing as his laugh was so contagious—and this was when he was alive—and make Elvis laughing bags and sell those suckers.

SP: Well, it's a wonder they haven't done that already!

JV: Yeah, I should probably do that, hold that thought, we're gonna work on that.

SP: What do you believe is Elvis Presley's legacy?

JV: The world. Look anywhere in the world and see Elvis. Let me tell you something, I just did the Dick Clark interview three days ago and what came to mind of course was how the very first satellite broadcast was Elvis. The *Aloha from Hawaii* special. We talked about that, about Elvis having the first satellite show broadcast to the world.

SP: Final question, Jimmy, if you had the chance—

JV: [Jimmy turns to my husband]—I just love her.

[We all start laughing.]

SP: I love you too. [Fits of giggles.]

JV: She's the best, you can't help but love her. Elvis should have met her, just to meet her would have cheered him up!

SP: Awww, that's the nicest thing you could ever say to me, Jimmy.

JV: Well, you are special.

SP: Thank you.

JV: That beautiful face and that beautiful smile she has.

SP: I'm not going to let you go home, you're staying here!

JV: I'll stay. [Laughing.]

SP: If you had a chance to give Elvis a message and you were sure that he would hear you what would you say to Elvis, Jimmy?

JV: Knowing where he is now?

SP: Where he is now.

JV: Well, I know where he is.

SP: What would you say to him, Jimmy?

JV: He's there where he knows everything now, so he knows that I love him and that his fans love

TOP: Elvis's grave in 2017, the fortieth anniversary of the King's death; **CENTER:** Shelly and Jimmy share a joke during the interview; **ABOVE:** Jimmy and Shelly bump into each other in a Vegas casino!

TOP LEFT: Elvis, 1955; **CENTER:** Elvis in *King Creole*, 1958; **ABOVE:** Elvis during the *1968 Comeback Special*; **TOP RIGHT:** Elvis signing autographs during the tour of Florida in 1955; **RIGHT:** Jimmy and Shelly; **OPPOSITE:** Elvis, publicity still for *Speedway*, 1968.

him, his family, everyone loves him, and he can't possibly not know now how many people love him.

SP: Yes, because he did say, "Who's going to remember me?"

JV: Yes, he did, and when he went into the Army he said they are going to forget about me. But no way.

SP: Well, I just want to finish this interview by saying, Jimmy Velvet, I love you to bits, and thank you so much for allowing us to take up so much of your time and for spending this time with me and sharing your thoughts and memories about your friendship with Elvis Presley.

JV: God bless you, Shelly.

"I will never forget this: Art Laboe said, 'And now we are going to hear a new sensation. His name is Elvis Presley, and he's going to sing this new hit called Heartbreak Hotel.' They played it, and I can remember where I was sitting on that stage. I froze. I probably looked like a startled deer in the forest, listening to his music for the first time. I had never heard that kind of music before, ever…"

LARRY GELLER ON FIRST HEARING ELVIS

INTERVIEW **TEN**

Larry Geller

Larry was Elvis's spiritual advisor and personal hair stylist from 1964. He played a key role in shaping Elvis's iconic look. He introduced Elvis to religion, spiritualism, and the supernatural. He wasn't always well-liked by Elvis's entourage, but has amazing stories to tell.

OPPOSITE: A portrait of Larry, taken during the interview.

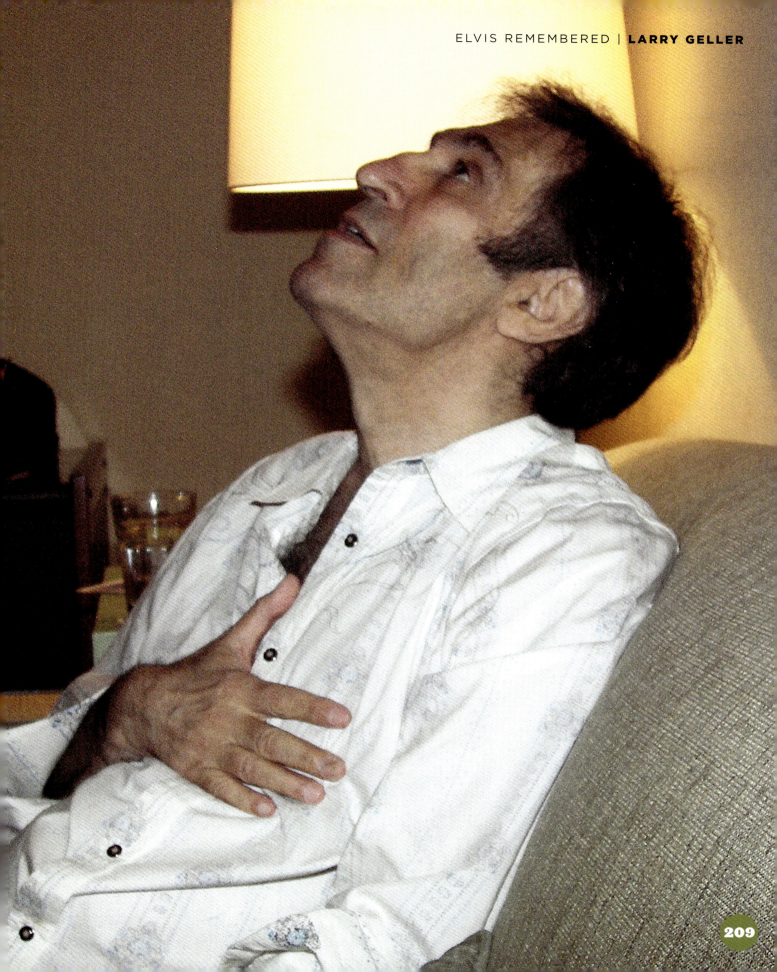

Interviewing Larry...

I wasn't sure what to expect when I was granted an interview with Larry Geller. I'd heard mixed opinions about his influence on Elvis as his hairdresser, friend, and spiritual guru. During our few hours together I found Larry to be overall a very gentle soul, the exception being when he expressed his feelings regarding untruths that were told about Elvis after his passing. Larry became extremely passionate and vocal about defending Elvis's good name but that just shows the genuine love and respect he had for his friend.

ABOVE: Larry and Shelly during the interview.

Larry appeared sincere, he took his time answering questions and although his interview was extremely long, much longer than I had anticipated—*which annoyed Patti Parry as we had a dinner date planned for after the interview and I turned up with the crew very late*—it was worth the rant from Patti to gain access to all the wonderful, captivating information Larry shared with me. He really opened up and at some point became visibly moved recalling some of his memories.

Listening back to this interview in preparation for this book I look at the conversation we shared in a totally different light. This interview, for me at least, is the greatest by far but I couldn't see that at the time. His answers were clear and concise, and he really thought about my questions. Larry can tell a great story recalling his time with Elvis with so much feeling, emotion, and at times

humor, providing us with a truthful insight into the years he spent with Elvis. His descriptions of incidents were so brilliant, you could have been there in the room with Elvis and Larry. Larry was ahead of his time with this New Age spiritual movement, and I believe he had a good impact on Elvis's life. He was a loyal friend to Elvis to the end. As a spiritual person myself I have the utmost respect for Larry Geller and will forever be grateful for both his time and his candor.

SP: Larry, it's so good to be here today! I am thrilled as I have been looking forward to doing this particular interview so much, and we have a lot of questions to get through.

LG: Wonderful.

SP: First of all, I would like to take you back to

the very beginning, so all the Elvis fans can get to know the real Larry Geller.

LG: All right.

SP: So in your new book, *Leaves of Elvis' Garden*, you talk about this early memory of your spiritual awakening, if you like, when you were very young. What inspired you, and how were you having these deep thoughts at a such a young age?

LG: I have a very unusual background. This opportunity is so wonderful for me to sit with you, Shelly, and to be able to have the fans get a chance to know me a bit better. It's taken many years for my voice and my ideas and the reality of my life and my relationship with Elvis to really come forth in a very cohesive, understandable way... because in a certain sense I am like a mystery man in the Elvis world, and I have been, but a lot of the fans have gotten to know me, and they're reading my work and they're starting to really get a frame around the picture... and it has taken thirty years. But we will get into that later because I want to answer your question.

LG: Where we are sitting right now [Los Angeles], this is where I grew up in this neighborhood back in the '50s, 1955, early '56, and this is before rock and roll. I went to Fairfax High School and directly across the street from me a kid moved in, and he and I got into music together... and his name was Phil Spector.

SP: Wow!

LG: Phil Spector is notorious, he started the sound of the '60s, he produced the Beatles and many other great musicians.

SP: Very talented.

LG: We had a little group. He played the accordion, and I played the drums, and during that period of time I was the president of the Fairfax Orchestra. I also played the kettle drums and the snare drum.

SP: You were a drummer?

LG: I was.

SP: How old were you then, Larry?

LG: I was 16 back then. During that period of time I got to be very friendly with Ricky Nelson. Ricky and I used to go to parties on the weekend, and I recall one weekend his parents Ozzie and Harriet picked him up to drive him home and they drove me home... and I was sitting in the back of this station wagon with Ricky Nelson and I thought I was on a TV show. Ozzie and Harriet in the front seat driving me home!

LG: At any rate, 1956 was a flash year, that was the year that Elvis became known to Planet Earth. He was an explosion, there was no rock and roll, it was rhythm and blues and some great music, but not rock and roll. I remember the day, right around the corner from here, where I first heard Elvis. There used to be a very famous DJ by the name of Art Laboe. Art Laboe is the man that coined the phrase "oldies but goodies." He started the first record company, [this needs clarifying. Obviously, many record companies started up before him] and he packaged all the great rock and roll bands of the '50s and '60s and it was called Oldies but Goodies. We used to have drive-in restaurants in the '50s.

SP: Gosh, I wish they had those things now!

LG: I know it! There were many of them along Sunset Boulevard. Anyway, after school we would go to one of the drive-ins, and Art was having his show, and he would come up to the car and take a request, and the girls would come out and deliver the hamburgers and the food and drinks. Then *American Bandstand* was so popular that he got the local *American Bandstand* show here, and he had his show every day at 4 o'clock, similar to the *American Bandstand*. So one afternoon I came with my conga drums, and I got to play for everybody, and I was on television, and I will never forget this: Art Laboe said, "And now we are going to hear a new sensation, his name is Elvis Presley, and he's going to sing this new hit called Heartbreak Hotel." They played it, and I can remember where I was sitting on that stage. I froze. I probably looked like a startled deer in the forest, listening to his music for the first time. I had never heard that kind of music before, ever...

SP: I can just visualize that. What a good description.

LG: I had never heard that kind of music ever, and in those days people weren't black, they were colored, and I thought. "Whoa! This colored guy is really good."

SP: Yeah, you couldn't say that today.

LG: Well, I'm saying it, but in context. All my friends thought Elvis Presley was a colored guy. But Art Laboe played this song and then he said, "We're going to hear this again," and he played it again.

SP: And that was it, you were hooked?

LG: I was hooked. That was the beginning. Elvis

ABOVE: Larry Geller. Although not part of the "Memphis Mafia," he still spent a lot of time with Elvis, especially in later years.

TOP: Elvis with adoring fans, around 1955 or 1956; **ABOVE:** The Harmonica Rascals. Larry's father was one of several harmonica players in the band.

handed us rock and roll on a silver platter. Then the next record came out, then the next. Then "I Want You, I Need You, I Love You," "Jailhouse Rock," in 1956, well, that was Elvis, and by 1957 he was already established, he was the king. And growing up in this area in Hollywood, I would see celebrities every once in a while. I remember right here on Hollywood Boulevard seeing Elizabeth Taylor.

SP: Oh, I'm going to ask you a lot about this.

LG: Well, I wanted to tell you about when I met Elvis as a kid.

SP: No, of course I'm going to ask you about that. But first can I take you way back to when you were little, because I think this is relevant to all this. What you wrote in your book, for example, on how your mother almost became dependent on you.

LG: Oh, yeah, yeah, right.

SP: Okay, so something happened. Didn't you have an experience, a spiritual experience? I mean what made you want to know more about life after death at such a young age?

LG: I hear ya, I hear your question. Well, my family… we moved out here to California back in the late 1940s because it was the land of opportunity. I was very ill as a child, I had asthma, and Elvis was an asthmatic person as a child too. Not a lot of people

know this, but I remember him telling me he used to get these allergies, he used to have to try and scratch his back, and he would take his shirt off, and he would get next to a tree and shimmy up and down until he was bleeding because he was itching. I used to go through that too.

SP: Oh, no, poor kid.

LG: But anyway, we moved out here, my grandparents moved out here, and my parent's friends. A few years later, it was around 1951, and my beloved grandmother was murdered. They found her body in the Pacific Ocean.

SP Oh, my goodness.

LG: That was the big tragedy in our family.

SP: Terrible.

LG: My poor mother, it was her first experience with death, and it blew her away. My father, thank God, was so beautiful to her, he comforted her but still, despite this she was on the edge of being so despondent and going into some kind of emotional breakdown.

SP: Like a deep depression?

LG: A deep depression, and some friend of hers said, "I know a good book you should read," and it was called *Science of Mind*.

SP: Right, I remember reading about that.

"He had the eyes, he had the perfect aquiline nose, the lips were famous. He had the voice, the charisma, he had the fans, the fame, the money. He had the soul. He was the perfect package..."

LARRY GELLER ON ELVIS

LG: Well, there are Science of Mind churches all over the world.

SP: Ernest Holmes?

LG: Ernest Holmes and my mother got involved. She read the book, then she read another book and another book. I have twin sisters, they are seven years younger than me, and my mother had no one to talk to during the day, my dad was at work, so she would talk to me and she would read to me from the books. I would be sitting there when I was 12 years old, and I would listen to all these ideas. My mother really, in retrospect, was talking to herself, and I became her student, and I would listen. During this period, my father, just to back her up and just to let her know he was with her all the way, he gravitated towards this very interesting procedure of spiritual healing. My father became a spiritual healer, on the side. It's not what he did for a living, but he did this for a while.

SP So he has a real gift, a talent, for this traditional healing?

LG: Totally.

SP: However, he never knew this gift until the tragedy took place?

LG: Yes, my father was originally a musician. He was in show business, traveled the country on tour, late '20s, early '30s. He was a harmonica player with some of the biggest groups in America.

SP: Like who?

LG: Larry Alder, Borrah Minevitch, The Harmonica Rascals.

SP: They were the first and most popular of the Vaudeville harmonica bands, were they not?

LG: Yes, they were.

LG: At any rate, I remember one night... because I was asthmatic, I would wheeze. I was on medication, and I had some very difficult nights where I couldn't breathe. So one night I was sleeping, and I woke up and my dad stood above me with his hand hovering over me and I said, "What are doing?" He said, "Well, I'm giving you healing, Larry." So I asked him, "Well, why didn't you do it while I'm awake?" My dad replied, "I didn't know if you would accept it."

SP: He thought it would freak you out?

LG: Yes, he thought it would freak me out, but I said, "No, Dad, that's fine, I want you to help me." At any rate because of that something was instilled in me whereby I had the freedom to search, to investigate, to probe ideas that perhaps maybe I wouldn't be able to if my mother didn't teach me what she taught me. I remember she always used to use this mantra with me. "Larry, always remember this: change your thoughts, and you can change your life, change your thoughts, and you can change your life," and that stuck with me. Now, I graduated high school, and that's when I began my search but I want to go back a bit.

SP: Yes, because before you graduated it was a time, I guess your early teenage years, where you became interested in girls and were hanging out with all the boys, and it was around the time you were living in L.A. and you had all these celebrity sightings, so can you tell me a little bit about that?

LG: Yes, I was in a department store, and I was walking around, and I literally bumped into this guy and I turned around and looked, and it was John Wayne.

SP: [I gasp.] No!

LG: Yeah, and he's six foot four, John Wayne... and I

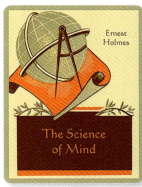

TOP: Ernest Shurtleff Holmes, author of *The Science of Mind*, 1926; **ABOVE:** One of the covers of *The Science of Mind*.

TOP: Paul Newman and Joanne Woodward, two of the many celebrities Larry would encounter; **ABOVE:** Larry expounds his philosophy in a previous interview situation.

look at him, he kind of grinned at me. I also saw Liz Taylor and Gregory Peck.

SP: I love Gregory Peck! Was this an everyday thing to you?

LG: Well, after a while it really was run of the mill. One day we went to this drive-in called Dolores's and everyone went there of an evening, and I remember I went there in 1956 and there was Paul Newman and Joanne Woodward, when they first started going together. But I had this celebrity encounter in 1957, and it was at the old campus site auditorium.

SP: This is the encounter that rocked your world, correct?

LG: Yes, and I'm still rocking. So at any rate Elvis was coming to town and that was it, we couldn't believe it, and we had to see Elvis. He was coming to this auditorium which was about four blocks from where I lived, so my buddies and I, we walked over there and we looked like Fonzie caricatures with pompadours, duck tails, tight jeans. I'm still wearing black jeans. This auditorium was famous for auto shows, kitchen shows, political rallies. So when we got there, there were thousands and thousands of kids just teeming in from everywhere. We were so excited. They all had tickets, and we

didn't. We thought we were so clever that somehow we were going to get in, someone is going to invite us in. Everyone went inside and the five of us were standing there, and we had to see Elvis! We tried to pry open a door and a window. We walked to the side of the building, and I said, "Look, there he is, there's Elvis!"

SP: He was just standing there?

LG: Elvis was standing in front of a car with about five or six guys in front of him and he was wearing a gold lamé jacket, and I said, "You guys, come on... let's go say hi." They froze in their tracks, and, by the way, these guys and I are still friends today.

SP: Wow!

LG: Fifty-one years on, and we are still friends.

SP: So they hung back?

LG: Yeah, so at any rate I said, "I'm going." Nothing was going to stop me. I ran up to Elvis, and I remember looking up at him because I was shorter than he was in those days. So he looked at me and as I'm looking at him, that face, those eyes, his nose, the sideburns, everything... to me he looked like a man from another planet! I had never seen anything like this before, and he had this energy about him, like this burning energy glowing from within, and he looked at me and saw that I was really nervous. So I said, "Hi," and he said, "Hi, I'm Elvis Presley," and I said, "I'm Larry Geller." At that point one of the guys said, "Elvis, they're calling for ya," so he looked at me and said, "Well, kid, I gotta go. See you some other time." And he walked off, and I stood there.

SP: You were spellbound.

LG: I started to imitate Elvis at parties, I was doing karaoke then, I got a guitar, I knew every song.

SP: It was a very special moment in your life that you will never forget.

LG: Yes, and now I want to fast forward three years.

SP: Okay, so you enrolled in college.

LG: Yes, I did a stint in college.

SP: So its now the '60s, and there are a lot of changes.

LG: Well, I want to tell you about it. I became a hairdresser.

SP: What made you want to become a hairdresser of all the other things you could have done?

LG: Well, one of the guys that happened to be with me that night, he and I were taking a walk one night—I was taking theater arts, I thought of going into acting or something so I could be part of show business in some way— and my buddy Christian said to me, "You're very artistic, a creative kind of guy, so why don't you become a hairdresser so you will have an occupation? You don't know where that will lead you to." I said, "Yeah, yeah, that's a good idea."

SP: So you didn't know you would be good at this and hadn't thought of this previously?

LG: Well, I was the only artist in school, and I used to be a sculptor, I'd paint quite a bit, and so I knew that I could do it.

SP: Hmm, okay.

LG: So I enrolled in the beauty school that was about four blocks from where we are now.

SP: Didn't you go to beauty school with Patti Parry?

LG: She went right before me. I think Patti might be a year or two younger but I'm not sure.

SP: Right, okay.

LG: At any rate, I took my state board examination, and I'm waiting for my results so I could be a licensed hairdresser in Beverley Hills to do women's hair. I'm walking down the street one day, and I see

a store and it looked very unusual to me. It had a stained-glass window, a kind of weird configuration. I didn't know what it was. What it was was an Egyptian ark. So I walked inside, and there was a guy on a ladder, and I didn't know what the place was because in those days men went to barber shops. The old fashioned barber shops where they would get the buzz-cut and they put the oil on the hair. But I walked into this salon and I saw shampoo bowls and I enquired about what it was to this man on the ladder, and he said he was opening the very first men's hair salon in America, and he was going to style the hair and shampoo it first. So I told him about myself and he said, "Do you know I do women's hair? Come with me. It'll be you and me."

SP: Now is this Jay Sebring?

LG: Jay Sebring. And I saw the opportunity and, in effect, we were the progenitors of a new industry. We were pioneers. Within the first three or four weeks.

SP: So you did your training with Jay Sebring?

LG: I did my training. I shampooed his customers, I swept the floors, I answered the phones, I took the appointments, and within a matter of a couple of weeks—as I already knew how to do men's hair a little bit—I'm styling men's hair and from the very beginning we had Frank Sinatra.

SP: In the very beginning? Frank Sinatra!

LG: People just heard about us right off the bat and the word spread like wildfire.

SP: So I read you did Steve McQueen's hair.

LG: Steve McQueen, Henry Fonda, Rock Hudson, every major star in motion pictures, television. Directors, producers, we were it! And when I see films of the Sixties I see my work. Here I am, a young guy, and I'm making good money. I call my own hours, and it was a wonderful life.

SP: They were all beautiful men, gorgeous men.

LG: That's right.

SP: But the most gorgeous man you were about to

ABOVE: Elvis onstage in 1958.

215

ABOVE AND TOP: Elvis and Larry in the early 1970s.

encounter right? He didn't actually step foot into that salon, did he?

LG: No.

SP: So it's April 30th, and the phone rings, and on the other end of the phone line is Alan Fortas?

LG: Alan Fortas, who used to work for Elvis. He passed away about 15 years ago, a very nice man.

SP: Okay, so you're just working away at the salon...

LG: Yes, just working away, and I have a wonderful clientele—Sam Cook, Roy Orbison, some wonderful celebrities, Robert Wagner—

SP: Cynthia Pepper likes Robert Wagner.

LG: He still looks great. I saw him the other night on TV. He looks fantastic. I've been around the most handsome men in motion pictures in history.

SP Steve McQueen was very handsome!

LG: Yes, and Rock Hudson, Warren Beatty, James Garner... but let me tell ya, Elvis was a notch above the rest.

SP: I bet.

LG: There was something about Elvis.

SP: What happened after the phone rings and it's Al, tell me about that?

LG: So I answer my phone, I hear this southern drawl, and Alan said, "Hey, Larry, Elvis heard about ya and he wants to know if you would like to

come up to the house to fix his hair. And it's funny because I can remember my thoughts right now as Alan said that to me, I thought to myself, "I didn't know Elvis's hair was broken." [Laughing.] At any rate working with Milton Berle, James Garner, and all these celebrities after a while, it was no big deal.

SP: So you weren't intimidated at all because it was Elvis Presley?

LG: Not at all, I was not starstruck. I was used to this. However, the thought of meeting Elvis, that was it, that was it for me. I was excited. So I drove up there to the Bel Air gates and there was somebody there to meet me, another guy that has passed away, Jimmy Kingsley. I followed Jimmy up to the house. I knew which house it was straight away as there were tons of fans and the gates opened up and the fans are screaming "Tell Elvis I love him!" and people are taking pictures, and I was like, "Wow!"

SP: Must have been a surreal experience for you. The first time you're going through the gates to his home, and all these young girls are screaming! You were probably thinking, "What the heck?"

LG: Well, I knew what I was doing, but, yes, it was something else, it was new. So I walk into the house, Elvis walks up to me. He says, "Hi, I'm Elvis Presley," and I said, "Hi, I'm Larry Geller, nice to meet you," but I'm having a flashback of that skinny little short kid, you know, from eight years earlier. Though I didn't say anything. So Elvis said, "Come on, man, let's go into my bathroom," and he said, "you can fix my hair, [Larry Geller starts laughing] and we can talk."

SP: Can I just say I know when you went into that bathroom you were there for a long time, so how long did you spend with him that day, all in all, would you say?

LG: Probably around two and a half hours. What happened is we walked into Elvis's bathroom, and I expected all the trappings of a Hollywood star—a salon-type chair and all that sort of stuff, but it was nothing of the kind. We walked into the bathroom, and he closed the door. He said, "Come on, man, just shampoo my hair right here," and he stuck his head in a basin. So I shampoo his hair, and I'm rinsing it out with water from under the faucet, and I'm almost done, and then all of a sudden he pulls his head up. He starts shaking it, and water is going everywhere, over me, over him, and he's drenched. He looked at me and he smiled and said, "Hey, man, what the hell, at least it's clean!" [We all start laughing.] When he said that, I knew Elvis, I knew his nature—he was so down-to-earth, so real, so spontaneous. He then said, "Come on, man, there's a sofa here, and you can do my hair there." We sat in front of this long mirror, and he explained to me he was in the middle of doing a movie [*Roustabout*]. It's so funny I'm talking to you and I'm remembering, and I'm drawn back to that moment, it's still so vivid, it's amazing, like it was yesterday! Now if you asked me about yesterday, I've got to think, furrow my brow and think [laughing] but I can remember that day, it's so fresh. So Elvis said, "I'm right in the middle of this movie, and they're going to film me so you can't change it too much." I said, "Don't you worry, I know exactly what you want." Now people that knew Elvis knew that he loved to talk, he loved to engage in conversation.

SP: A bit like you Larry.

LG: Yeah, I'm that way too.

SP: I love that, when people can sit there engrossed in conversation and can talk for hours, especially when it's something so interesting like this.

LG: Well, at any rate I didn't know he was really a talker, I didn't know that yet. So I'm doing his hair, and as I'm doing his hair, I'm looking in the mirror, and I see his eyes darting back and forth following every move I make, and I'm not going to invade his privacy. I work with celebrities all the time, and

I understand he wants to talk, I'm there, and I'm available while I'm doing his hair. So I do his hair. It was so easy... here's the thing, Elvis, as I was saying a few minutes ago, he was a notch above the rest. I mean there were major stars that would come to the studio or to Vegas. They would stand next to Elvis, and they would pale next to Elvis, and they knew it! [We all start laughing.] He looked like he stepped out of the pages of mythology

SP: Like a Greek god.

LG: Like a Greek god, or the face of King David himself [More laughing.] And that's what he had, that was Elvis. He had the eyes, he had the perfect aquiline nose, the lips were famous. He had the voice, the charisma, the fans, the fame, the money. He had the soul. He was the perfect package.

SP: Without sounding too farfetched, was he like he was a gift from God, would you say?

LG: He was, he is a gift from God, there are no questions about it.

SP: Well, yeah, he was put on this earth for something and wasn't just your average human being, he was a very special person.

LG: In the history of entertainment and show business he's number one, no one comes close, and we will talk about that later but let me get back to the story. He also had the hair, he had beautiful hair, but it lacked some body, it really did. I had to create my own special shampoo for him, which I did. It was a very very basic pH-balance use, and I would add vitamin E capsules and in those days people didn't know what Vitamin E was. I'd puncture holes in it and squeeze the gel and add 99% aloe vera and a few other goodies, and I would shake it up.

SP: This was a special shampoo just for Elvis?

LG: Yes, yes.

SP: You wouldn't use this on all your clients?

LG: No, just for Elvis.

SP: You should do that now [special shampoo]!

TOP: Elvis and Alan Fortas; **ABOVE:** Elvis with Larry, amongst adoring fans.

"Larry, there has to be a reason why was I plucked out of all the millions and millions of people living, to be Elvis. There has to be a reason. There's got to be, I've always known it, I've always felt this unseen hand guiding my life ever since I was a little kid. Man, you have no idea what poverty is all about, trust me, man, trust me, where I came from and what my family and I had to go through..."

LARRY DESCRIBES HOW ELVIS OPENED UP TO HIM

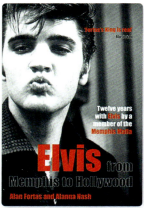

TOP: Elvis, in the late 1960s; **ABOVE:** The cover of *Elvis: From Memphis to Hollywood*, by Alan Fortas and Alanna Nash.

LG: Well, Shira and I are in the process of doing that, and I'm going to create something that is so wonderful and so advanced because I've studied this my whole life. We've come up with something called Nutrastar Shampoo and it's hot but that's for maybe the next time. So he had the hair but it lacked a little bit of the body, so I would massage Elvis's hair over the years to increase the blood circulation to the roots. He said, "Look, you can do whatever you want with my hair." He said this over the years but added one thing more—"You just make sure I keep it."

[All laughing.] Elvis is known for his hair, right?

SP: Right.

LG: At any rate, I blow dry his hair that day, and I spritz it, and I'm standing behind him, and then I say, "What do you think, Elvis?" and he says, "Yeah, yeah, that's great." Then he turns around in the chair, and he looks at me and says, "Larry, let me ask you a question. Who are you? What are you into, Larry, what are you really all about?"

SP: He really put you on the spot, didn't he! How did you respond?

LG: On the spot and totally straightforward, and what ran through my mind in those few seconds I knew right then and there he was going to either accept what I say and appreciate it or just think I'm another Hollywood nut because in 1964 no one spoke about what I started telling him. I said, "Well, as you know I work at Sebring, I work with celebrities every day for a living, but what's more important to me, more than anything else in life, beyond money, beyond career... and what we are born for, what everyone is born for, is to reconnect with God. To find out who we really are. Where do we come from? Where do we really go? Do we really have souls? Is there really life after death? I know you're Elvis Presley, you're the biggest star in the world, and it probably sounds corny to you." He said, "Whoa, wait a minute, man. Larry, you have no idea how much I need to hear what you have to say. Please, man. Keep on talking." So I said to him, "Elvis, I read a lot of books, books from every religion in the world, my mind's open. I want to learn, and they all have something to offer about the soul and about what this is really all about. I meditate, and I pray, and I do yoga, and I eat healthy foods... I'm a vegetarian." So the conversation at that point got even deeper, and Elvis opened up. What happened really, Shelly, essentially, is a synergy between us. It's like when you meet someone and you say, "Hey, I really like this person," you know, we are going to be friends forever. It's not like when you meet someone, and you go, "Hey, what is this?" You know you have to question stuff.

SP: Yes, I know like, "Well, I'm not too sure about this person." There was this instant connection with you both at this point.

LG: Yeah, and there was this bond that was there, and it was obvious, and I started explaining certain principles of the books that I was reading, and I started talking about my background like I was telling you earlier and about my Judaism.

SP: Yeah, because can I just ask you this?

LG: Yes.

SP: Is it correct that Elvis once told you that his mother Gladys had Jewish relatives?

LG: Oh, yes, absolutely.

SP: Okay, so where in his family?

LG: On his mother's side, and according to Jewish law it cuts through the mother, his bloodline, but I'll tell you about that in a little bit.

SP: So he volunteered that information?

LG: Oh, yes, he volunteered that, and two weeks later… I'll tell you what happened. Something very interesting happened in relation to this but let me just finish this part of it.

SP: Okay.

LG: So I told him a lot about myself, and he started telling me about himself. About Tupelo, Mississippi, and when he was born, about his twin brother Jesse Garon. We are about an hour into this conversation, and I'm realizing he doesn't know me, yet he's opening up about some very intimate things, about his mother and his father and about certain feelings he had about the Jews and growing up in Tupelo. He continued talking about his mother and his twin brother and he started crying and he had tears rolling down his cheeks. I'm looking at him, and I'm thinking, "Wow, what is going on here? He doesn't know me, does he do this with other people?" I didn't know, and like I said a moment ago, something clicked. It was synergistic. I triggered something in him, and he did the same with me. We just opened up and talked about how nothing is a coincidence, everything happens for a reason, every person you meet, every incident in your life. I remember him saying—and, Shelly, as we are talking I can see Elvis exactly how he looked— "Larry, there has to be a reason why was I plucked out of all the millions and millions of people living, to be Elvis. There has to be a reason. There's got to be, I've always known it, I've always felt this unseen hand guiding my life ever since I was a little kid. Man, you have no idea what poverty is all about, trust me, man, trust me, where I came from and what my family and I had to go through…" and he

told me, "I was born at home," and then he told me his whole history. So this conversation went on for several hours, and I told Elvis about several books that I thought he would really, really connect with and one of them was called—

SP: *The Impersonal Life*? Which became his favorite.

LG: *The Impersonal Life*, yes, which was his favorite book, apart from the Bible, of course, his Bible. It became his favorite book. In fact we made a film at MGM once, well many times, but this one time after a movie, Elvis would give every crew member and every costar and the director and the sound crew, every person that was involved in the movie, a gift before the movie was over. Elvis said, "Larry, go buy a hundred copies of *The Impersonal Life*." So I did, and he gave everyone a copy. He would say, "Read this, you gotta read this." In fact, after Elvis really got involved in books, I would bring him book after book after book, all of his costars received many, many spiritual books. Elvis was a ferocious reader. So, to finish this portion of the story…

TOP: Alan Fortas worked for Elvis until right after the '68 Special. He left because of the heavy traveling involved; **ABOVE:** As Elvis's personal hairdresser, Larry was credited with creating some of his most iconic looks.

"'I want a Star of David here, this is what my mother would want, and this is what I want, so let's find a stone cutter.' The following week the most beautiful Star of David was placed there..."

ELVIS TALKING TO LARRY AT HIS MOTHER'S GRAVE

TOP RIGHT: Promotional portrait of Elvis that was used for the cover of "The California Sessions"; **ABOVE:** Larry, circa 1990.

SP: Okay.

LG: I remember it was about two and half hours into this, and there is this knock on the door, and I hear, "Hey, Boss, are you all right in there?" and Elvis shot back, "Hey, man, I'm fine, I'm fine. I'll be out soon."

SP: It was one of his entourage?

LG: Right, one of the guys. [Larry cracks up laughing.] This hairdresser, this Hollywood hairdresser is here two and a half hours in the bathroom with Elvis! What the hell is going on in there? Right! Hey, let me tell you something—if I was one of those guys I'd be wondering what in the world was going on in there. [Laughing.]

SP: [Laughing.] Right! A long time to be in the bathroom with Elvis.

LG: Yeah, so I realize time is going by, so I have to get back to the shop. So I say, "Hey, Elvis, I got to get back to the shop. I have an appointment, but if you want me to come back, if you want to talk, I'm available. I can bring you some books if you want to read some of the books that I told you about." Elvis said, "Hey, I got a better idea. Go back and tell them you quit, and come and work for me full time. Come back and meet me tomorrow morning at Paramount Studios. What do ya think?" Well, it's interesting because I was supposed to be opening a second salon with Sebring at Palm Springs. I was going to move there, and I was just going to work with Kirk Douglas, Frank Sinatra, and Robert Mitchum, all those people, but when Elvis asked me that, I said yes.

SP: You said yes straight away?

LG: Straight away.

SP: So you went back to work that day?

LG: I went back to work.

SP: So how did you explain this to Jay Sebring?

LG: Well, we didn't have cell phones in those days, so I couldn't call him. So I drove back in my little VW convertible.

SP: I have one of those.

LG: You do?

SP: Yes. [We laugh.]

LG: So I drove back to the salon, I had my bag, and I was excited. I get out of my car, and I go to jump up on the curb but as I do my foot hits the lip of the curb... and I fell over and fractured my arm.

SP: Oh, no!

LG: Yeah, and I was meant to be at Paramount Studios the next day. Elvis said, "Your name will be at the gate, just be there."

LG: So I go in and I tell Jay, and he was not pleased.

SP: I bet he wasn't!

LG: He understood.

SP: So you just said, "Hey, I'm leaving?"

LG: I said, "Hey, I'm gonna work for Elvis. I gotta do this. I have to do this for Elvis," and in my heart I knew it was right. When you know something is right, it's right. And it was an opportunity, and I realized that Elvis is hiring me as his hairdresser but he wants me there for a deeper reason, and that's what was most important to me. I could do his hair but to be friends with a person like Elvis? There's not a person like Elvis, there's only Elvis.

SP: Well, you were hired as his hairdresser, and everything happens for a reason.

LG: It was destiny, there was a purpose involved in all this. So I went home and by the time I got home my arm had swelled up three times its size, and I was in trouble. How am I going to hold a hair blower the next morning? How am I going to do Elvis's hair? I was going to go to hospital but then I realized if I went to the hospital they would put a cast on it then I would be in trouble as I would be immobile.

SP: Hmm, yes.

LG: I sat in the chair, I prayed, I meditated, I did everything I could to heal myself, and I was up most of the night. The next morning I put a long sleeved shirt on. I was in terrible pain but I didn't want anyone to see it. So I went to the studio, I went in and my name was at the gate, and when I drove in Elvis drove in at the same time. I'll never forget, he was in a black Rolls Royce. We went into the dressing room, and Elvis said, "Hi, man, have you got those books?" So I'd brought him *The Impersonal Life* and another book called *Autobiography of a Yogi*. So Elvis sits in a chair and in those days Elvis was very kinetic, in those days he moved around a lot, so he sat down... and my arm is killing me. I remember standing there with my hair blower, and I spray his hair, and I'm blowing his hair, and I get my dryer to do my thing but I'm starting to get dizzy now.

SP: Because of the pain...

LG: The pain was horrendous, and I remember the room started to spin a bit, and I thought, "Oh, my God, this is embarrassing, don't let this happen to me!"

SP: You were so desperate to be there and do his hair though.

LG: You know you do what you have to do.

SP: Yeah, yeah.

LG: I was not going to allow my nervousness, my

pain, the spinning of the room to prevent me from doing Elvis's hair that day, and I did his hair. So that kicked it off and, Shelly, it's not stopped! Its still going on like right now.

SP: Can I ask—

LG: —and by the way I just wanna tell you, we are talking a lot about me but this is about Elvis. Let me tell you what happened at the end of the day, filming had finished and we were going home, and Elvis said, "Come on, let me show you my car." We went outside to his Rolls Royce, and I said, "Oh, Elvis, it's just beautiful." Elvis said, "Follow me to the house, you can take it for the night." [Larry laughs.] And I said, "Oh, no, Elvis, that's okay." He wanted me to take his car!

SP: He wanted to just give it to you, his car?

LG: To use for that night, to drive around and go out.

SP: Oh, my goodness.

LG: I said, "No, that's okay," you know. So two weeks later the first thing Elvis would do after a film, he would say, "Let's get out of Hollywood, man. I can only handle Tinsel Town for so long, there's no reality anymore, and I gotta get back to Graceland. That's where my reality is, and that's where I'm sane."

SP: So you hadn't visited Graceland yet?

LG: No, not yet. He said, "After a while even

TOP: Elvis with Larry in the early Seventies; **ABOVE:** Elvis loved the look Larry styled for him.

these buildings look like movie sets to me, and the people out here... ya know? Anyway what we do is [Larry pauses] we make three movies a year, as all the Elvis fans know. So, we travel back and forth from here to Memphis and from Memphis to LA, as Elvis didn't fly during those years. So I made about fifteen trips over the years. So we drove back, and Elvis had about ten books that I had brought him, and he's reading every day. Elvis read every day! He used to read sports magazines and other things, but now he's getting very serious and every hour or two on the road Elvis would drive this Dodge mobile home that he had, and I would ride shotgun with a few of the guys in the back, three or four guys in the other vehicles, and we traveled across [the country] to Memphis. What happened was on the very first trip we pulled into a gas station in Holbrook Arizona, it's about three in the morning, whatever it was—Elvis always traveled during the night, by the way.

ABOVE: Elvis, circa 1968.

SP: Why was that?

LG: Well, because this was Elvis's chance to breathe and not be Elvis Presley and just have that freedom to be on the open road and just not be hassled during the day by people. He had just got off from working for a couple of months on a film.

SP: And he just wanted to relax?

LG: He just wanted to relax, yes. So we pull in for gasoline off the open road, and Elvis, he never got out of the vehicle because he would be sitting in the back and he would be reading one of these books, and one of the guys said to me because I stepped outside and he said, "You went to college, didn't ya?" and I said, "Yeah, I did," and then he said, "You must have studied psychology because you're using some psychology on Elvis."

SP: Oh, dear.

LG: And I thought, "Oh, wow. Well, that's not what's going on here." I said, "No not really, I didn't study psychology," at any rate.

SP: The thing I wanted to ask you was Elvis was open to all types of religion, wasn't he? And you introduced him to a lot.

LG: Yes, he was; I introduced him to the whole shebang.

SP: Yeah, so when you first started working for Elvis, okay, I just want to ask you about the fact that you were Jewish.

LG: Yes.

SP: Is it true that Vernon Presley... would you say he was prejudiced? I've read somewhere that he was quite prejudiced, and he was kind of upset when he found out that Elvis had hired you to come work for him, just because of the simple fact that you were Jewish.

LG: Well, let me just say something about that.

SP Okay.

LG: First of all, George Klein, who went to high school with Elvis, was Jewish, Alan Fortas was Jewish, Marty Lacker is Jewish, so it's not like a new Jew came on the scene. However, this is interesting, and this is a porthole into that, or into Vernon, so to speak, and the whole Jewish thing.

SP: Okay.

LG: We went back to Memphis and after three or four days, the very first thing that Elvis did when we got there, he said, "Come on, we are going for a ride. I want to show you something." We get in the limo and we sit in the back seat, Alan Fortas drove with one to two other guys for security. We drove to Forest Hills Cemetery, where his mother was buried, and I didn't know where we were going. So we pull into the cemetery and he says, "This is where my mother is," and we drive up to it and he tells the guys, "You stay there." He gets out with me, and we walk up to her graveside, and we stood there for about ten minutes perhaps, very quiet, very solemn, and he looks at me and he says, "I want a Star of David here, this is what my mother would want, and this is what I want, so let's find a stone cutter." The following week the most beautiful Star of David was placed there. In fact there is a picture of it in my new book. After Elvis died, Vernon had it removed. [Larry raises his hands in despair.]

SP: Ahhh, so this is where all this has come from! People who knew Vernon say that Vernon was prejudiced.

LG: He didn't want it there, for sure.

SP: Okay, so how did Vernon react when Elvis had the Star of David put on his mother's headstone?

LG: This is what Elvis wanted. Vernon is not going to go against Elvis, no way.

SP: So Elvis always had the last say?

LG: Elvis had the only say, the first and the last.

SP It's a well-known fact that there were the few of the guys that didn't particularly take to you?

LG: Ya think?

SP: [Laughing.] Yeah, which I don't get.

LG: Get outta here! [Laughing.]

SP: I mean, you're such a nice guy! [Larry laughs.] Maybe they were a little envious because you had that special relationship with Elvis that they might have wanted? However, some of them were a little bit stand-offish with you, maybe a little bit hostile towards you, am I right? And a few of them went so far as to accuse you of being a phony. Why do you think, why do you think they resented you so much?

LG: [Larry claps his hands together.] Well this is quite a subject, this is quite a subject. Errr, well, of course never in front of Elvis would they say anything like you just intimated, and nobody ever to my face called me a phony or anything like that.

SP: Really?

LG: Never. They would say, "Here comes the guru, here comes the wandering Jew, here comes the great teacher," things like that, but never in front of Elvis. But Elvis knew this was going on, and we would talk about it all the time. I spent more quality time with Elvis every day for years alone, and I would do his hair. Every day if we were at Graceland or the studio, wherever we were, we would go by ourselves and go and hang out together for an hour, for two hours, for three hours every day, and I suppose there might have been some resentment, and some jealousy, and I know because I've seen some things written in books like, "Larry would fill Elvis's head with all this garbage and all this crap" and remember I'm doing this for years and years with Elvis. Okay, let's look at his for a minute... remember, I see this happening a lot politically and the easiest thing to do is to smear someone and make an accusation, but it's been almost thirty-one years, right? And in several of these books, not all of them but several, some people said, "Larry was filling Elvis's head full of crap and tearing his head up and doing this."

SP: It's kind of a bit old now, don't you think? Don't you agree that's a bit old in this day?

LG: It's beyond that, it's imbecilic, because never once do you hear what I was telling Elvis. Well, what? What was I telling Elvis? Nobody ever says, because they don't know.

SP: Yes, why was it that they thought you were filling Elvis's head with nonsense, and how did you deal with that, calling you "a Wandering Jew," etc.?

LG: I would just laugh it off because I was there for a reason. Elvis and I would talk about this, like I'm talking to you now, Shelly. Elvis would say, "Hey, I always liked being misunderstood, and you know why you're here, and that's the important thing." But here's the thing, two things basically: Elvis was a very bright human being, brighter than anyone around him. He was very insightful, and he developed over the years. What kind of a commentary is this on Elvis to say that this guy Larry Geller was feeding Elvis's head with all this crap and nonsense every day, what is that saying about Elvis? What, that Elvis is some kind of schmuck, sitting there listening to this guy filling his head with garbage?

SP: Exactly!

LG: Elvis was a brilliant man, he was a musical genius, he was a very creative and intelligent human being. A highly developed, spiritual person. So what is that saying about Elvis? Now you ask me how I take it... when people project things like that on me, they're not talking about me, because I wasn't feeding Elvis's head with any nonsense or garbage. So they're projecting their image of who they think I am. So it really, in the ultimate sense, doesn't bother me because they're not talking about me; they think they are but that's not me. Anyone who knows me, can see that, understands that recognizes that. Elvis certainly did.

SP: They could actually be talking about themselves.

LG: I was hoping you would say that and not me, but okay! [Larry laughs.]

SP: Well, it's so obvious, it really is.

LG: I mean, I could go on, down this line but do you know what Elvis said to me several times in the last year of his life? He knew a book was coming out about him, and he said, "You know I'm not worried,

TOP: Larry during the interview; **ABOVE:** A uniformed Elvis with a loyal fan.

I'm not worried. My fans are smart, my fans will know the truth about me and who I am. My fans are not going to believe things that are not true. I am not concerned. My only concern is my dad and my little girl, that's my only concern. I am not concerned about myself or my image or my career, not anything like that." So Elvis had that same attitude when people were speaking about him in any terms that were not cohesive.

SP: Yeah, because I believe a few of his guys—and I'm not going to mention any names—but purely by what they have written, made out that Elvis couldn't think for himself.

LG: I know about this.

SP: He had this need to improve his mind constantly, like if he didn't understand something he would reach for his dictionary.

LG: Exactly!

SP: He would look things up, break words up, and in fact he was so into learning he wanted to teach as well. Is it true, Larry, that he bought all the guys dictionaries so they could have this word right?

LG: He didn't buy them all dictionaries but he would teach all the time. Let me tell you something. This is in Las Vegas 1973, and we are all sitting, all the guys are sitting, and Elvis is talking and something is said about one of the books that Elvis has in his hand. Elvis said, "Guys, tell me that you really love me, and you want to make me happy. You know I'm going to tell you the one thing that you can all do that would make me happier than anything else you could do, find out who you really are, find out the truth about your existence. When you start to do that, that's how you're going to make me happy, that's what it's all about."

SP: So he would not only bare his soul to you, maybe in some ways to the other guys too, because he wanted them to know that he wanted them to find out what life was really all about.

LG: Totally, and we talked about this many times over the years in different ways. He would say, "Look everybody comes to the truth in their life, and they start to search when they're ready. You can't make anyone, you can't push anyone, otherwise they're going to go further away from it."

SP: He was right, that's absolutely true.

LG: Each one of the guys in their own time and their own way, and all we can do is plant the seeds, we can plant the seeds.

TOP: Elvis in a publicity still for *Jailhouse Rock*, 1957; **ABOVE:** Elvis onstage at the International Hotel in Las Vegas in the early 1970s.

SP: Okay, well, because you were so close to Elvis and he would confide in you, what would you say Elvis's greatest fear was?

LG: That's a great question, Shelly.

SP: I don't mean about his fans not loving him anymore, or anything to do with the fact that he didn't like his movies. I mean something deeper.

LG: I hear your question. Elvis didn't have many fears, he was a fearless person, he certainly didn't fear death, he feared failing, failing. I remember he said, "If I have one regret in my life it would be not living up to my potential of whc I am as an actor, as an entertainer, and I know, I know that I can do films that are really Oscar-worthy and I'm afraid that I'm not doing what I can do, for myself, for my family, and my fans." When it comes to being fearful that's the only thing that Elvis feared. Not living up to his potential, and that's a very big subject about his potential because there are a lot of erroneous stories about the end of his life, and I really go into this in my book *Leaves of Elvis' Garden* and you know because you've read my book.

SP: Yes.

LG: And it is in there.

SP: I know, and I want to touch on that in a minute if I may.

LG: All right, we will get to that, I'll wait then.

SP: Because when I read that last chapter—and I have read many Elvis books—but your book moved me in a way that I have never been moved before through an Elvis book.

LG: That is music to my ears.

SP: Well, it's true.

SP: Didn't he have this desire to escape as well?

LG: I hear your question, I know your question, and the answer to that is yes and no!

SP: Yes and no?

LG: Okay, let me explain what I mean. At the end of Elvis's life he was at the crossroads, many things were emerging from his inner being, frustrations and problems that he had in his relationships with other people in the group in terms of what he wanted to do with his life and his career. This had to do with his manager and several other people in the group. We know how some people were let go the year earlier. Elvis was planning a new life, he wanted to transform his career and his lifestyle. He would never stop working, but at the same time he knew he needed balance. This is what he read about

in books, that his key in this life was to find the balance between harmony and peace and relaxation and work and career.

SP: And that's what he struggled with.

LG: And that's what he struggled for and he never did find, but he knew it, he woke up to it, and that's the point and that's what I bring out in my book, and this is what fans need to realize. Elvis woke up to the fact that he outgrew a lot of people and old friends. He woke up to the fact that he was unhealthy and had health problems. Glaucoma, hypertension, his blood pressure shooting up to 180 every night, a spastic, twisted colon. He was taking medications from different doctors, poison, pills, and finally he got to the point where he said, "That's it, that is it," and I remember the night, well it was the afternoon when it all came to a head. We were in Louisville, Kentucky, and I was sitting in the suite, and the night before Elvis had had a very difficult night. He had a sore throat, he felt he had a fever, and he was nauseous, he couldn't sleep. Finally it got to be about five or six in the morning. He took

a bunch of sleeping pills, and I'm sitting in the suite and the doctor's in the bedroom with him, and it's now four o'clock in the afternoon. Never once did Colonel Parker come to see Elvis after work. It didn't happen.

SP: He never came to see him?

LG: He would never come to see him. Next thing there was a pounding on the front door—and that shouldn't happen, we own the floor. You can't get off the elevators unless you're one of us. I run to the door and look through the peephole and there's Colonel Parker. I open the door and the first thing he says very gruffly is. "Where is he?" I say, "Well, Colonel, he's in the bedroom. Let me tell him you're here," and he says, "No, I'm going right in!" And he walks right past me and goes to the door and he opens it, and what you see is Elvis semi-conscious, and this is so painful for me, very painful for me to tell you this but this is what happened. The doctor was holding Elvis's head over a bucket of water, and then Elvis lays back moaning, and the Colonel slammed the door shut and I thought, "Damn it!"

TOP: Elvis performing in Tampa, Florida in 1956; **ABOVE:** Elvis in a publicity still for *Jailhouse Rock*, 1957.

225

SP: So now you're on the other side of the door?

LG: I wasn't invited in, as the manager he shut the door on me, and my first thought was, "Wait a minute, finally he's going to see reality and the tour is gonna stop, and Elvis is going to get the medical attention that he needs." I would say approximately a minute, two minutes later, the door opens and the Colonel walks out, and he walks up to me. I stand up and we are toe to toe, and I will never forget it, he had his cane in his hand, and he raised it and looked me right in the eye, and he said, "Now, listen, I was just in there, and I saw him. The only thing that is important is that that man is on the stage tonight, do you hear me? Do ya hear? Nothing else matters here, nothing. He's got to be on that stage. That's it!" And he walked out. It was very, very painful. The doctor leaves and I walk in, and Elvis says, "What the hell? Why did you let him in?" I told him what happened, and he said, "That son of a bitch," and he started to cuss. "I've had it, man, I've had it with that man, that's it. I almost fired him in '74, this is it, man, that guy has lost touch, he doesn't give a crap about me, I know he doesn't, I know he doesn't. I know what he wants, and I know what his deal is and what he lost in Vegas, he lost a million and a half dollars in one night... and he uses me, and I'm his bait... and I get it!"

SP: Why do you think it took him so long to realize the truth about Colonel Tom Parker?

LG: It wasn't just Colonel Tom Parker, it was Elvis's life in total, it was the complete thing. He was going through an inner revolution and a lot of things emerged. His romantic life, people around him who he felt he outgrew. His lifestyle, he just didn't want to tour anymore. He loved singing, he just didn't want to tour anymore. He wanted to be an actor. He said, "Larry, here's what's gonna happen... A, B, C, D, and E, they're gone, that's it. I've carried a lot of these guys for too long. I'm only gonna keep two or three people and we're gonna go to Hawaii for a year and, man, I'm gonna get on a diet and we're going to exercise every day. Hey, I'm not kidding myself," he said, "I know it's not going to be easy, but I know I can do whatever I put my mind to." He said, "I'm going into unchartered waters." That's exactly what he said. "I'm going to get off those f...ing pills, I don't want doctors anymore, and we are going back to Hollywood, and I'm going to make movies as an actor, and I'm going to find a new manager. I really would like Tom Hewitt to be

my manager." Tom Hewitt was Jerry Weintraub's partner; they were the promoters of Elvis's concerts. I'm giving you the—even though, Shelly, you and I are talking—I'm giving you a shorthand version of many conversations that went on for a long time, about what Elvis wanted to do with his life.

SP: The drastic changes he so wanted to make.

LG: The changes, he said, "I'm gonna do it, this is it, this it. My life is on the line, and I know it's at stake and I'm gonna do it, only I'm going to do it in September." Elvis told me, "My contracts are signed, and I can't disappoint my fans." And I bring this out in the book, this is right now the crux of the tragedy of Elvis's life, because his life was magnificent, his life was over the top, a fantasy come true, and it ended tragically because he realized what he had to do to keep it going. To go on and to achieve greater vistas. He procrastinated, he didn't pick up the phone and say, "Colonel, adios, you're out of here. He didn't tell A, B, C, D, and E "I'm sorry, I have to let you guys go." He didn't call Elwen our pilot and say, "Crank up the plane, let's get our asses to Hawaii tomorrow."

SP: So why didn't he do that?

LG: Because he thought he had contracts until September, and he did, he didn't take the power that was really his all along. All along.

SP: He always thought of other people before he actually thought of himself.

LG: First of all it was very difficult for Elvis to say no to anyone, very difficult, he didn't want to hurt anyone. Elvis wouldn't hurt anyone. He was such a good guy! Shelly, if you came over to the house tonight I promise you, you would not leave without a new car or a bracelet, he would do something for you. That's what Elvis was like. Every day he would do something for someone. He was a beautiful man.

SP: A big heart for sure. Well, Larry, I have some questions I want to put to you from some of his fans from Elvis International and get some answers to some of the questions that have been emailed to me, too, from his fans.

LG: All right.

SP: I want to start with a question from a lady, a lady called Aileen from Dublin, I believe.

SP: My Dad's Irish.

LG: Really?

SP: Yes. So, Larry, Aileen wanted me to ask you,

TOP: A sombre looking Elvis during an interview, circa 1960; **ABOVE:** Elvis: Recording the *That's The Way It Is* album, ten years later, in 1970.

"Did Elvis believe in reincarnation and if so did he give you any insights as to whether he thought he would come back as an entertainer or did he think he would come back as someone else?"

LG: [Larry laughs.] Elvis, as I mentioned earlier, read a lot of material. He was a ferocious reader, he read from every wisdom teaching on planet Earth. Things that people had not even heard of before. He was bright, and he read a lot of concepts, along the lines of reincarnation, and his end result on the subject was, I don't know for sure, but I am certainly hoping as that would explain a lot of things... as why are some people born with certain disabilities and what did they do in the past? Why do they come here in such horrible situations? You know.

SP: Yeah, he was totally open to the idea.

LG: Yes, he was.

SP: Lorraine from the U.K.'s question is similar to that, she wants to ask about life after death, and she goes on to say, "Have you had any signs that Elvis is still with us in spirit, and if so what are these signs? [Giggles.] And when was the last one?"

LG: Well, okay, let me ask you a question.

SP: Okay.

LG: Well, personally there is not a doubt that the soul goes on, this is just one of a succession, the soul is eternal. The soul is eternal. It wasn't four

five or six weeks since Elvis had passed away, and something major happened in my life when Elvis came to me.

SP: He came to you?

LG: Yes, and what happened was, I was sleep dreaming, and I woke up in my dream, and I woke up from my dream.

SP: Sleep dreaming?

LG: A regular dream like we all have, and in the dream Elvis appeared but it wasn't a dream anymore.

SP: So it was more like a visitation?

LG: It was a visitation, and he took me by the hand, and he looked fantastic. He was wearing a black suit, he looked radiant, just beautiful. And I took that man's hand right there, I took him by the hand—and my son—and he was about this big at the time, [Larry motions and raises his hand to show me the height of his son.] and the three of us walked into a chapel like I have never seen before... and I have seen some places. I've been to the Vatican, I've been to Europe, and I've seen some Gothic cathedrals and they're amazing. He led me into a building that I have never entered into in the real world. Ceilings that must have been 80 to 90 feet tall. Huge stained-glass windows with shafts of light. Groups of two or three people walking, and everyone was silent, and there was this peace and serenity, a radiance, a luminous essence about this building, and

TOP: Elvis during the *That's The Way It Is* sessions, 1970; **CENTER:** Elvis at the piano— the sheet music for "Love Me Tender" is on the music stand; **ABOVE:** Elvis onstage in the early days.

TOP: Elvis taking the keys to his white BMW 507 Two Door Coupe, during his U.S. Army Service in Germany; **CENTER:** Elvis Presley in *Charro*, 1969; **BOTTOM:** Elvis, circa 1960.

Elvis looked at me and he said, "Now, Lawrence."

SP: Did he always refer to you as Lawrence?

LG: When he was serious, and he really meant it. He said, "Lawrence, I am going to reveal to you everything we have been studying for all those years. I'm going to tell you the truth in these mysteries, only when you wake up, you're not going to remember a word I told you." And the next thing I know my phone is going off, and it's my sister, and I was pissed! [Laughing.] I said, "Why are you calling me?" [Larry starts laughing again.] And I don't remember a word that was spoken. All I remember was it was not a dream.

SP: So in the dream you believe he shared revelations with you?

LG: [Laughing.] I don't know! He might have even told me the next week's lottery numbers, I don't know. [We all start laughing.] And now I'm going to tell you another dream, and this is amazing!

SP: Okay, so these visitations, if you like, are happening over time?

LG: Well, this was two years later, approximately February or March, no it was more like April or May of '79. The last time that Elvis ever sang in public was on the date—and this is very interesting—because Elvis was very much into numbers you know, and his

basic primary number was eight and so was Colonel Parker's. Colonel Parker's birthday was June 26 and that's an eight, two and six. That was the last time Elvis ever sang on Colonel Tom Parker's birthday. A few years later I had a dream, I can't believe I'm telling you this, because I've never told anyone this.

SP: Well, this is great! We're all ears.

LG: I'm sitting with Vernon Presley and a few of the guys, and we're chatting, and all of a sudden the door just opens and there's Elvis, and he looked very slim. He didn't look at any of us, he looked at his father. His father stood up, and they walked together, and Elvis took his hands and placed them on his father's cheeks and kissed him on the lips, and Vernon fell over holding his heart.

SP: [Gasps.] Oh, no.

LG: Vernon dies about six weeks later.

SP Oh my goodness! That was like a premonition.

LG: June 26th and that date was the last time Elvis ever sang at Colonel Tom Parker's birthday.

SP: I believe in premonitions and signs myself.

LG: Well, when I first met with Elvis, Elvis said to me, "There are no such things as coincidences, there are no coincidences, things coincide."

SP: Well, when was your last one? Have you had any more signs? Or do you just get feelings?

LG: I get feelings all the time.

SP: Where you feel Elvis is around?

LG: I do, well, you know something will happen, and I'll almost hear Elvis laughing because he had the most infectious laugh.

SP: Well, do you think he might be here today with us? [Giggling.]

LG: Well, I don't know, who am I say to say?

SP You're Larry Geller, that's who you are.

LG: Elvis was like you said Shelly, "a gift from God." He touched the hearts and the souls of humanity in a way that goes beyond the confines and the borders of show biz, because a lot of people are connected to deeper things in life and to God because of Elvis Presley. Elvis Presley went all the way down to animalistic sexual gyrations, where preachers were burning his albums. He had physical beauty, and yet he also had a soul that went out to the highest regions. He spanned the whole spectrum of the human condition. He is a reflection of America, of someone who became obese and took pills, to someone who was trying to connect with God. Elvis was a gift for us to learn from. We learned that we should not procrastinate, that if there's something that we are supposed to do in our life, we better do it now and don't wait. Doesn't matter if you're Elvis Presley, you could die. Even if you're Elvis Presley, he knew the first night I was with him, he told me, "I've got it all, man, but there is something missing, and that's the most important thing in life, and I learnt that from my mother." He said, "I learnt that from my mother, she was a very spiritual lady, and that is to keep your relationship with God... and I want to find out why I am on this planet." And he found out, he did find out, and that's why he was making plans to expand his career and his influence... Another question?

SP: Yes, Helga from the U.K., she has sent in quite a few questions but I'm just going to pick out a few good ones here. She says, "Larry, what real regrets do you know that Elvis had career-wise and also maybe of a personal nature?

LG: Okay, that's a question that I have answered partly... one, that he regretted that he allowed Colonel Parker, Hal Wallis, and others, people in power, not to give him movie scripts for pure dramatic roles, for him to activate his potential as an actor. He said, "I'm an actor, man, I don't know how I got through high school. I remember sitting

there just gazing out of the window, visualizing myself on the big screen. I would think about Mario Lanza, Tony Curtis, that's all I wanted to do."

SP: The films were probably one of his biggest regrets. He wasn't taken seriously.

LG: Exactly. He said, "Hey, I was in it to make money too, but I'm not in this just for the money. I'm an artist, and I'm in it for reasons that go way beyond the almighty dollar." Now, I'll never forget this. [Larry laughs.] I'll never forget a lot of things, every moment with Elvis was historical, you know. We were talking early one morning when the sun was coming up, and we are talking about certain things about his life, and he said, "Man, I'm just like anyone else, I've got feelings. I've got feelings that run through my body." He said, "Put yourself in my shoes... do you realize how difficult it is for me to realize the trust for a woman to love me—me or Elvis? How do I know for sure? Think about it."

SP: Okay, just briefly I'd like to go over the details that led up to you leaving Elvis, because you did leave him for a while.

LG: I did.

SP: Through no choice of your own?

LG: No, no, it was my choice.

SP: It was your choice?

LG: Absolutely.

SP: Well, let me just put this to you because I heard during the making of his movie *Clambake* that Elvis had fallen, and had a concussion, and Colonel Parker went on the rampage and was accusing all the guys of not looking after Elvis properly, and saying there was going to be some changes.

LG: That's true.

SP: And one of these drastic changes was Larry Geller had to go, and all his religious books had to go with him, okay?

LG: Not exactly.

SP: Was that not the way it was?

LG: Well, yeah, sort of. Let me tell you briefly, it's a long story. What happened was it was the very first day of filming *Clambake*. We had just come back from Memphis, and Elvis came out of his room and he's holding his head. He sits in a chair, and he says, "Wow, man, I don't know what happened. I don't know if I fell or if someone hit me." He said, "Come

ABOVE: The King.

here, feel this." I came over and everyone felt it, like a golf ball right here. [Larry points to the back of his head.] And he said, "I feel dizzy and all that." Colonel Parker came in—and all those years Parker gave me nothing but surface respect. Now there was a problem. Doctors came in, he was taken to the bedroom, and the Colonel said, "I don't want him reading books. No more bookstand, you get rid of those books!" Several days later Elvis was feeling a little bit better, there was a big meeting. Colonel Parker, Elvis, Priscilla... and Elvis never said a word. Colonel Parker gave the talk. "There's going to be a few changes around here. I got to take care of Elvis, and from now on I don't want him reading any more books, and I always want two people with Elvis now, not one."

SP: So you were not allowed to continue seeing Elvis and do his hair on your own?

LG: That's right, someone had to be in the room.

SP: Now that wasn't just against you, was it?

LG: It was against me, of course it was.

SP: He didn't want you to be alone with Elvis?

LG: That's right.

SP: So the Colonel blamed you for what had happened?

LG: No, he didn't blame me, he just didn't want me there anyway. This was just a device, a ploy, he used it.

SP: So he wanted you out?

LG: Of course, yeah. I did leave but not because I was asked to leave.

SP: So why did you leave?

LG: So, I was not allowed to be with Elvis alone. Elvis was taking some medication, something, and I don't know what it was he was taking. He was very different every day, at the studio, and there was something, I don't know, I just knew it would be better if I leave. I just felt that it would be better, and I knew that if I left, I'd come back in the future. Maybe in a year, ten years, maybe twenty years, whatever. So I went to Yosemite National Park.

SP: Yes, I know it, but I've never been there.

LG: Well, I went there, and I spent a couple of days, and I really contemplated and thought about it. I wrote a letter, and I gave it to Jerry Schilling. What happened was, it was the night before, it was April 30th, and Jerry Schilling called me up he said, "You better get over to the house, we are going to Vegas." So I said, "I don't think so, Jerry. I think I'm quitting," and a couple of weeks later I met Jerry, and I gave him the letter explaining why I felt it was better if I leave. He [Elvis] was going through changes.

SP: Did you perhaps feel like you were being alienated?

LG: I felt like my influence would turn into something I did not want it to be.

SP Okay, it might have gone ugly?

LG: It might have gone ugly, it might have gone weird, it might have gone off the rails, and I didn't want that to happen so I sacrificed myself.

SP: Okay, because in Jerry Schilling's book, *Me and a Guy Named Elvis*, he actually wrote about this incident and he told it in a slightly different way. He said he actually felt kind of sad that you weren't going to be around for much longer because he liked you. He liked listening to you and your take on the spiritual side of things.

LG: Yeah, there were a few in the group. Charlie Hodge was another.

SP: Who would you say out of the group were the ones that were nicer to you and kind of understood you more?

LG: Jerry Schilling, Charlie Hodge.

SP: Jerry Schilling?

LG: Yeah, Jerry Schilling and I were friends, and I don't want to mention names because if I say this about one person then I don't want to leave people out.

SP: Okay. I get that but those were the two main ones that spring to mind.

LG: Well, yeah, and George Klein, definitely George Klein.

SP: Okay. So how do you think, deep down, Elvis really felt about this halt that was brought to your relationship? I mean when you decided to leave was that it, was it a clean break?

LG: Totally, totally.

SP: So you didn't make contact with him?

LG: Not once and what happened was... you know Jack Rivers [Johnny Rivers], the singer?

SP: I don't actually.

Jason Edge: She's English. [We all start laughing.]

[Jason was the president of Elvis International and he was the photographer for this particular interview, as Rudy was not available.]

LG: He was a big rock and roller in the '60s and '70s.

SP: Okay.

LG: He had hits like "Poor Side of Town", "Summer Rain." He sang the theme Secret Agent Man for the TV series. Anyway, he called me up and he said, "Larry, you have to go to Vegas to see Elvis. We're going to see the show." I said, "Really, I don't know if I should, Jack," and he said, "No, no, he needs you. He really needs you—he just broke up with Priscilla. She just left him, and he's going through a lot." I said, "Have you spoken to him?"

SP: This is after you have had a break from him?

LG: Yes.

SP: Okay, sorry, so this is why you came back?

LG: Yes. So I said, "Okay," and I went to the show. It was an interesting show. I hadn't seen him for a few years, saw some physical changes.

SP: Were you shocked?

LG: I was surprised, a little bit, a little bit. When

the show was over I was asked to go backstage, and there were people there and Elvis was in the dressing room. He comes out, and he comes right over to me, and we just hugged. He said, "Come on, man, let's go upstairs." We go upstairs and we go to his bedroom, and in the bedroom there are stacks of books I gave him. On the floor, on his nightstand. Now they were really used books, dog-eared, you know?

SP: He had got them all back and they were well read. [Laughing.]

LG: I picked one up and said, "Elvis, this is falling apart, let me get you a new copy." He said, "No, no, I like them that way."

SP: So this was it, this is how you came back?

LG: Well, I didn't go on tour, but, yes, I was back. And then what I did was—I was right in the midst of creating a magazine called the *New Age Voice*, I was the editor, I did everything, the layout. So Elvis said, "I'm going to Hawaii to do the big Hawaiian Special, so come out with me." I said, "I can't, I'm going to Europe with Johnny. I promised him I would be his manager for a tour." So after the tour I gave Elvis a copy of the *New Age Voice*, and he gave everyone a copy. He was so proud. Elvis said, "I want your permission to use the title of your magazine for my new group and call them The Voice."

SP: Yes, The Voice, they would come on before Elvis.

LG: Yes, they did.

SP: Okay, I just want to ask you about Elvis and Priscilla. Did you see any signs? I know that there was a gap where you didn't see Elvis, but prior to this did you see any signs that indicated Elvis and Priscilla would not stay together?

LG: I can't really talk about that, because when I was there they were together 100 percent.

SP: Okay so let me put it this way, Larry, were you surprised when you heard they had split up?

LG: No.

SP: You weren't surprised?

LG: No, because I knew Elvis.

SP: Did you ever try to offer up any advice or guidance regarding the mistakes he made while he was married to Priscilla?

LG: No, I did not. No, no.

SP: Okay, well I imagine it was quite a challenge to be married to the King of Rock and Roll anyway, you know.

TOP: Larry; **CENTER:** *That's The Way It Is*, 1970; **ABOVE:** Elvis, with Larry behind him, mid-1970s.

8888777

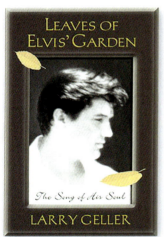

TOP: Elvis and the band getting down during the making of *That's The Way It Is*, 1970; **ABOVE:** Larry's book, *Leaves of Elvis' Garden: The Song of His Soul.*

LG: Of course. Naturally.

SP: I just want to say—and this isn't a question, it's something I want to say myself—I admire Priscilla so much. She's just fourteen years of age, she's swept off her feet, and I honestly believe she never stopped loving Elvis, she's so in tune. They came out of court holding hands.

LG: Exactly, she does. I met Priscilla for lunch, and we had quite an interesting conversation last year and her feeling for Elvis has blossomed and deepened over the years to the point where she totally understands things that she said she didn't understand then, but she does now, and she gets it.

SP: Well, the thing is she was so young, and a lot of the fans failed to acknowledge this, the things that Priscilla had to deal with.

LG: Sure, of course it wasn't easy.

SP: She has gone on to do so much for Elvis's memory, everything that she has done, like opening the gates of Graceland to the public, she's joined forces with EPE, she's allowed more access into Elvis's life that any fan could ever hope for.

LG: Absolutely, and it's only going to get bigger. There are so many great things that are being planned right now and, yeah.

SP: So, I think like we were talking about fate before, I think it was all meant to be.

SP: How do you feel, Larry, when you visit Graceland now?

LG: Here's what happens when I'm there—two things. Basically it's surrealistic because whatever I'm seeing, I'm flooded with memories of how things used to be. Incidents, riding our horses in

the back. When Elvis and I created the Meditation Garden. Marty Lacker had a lot to do with that, as well, not the other people. Elvis and I became spiritual. This was now the big change in his life, he got spiritual, he was reading books, and he wanted a meditation garden.

SP: So that's why he wanted the meditation garden?

LG: Yes, simple as that, and never, ever in the wildest imaginings of what's occurring today. So when I go into the Meditation Garden, I remember sitting there with Elvis just talking, just sitting outside talking about life, and his father would come or someone else, and we would sit there for an hour or two drinking lemonade or whatever. Now look what it is. Elvis is buried there with his family. That's what it is. My feelings when I go there are very mixed because I appreciate what happened to me, and yet I have so many feelings and memories but I love it. I love it. I appreciate it, I understand it.

SP: Okay, Larry, one of the last few questions, and I know some people avoid this question, but I know you went into great detail about this in your book. Those last few weeks leading up to Elvis's death… did you ever think to yourself that the end was near? Did you know in your heart that he wasn't going to be around for much longer?

LG: Yeah, I did to be honest with you.

Elvis knew it too, deep down inside, but not consciously, and that's how life works. Two realities were happening in Elvis's life. Life and death, they were paralleling one another, and I remember when Elvis would sing "Unchained Melody," every time he would sing it, and when he sang it the last year of his life by himself at the piano, when we hear it now you know, they put the music in, but it was just Elvis at the piano with a blue light on him… and every time he sang it, everyone just had chills. We knew that this was something special, and I thought, "He is singing to his mother, he's singing to death," and then I thought, "No, no," and I'd push it out of my mind. I was in town here and the last week of Elvis's life [Larry hesitates]… I don't even believe I'm telling you this because I don't talk about it, but because it's you and the importance of who you are and who it's going out to, I'm going to be open.

SP: Well, I really do appreciate that Larry.

LG: All right, about… well, it was the night of my

birthday, August 8.

SP: Another 8.

LG: Yes. So I'm born in the 8th month, the 8th day, and Elvis dies eight days later on the 16th. So I'm in town, and I'm driving, and it's a warm summer night. I'm driving with the top down, and I drive up to Mulholland Drive, and I'm overlooking the city lights below. All of a sudden, I had a flash that Elvis died, and then I'm thinking, "That's crazy, what are you thinking?" I sped home, I called Graceland, and it's about 3 o'clock in the morning. One of the maids answered. I said, "Hi, Pauline, it's Larry. How ya doin', hon?" She says, "I'm doin' fine, Mr. Larry." I said, "Anything new?" and I just started chatting.

SP: But you wanted to make sure that wasn't a premonition?

LG: Oh, yeah, so I just dismiss it. Then two days later Elvis calls me up, and we have a very interesting conversation about his life, about Ginger, and about this book that's coming out and various things. Then he said, "Don't forget you got to get me those books you were talking about," and I said, "Yeah, of course, Elvis." He said, "Well, come in tomorrow." I said, "Elvis, I can't. I have some business, and I have some things I must attend to." So two days later he calls again and he says, "Come in tomorrow," and I say, "No, Elvis. I'll be there on the 14th." So my father drove me to the airport, and he said, "You're so quiet, what's wrong?" I said, "Dad, I just hope he is alive when I get there." And I don't know why I'd said that! So, I got there on the 14th, 15th and then we know what happened don't we? Elvis went. [Larry becomes visibly emotional.] He went to—you know I talk about this, and I dissolve back into this. If I get emotional, I can't help it. Now in reality, when it comes to relationships there is no such thing as time and space, it's alive, it's real. You've never met him, and you feel his influence.

SP: Absolutely.

LG: Everyone does. This is what happens, and I'll walk you through this, this will be the conclusion, I guess. It was the night of the 16th. Elvis wanted to go and see the movie *MacArthur*. We are leaving the next day to go on tour, and Elvis wants to go to the movies. This man wouldn't stop, he was a driven person, God bless him. So Joe and I got on the phone. [The phone literally starts ringing in our hotel room as Larry says this.]... And there it is now, [we all laugh] answer it. It was Joe; we were trying

to set up to see the film *MacArthur* with Gregory Peck at the Memphian Theater. Elvis was going to come back around one o'clock after the dentist. Elvis was on Elvis time, he went to the dentist at one in the morning. It didn't matter, it was Elvis's right. Something happened with the projectionist, there was a crisis, and he couldn't do it. So we had to tell Elvis when he came back no movies. I was kind of glad as we were going on tour for a couple of weeks. This man needs his strength, right? I hear the front door open, and Ginger comes in, and Dick Grob comes in, and I think another person, it might have been Billy Smith, but it really doesn't matter. Elvis was in a black jumpsuit, his sunglasses, and a big belt. Elvis spoke with his eyes, he was a communicator to the hilt, so I remember I heard the front door so I go to it, and Elvis is standing there. He takes his glasses off, and he looks at me, and he sighs. He puts his glasses back on, and he goes upstairs, and he said a mouthful when he did that. What he's saying to me is, "Man, I'm going through it." I felt horrible, and I thought, "Why are we going on tour? This is insane." I go in, and I sit down, and about five or six minutes later someone says, "Larry, Larry, its for you"—they have the phone—"it's Elvis, he wants you." There's a phone in the kitchen and in the den, you know the layout. I pick up the phone, and Elvis says, "So what do you think, man?" and when I heard his voice it struck me so oddly. He sounded like he was 15 years old. Pure and young, joyful, and he sounded so good. I said, "I don't know, Elvis, I mean it's late." And he said, "Well, maybe you should come upstairs and talk," and I'm thinking to myself, "His voice. What am I hearing in his voice?" I put two and two together, and I thought, you know, what... he's okay, he sounds so vital, so young. I didn't feel bad. I thought it's all right, it's just a passing thing. He said, "Hey, man, we've got a lot to talk about." I said, "Elvis, I know, but we are going on tour tomorrow. If I come upstairs, we will spend the whole night talking."

SP: You wanted him to get some sleep and sleep for yourself?

LG: "Yes," I said. "Tomorrow we are going to be on the road." I said, "I'll come tomorrow. We can do your hair and we can spend two weeks talking, you know?" So he said, "Well, whatever's right." And he started to laugh, and I started to laugh because his laugh is infectious... and we are both laughing. And then he said, "Don't forget now. Angels fly because they take themselves so lightly."

TOP: Larry during the interview; **ABOVE:** A rare photo of Elvis—with cigarillo.

TOP: Elvis and the band recording the title track of the movie, *King Creole* (Paramount, 1958); **ABOVE:** A young Elvis in 1954.

SP: Wow.

LG: I go to my room at the house where Joe and I, Lamar and Priscilla and Jerry sometimes used to stay. I go to my room, ten minutes later I get the call: Elvis wants his book. There was a special book he wanted, and it was the scientific search for the face of Jesus, and it's all about the holy shroud of Turin. I clipped a couple of the pages that I thought Elvis would really like and two other books, one was called *Music: The Keynote to Evolution* and another book I don't want to talk about right now. So that was the last thing Elvis ever said to me, "Angels fly because they take themselves so lightly." His body was found the next afternoon on the floor in the fetal position with that book clutched to his chest. I drove up to Graceland [without knowing]. Someone drove me, and I noticed when we were driving a lot of cars and a lot of people... and I thought, "Well, that's weird. What's going on?... but we are leaving tonight." Then I saw three helicopters. I get to the gates of Graceland, and Uncle Vestor opened the gates. I said, "This is the van that's going to drive me up, Uncle Vestor." He said, "Didn't you hear what happened?" I said, "No, what happened?" He said, "Elvis just died." I said, "What did you say?"

and he repeated, "Elvis just died, Larry." I remember looking up at the bedroom. They drive me up there, and I jump out of the car, I run into the room and Vernon is crying, "Larry, Larry!" I run over to him, and he sobs, "What am I going to do? He's gone, he's gone." Lisa is walking around crying; it is a scene that I will never forget. I can't really describe that now because I'm going to tell you something else. I'll tell you one thing that was really bizarre— little Lisa Marie. That afternoon people were crying, and they were in shock, and she was walking and she had her hands in her pockets, and she said, "You know what? I can't believe it, Elvis Presley is dead!"

SP: Oh, bless her.

LG: We look at each other, wait a minute, what? So Vernon said to me that the head of the mortuary had come over to make arrangements. They call me in, and Vernon says, "Larry, I want you to go to the mortuary. Elvis would want you there, you know how he should look. I want you to oversee everything, do his hair." Charlie Hodge said, "I'll go with you, you can't do this alone." So I said okay and so the next morning, at eight am, I had to be there. I was in the worst shape of my life. I remember crying so much, I didn't know the body held so much water. We are made up of 75 percent water.

SP: I didn't know that either.

LG: At any rate, I didn't go to bed that night, and I went to the mortuary, and thousands of people are there. I remember they opened the doors for me, and Charlie came in and police officers and Robert Kendall, the head of the mortuary. I remember walking through this brick building, I understood what the building was anywhere I was going. I could hear the whirring of the helicopters and the silence out there. I could see tears and people holding each other, black people and white people. I'm looking at all these people, and I felt like I was inside of a movie. I walk inside this building and this police officer follows me. He takes me by the arm, and he takes me to this long corridor, this dark dank long corridor, and it's weird, all I can hear is the vibration of our footsteps against the brick, and my heart is pounding in my chest. So I suddenly stop, because I saw what was at the end. There was this table with a sheet, so I stopped and this police officer grabbed me, and I said, "Just leave me be for a minute." I was getting a little freaked out but I gritted it, and I walked into this room. I walked up to Elvis, who was laying on this table. He was sleeping. This is Elvis, and he was just sleeping. I wanted this to be a joke but it wasn't. It wasn't a joke. That was the corpse of Elvis Presley I had to honor. There was a sheet up to here, [Larry points to his chest] and I don't know how long I stood there, but it was a while, and I looked at that face, that nose, those lips... and all those memories from when I was a kid, they all came flooding back to me of when I first met Elvis. How could this be? And he had a look on his face of peace, peace that's all I can describe. I almost felt him in the room with us, you know, and now I had to work on him. It took me a long long time to do his hair because first of all he was positioned horizontally, and his hair had already been shampooed and the life force had left his body. His hair had no life, nothing, and with the effect of gravity it wouldn't do anything, so I had to do it over and over again. Inside I'm talking to him, I'm talking to him, communicating, trying to keep the connection with him. "Elvis, I know wherever you are, you are okay." Finally I said to one of the morticians, because I realize I didn't bring my dyes with me, that I used to dye his hair black. He had a regrowth of white, but this lady, thank God, had some black mascara, so I did my thing and blended it in, and as I'm doing this they pull the sheets down and there's autopsy scars. Charlie screams, "How can you do this to us?" They quickly say, "Sorry, sorry," and they pull the sheet back up. So I got the hair looking the way it should, and this is the remains of Elvis Presley. They brought his body to Graceland at noon. Wow, this is very difficult for me to talk about this but let me conclude by saying the next day was the funeral. When the funeral was over, the guys and Vernon went into the back room where the casket was, and this is the last time that Elvis will be seen by anyone. Joe took the TCB ring off, and he handed it to Vernon. Vernon said, "Goodbye, son," it was just a scene, you can imagine, and I did something that I had to do. Thank God I had the guts and presence of mind, as the lid was going to come down I put my hand inside on Elvis's forehead, and I said something to him silently, and then the lid closed. [Larry claps his hands together to imitate the lid of the casket closing fast.] I was the last person to ever touch him, and it had to be that way. It had to, and that's the way it is.

SP: Now for one final question, Larry. Given the chance, what message would you give Elvis today, what would you say to him?

LG: Well, first of all it's kind of unrealistic.

SP: Not really, for a spiritual person like you?

LG: I know, I know. I would thank him, I would thank him so much. I wouldn't ask him, "Well, what is it like to be dead?" [Larry starts laughing.]

SP: No, well, obviously I didn't mean that.

LG: Yeah, I know. Listen, talking like this for the last few minutes... I don't know how long has it been?

SP: A long time.

LG: There's so many feelings and realities, you know?

SP: Is there anything you would say to him that you didn't say to him when he was alive?

LG: You know we told each other we loved each other, we did, on several occasions, and you know, oh boy, we will have to do this again. I have some very dynamic, intimate things that I have to tell you. I told him the truth about some things and I told him in front of Doctor Nick, in front of Joe. I said, "Elvis, no one tells you the truth, no one around you tells you the truth, and if you want to just put me on a plane right now that's fine, but I got to tell you"... and I did. Something really heavy duty, and some major stuff happened because I told him. We went into the bathroom, and we cried, and we told each other we loved one another. So a lot of things like that happened. So what I would do, I would thank him profusely for everything that he has done and I appreciate everything. But one more thing, something pissed me off while I was in Memphis. A fan approached me, and I got an email from another fan about the same thing. Two people who both worked for Elvis said something that is so erroneous, and I must speak out.

SP: Okay.

LG: They said that Elvis was fed up with being Elvis, he was fed up and didn't want to be bothered anymore. He didn't want to be Elvis Presley, fed up with the fans, with his life. Nothing could be further from the truth. The very antithesis of that is the reality, 180 degrees. Elvis loved his fans so deeply, profoundly. I've never seen a performer love his fans as much as Elvis Presley. How many times did I hear him say, "I wouldn't be here today if it wasn't for them. They're the ones who put me here, I owe them everything, what they did for me and my family! It's the fans, it's always been the fans." We were in Oklahoma City and someone in the know that worked for the Colonel came up and said, "Elvis, I got some great news. They're raising

TOP: A white-suited Elvis in 1970; **ABOVE:** Elvis checks out the competition in his local record store.

the price of tickets for your show," and Elvis said, "No, they're not, no way, man. No way. No one knows better than me what it's like to struggle. My fans struggle, it's hard out there. I'll never forget, it's been instilled in my brain, and my mother told me never forget where you came from. My fans have to save up their money to come to one of my shows. I'm not in this just for the money, I'm in it for them, and that's why God put me here. They're not raising tickets for my fans." I told you earlier how he had a plan and a vision for his future. He loved his life, and he loved being Elvis Presley, and I am so honored to have known him. It's more than honored, it's a blessing. It's a blessing to have this opportunity to be with you, Shelly, and I hope some value has come out of this. Everyone should read my book because this is the book that Elvis wanted me to write. Elvis gave his life, and this book, *Leaves of Elvis' Garden*—Elvis is buried in the Meditation Garden and "leaves" means pages of Elvis's book—so these are the pages of Elvis's life. Elvis being on that show, being at his concert, that was his reality show, he had a message for every person... and according to who you are and where you are in life you'll get his message. This book is the quotes and passages of what he was into, what he saw.

SP: Well, Larry, I could listen to you all night.

LG: Shall we do it again?

SP: I will say, "To be continued," okay? But I just want to thank you from the bottom of my heart, and on behalf of all of the members of Elvis International and Elvis fans worldwide who will listen to this, thank you so much for everything you have shared with us today. You have given us a real insight to your life with Elvis, and you're a lovely, lovely man.

LG: Thank you, Shelly.

ABOVE: Elvis carefully signs a 45 Single bag for a little fan; **RIGHT:** *Elvis: That's The Way It Is*, 1970; **OPPOSITE:** Publicity still for *Jailhouse Rock* (1957), directed by Richard Thorpe (MGM).

"He loved his life, and he loved being Elvis Presley, and I am so honored to have known him..."

LARRY GELLER

The Fans

Elvis's popularity and fanbase is as strong now as it ever was. A theme of every interview was to ascertain the importance of the fans to Elvis, and it turns out that his adoring fans meant as much to him, as he did to them. Elvis never took his fans for granted. He always had time to talk to them, sign autographs, or buy them a Cadillac...! I recall Larry Geller telling me of a time when—at the peak of his fame—it was suggested to Elvis that he could double the price of his concert tickets, and the venues would still immediately sell out. Elvis, wouldn't hear of it, simply saying "You're not doing that to my fans."

These pages are a celebration of those fans—a small selection of the images I've received in the past months.

If you'd like to see your own photograph featured in a future edition of this book, send a pic to me at: *shellypowersfanpage@gmail.com,* and maybe you'll be one of the lucky ones selected to share space with the King!

Elvis often asked the question, "Who's going to remember me?" Well, quite simply, Elvis—everyone remembers you.

SHELLY POWERS

May 2023

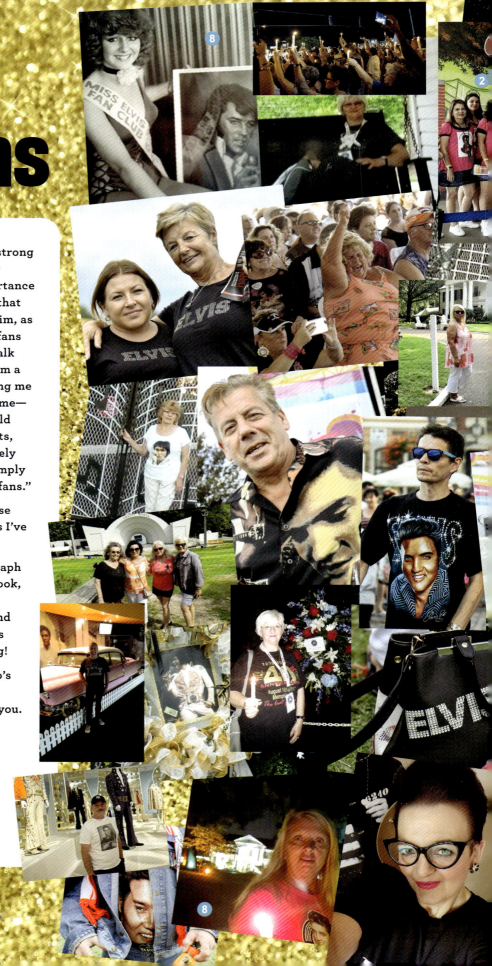